Eastern Africa Series

THE AFRICAN
GARRISON
STATE

Eastern Africa Series

The African Garrison State

Human Rights
& Political Development
in Eritrea
Revised & Updated

KJETIL TRONVOLL &
DANIEL R. MEKONNEN

JAMES CURREY

James Currey
an imprint of Boydell & Brewer Ltd
PO Box 9, Woodbridge, Suffolk IP12 3DF (GB)

and of
Boydell & Brewer Inc.
668 Mt Hope Avenue, Rochester, NY 14620–2731 (US)
www.boydellandbrewer.com
www.jamescurrey.com

First published in hardback 2014
First published in paperback 2017

The publisher has no responsibility for the continued existence or accuracy of URLs for
external or third-party internet websites referred to in this book, and does not guarantee
that any content on such websites is, or will remain, accurate or appropriate.

British Library Cataloguing in Publication Data
is available from the British Library

ISBN 978-1-84701-069-8 (James Currey Cloth)
ISBN 978-1-84701-167-1 (James Currey Paperback - revised & updated)

This publication is printed on acid-free paper

Typeset in 10/12pt Cordale
by CPI Typesetting

Contents

Acronyms & Abbreviations

ACHPR	African Commission on Human and Peoples' Rights
African Charter	African Charter on Human and Peoples' Rights
AFP	Agence France-Presse
AI	Amnesty International
AU	African Union
BIA	Border and Immigration Agency
CPJ	Committee to Protect Journalists
DMLEK	Democratic Movement for the Liberation of the Eritrean Kunama
EDRM	Eritrean Democratic Resistance Movement – Gash Setit
EIJM	Eritrean Islamic Jihad Movement
EIPJD	Eritrean Islamic Party for Justice and Development
EIRM	Eritrean Islamic Reform Movement
EISM	Eritrean Islamic Salvation Movement
ELF	Eritrean Liberation Front
EPLF	Eritrean People's Liberation Front
EU	European Union
HRW	Human Rights Watch
ICCPR	International Covenant on Civil and Political Rights
ICG	International Crisis Group
IGAD	Inter-Governmental Authority on Development
MDG	Millennium Development Goals
NDFLDS	National Democratic Front for the Liberation of the Eritrean Saho
NSO	National Security Office
PFDJ	People's Front for Democracy and Justice
RSADO	Red Sea Afar Democratic Organisation
RWB	Reporters without Borders
UDHR	Universal Declaration of Human Rights
UNDP	United Nations Development Programme
UNHCR	United Nations High Commissioner for Refugees
UNOVER	United Nations Observer Mission to Verify the Referendum in Eritrea
USCIS	US Citizenship and Immigration Services
USSD	United States State Department
VOA	Voice of America
WB	World Bank

Preface

This book is based upon the authors' long-term research and advocacy work for human rights in Eritrea. The direct inspiration for the book is a commissioned study undertaken by Kjetil Tronvoll on behalf of the Oslo Centre for Peace and Human Rights in 2009. The President of the Oslo Centre, Mr Kjell Magne Bondevik, former Prime Minister of Norway, had at that time just stepped down as a UN Special Envoy to the Horn of Africa and wanted to continue his human rights engagement in the region – thus commissioning a report on the dire situation in Eritrea. Thanks are thus due to Mr Bondevik and the Oslo Centre for commissioning the initial report. This book, however, is based upon an expanded and updated manuscript.

Several individuals have served as research assistants to this work, and special thanks go to Annie Golden Bersagel, Anette Frölich, Dag Rune Sameien, Tarana Riddick, Ann-Therese B. O. Kildal and Natasha Telson.

Oslo Analytica, a subsidiary policy research and advisory company to Bjorknes University College, has a dedicated Eritrea research group of some of the world's leading experts on human rights and political development in Eritrea and the Horn of Africa. Oslo Analytica is obliged to closely research and monitor the situation in Eritrea, in order to provide analytical works and policy advice to the international community for the purpose of conflict mitigation and alleviation of the long-term plight of the Eritrean people.

This book is dedicated to the many thousands of victims of human rights abuses in Eritrea under the PFDJ regime.

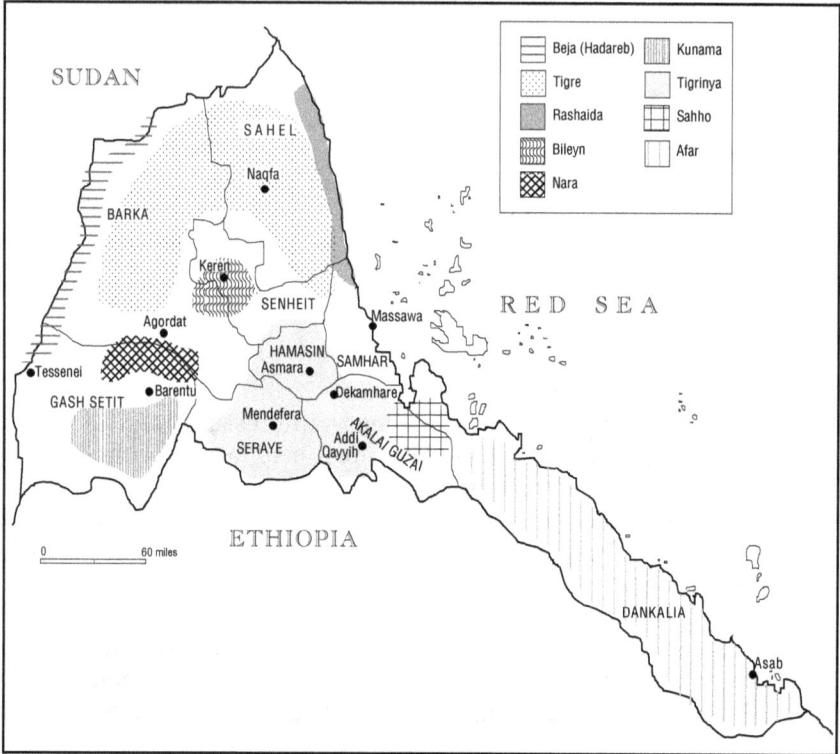

Map 1   Provinces, main towns and ethno-linguistic groups of Eritrea, pre-1996
(Map reproduced from David Pool, *From Guerillas to Government*, James Currey, Oxford, 2001)

I

Introduction:
The Eritrean Garrison State

The People's Front [EPLF/PFDJ] struggled for the independence and liberation of the Eritrean people. If it does not ensure human rights of the people of Eritrea, independence alone has no meaning.
Yemane Gebremeskel[1]
Director of the Office of the Eritrean President

It was better during the Derg [the Ethiopian military junta ruling Eritrea until 1991]. At that time the Ethiopians tortured us, but that made us only more determined in our struggle to become independent. Today, it is our own people who torture us, something which breaks down our spirit, as there is no hope for the future.
Eritrean refugee in Sudan

INTRODUCTION

A perennial issue in the study of civil-military relations is the under-standing of why and at what point a government perceives the need to militarise its structures of administration, leading to a perversion of civilian rule and a gradual slide towards military autocracy. This book's objective is to address this issue and assess the political context and human rights situation in Eritrea to attempt to explain why the country, since its liberation in 1991 and *de jure* independence in 1993, has developed into one of the world's most authoritarian states, militarised with a reputation for human rights abuse.

As early as 1937, the American sociologist George Lasswell presented the *garrison state* theory, which projected that a military elite could rise to power in response to long-term international tension, under which condition freedom is curtailed while preparation for war becomes the dominant thrust of a society. As Lasswell describes it: 'In the garrison state the specialist on violence is at the helm, and organized economic and social life is systematically subordinated to the fighting forces.' This means that the predominating 'influence is in the hands of men who specialize in violence' (Lasswell 1937: 43; Stanley 1997: 43). Although initially developed as an approach to the understanding of the industri-alised nations' turn to authoritarianism and militarisation, the theory

[1] From the official website of the government: 'Public Dialogue: Human Rights in Eritrea', posted 6 June 2006, at: http://www.shaebia.org/cgi-bin/artman/exec/view.cgi?archive=14&num=4553, accessed 5 November 2008.

may today be useful as a conceptual framework to the understanding of events unfolding in Africa and other developing countries.

Recent research has also made clear that elites who have come to power through violence are disposed to maintaining their positions through violence and responding violently to any future challenge (Gurr 1988). There are political, social and psychological reasons for this; first, a successful strategy is always easy to repeat, but also important is the socialising effect the use of violence has on both leaders and their subjects. Elites who successfully use coercion to achieve their objectives become habituated to the political use of violence – coercion and terror morph into political culture. Likewise, the subjects on the receiving end of coercion develop a culture of fear that lessens resistance and reinforces the impression among the elites that the use of violence is the appropriate strategy to keep protest and reform at bay and thus perpetuate power. Finally, a growing body of research confirms that domestic threats – in particular dissident demands – provoke government authorities to apply repression as a regulatory mechanism to maintain control. The type and level of repressive mechanism applied will correspond to the perceived seriousness of the threat posed (cf. Davenport 2000; King 2000).

It is no exaggeration to state that Eritrea today is imprisoned by an elite which 'specializes in violence' and terrorises its population, and the country can thus aptly be portrayed as an *African Garrison State*. The aspirations and hopes for democracy and respect for human rights as expressed at the time of independence in 1993, are today only bleak memories. The myth of Eritrean 'exceptionalism' – the unique dedication, skills and leadership qualities of the Eritrean People's Liberation Front (EPLF) – ought to be consigned to the dustbin of history, as the trajectory of Eritrean political development has followed a predictable path of increased authoritarianism since independence. Taking into account EPLF (and its subsequent civil 'replacement' the Peoples' Front for Democracy and Justice – PFDJ) political ideology and culture, the three factors advancing the militarisation of society mentioned above, are all relevant in explaining the Eritrean trajectory.

Eritrean society has been at war for the better part of the last five decades, including the 30 years independence war (1961-91), and subsequent border conflicts with the Sudan, Yemen, Djibouti and Ethiopia. The Eritrean-Ethiopian border war, which was actively fought between 1998 and 2000, is still being trotted out by the Eritrean government as an excuse to sustain a full war-footing mobilisation. The Eritrean leadership was thus socialised into warfare from a very young age, many being recruited to the liberation struggle in their late teens or early twenties and having served in combat leadership positions in the EPLF throughout the 1970s and 1980s. Hence, when Eritrea's 'Arab Spring' evolved in 2001, where both government and military leaders, as well as students, journalists and civil society activists, demanded the liberalisation and demilitarisation of society and respect of human rights, this was perceived as a serious and imminent threat to the survival of the regime. As a response to this threat, President Isaias Afwerki ordered a broad and ruthless crackdown in September 2001, closing down Eritrean society permanently.

The purpose of this book is to assess the state of human rights and political development in Eritrea since its military liberation in 1991 and *de jure* independence in 1993, while simultaneously casting light on the country's development along the path it followed. The human rights crisis in Eritrea is so dire, widespread and systematic that to cover all its facets in one book is a Herculean task; and particularly so since Eritrea – next to North Korea – is one of the world's most secretive and closed states. Nevertheless, this book provides comprehensive and updated understanding of the human rights and political situation inside Eritrea today. It provides analysis of some core issues of concern and aspires to serve as a stepping-stone to further and more specific works to be carried out in the future.

We start below by discussing the pre-colonial, colonial and post-colonial history of Eritrea up to the present, including a discussion of the ethno-linguistic and religious make-up of Eritrean society. This will help in understanding the formation of the Eritrean statehood and its contemporary history. In this chapter, we will also discuss the major definitional parameters and theoretical constructs that serve the purpose of an overarching conceptual framework for the analysis that follows in the remaining chapters, as well as the methodological constraints of the study.

THE FORMATION OF ERITREAN STATEHOOD: PRE-COLONIAL AND COLONIAL PERIOD

Eritrea is Africa's second youngest state, the youngest country being South Sudan. Eritrea achieved formal international recognition as an independent country in 1993.

Before the advent of colonialism in the Horn of Africa, the area known today as Eritrea generally fell under four different political domains.[2]

The Mereb Melash (The Land Beyond the river Mereb) as it was called by the Abyssinians, or *Midri Bahari* (Land of the Sea), was the highland region. The inhabitants of this region were Tigrinya-speaking, mainly Orthodox Christians from the three traditional plateau districts of Hamasien, Seraye and Akele-Guzay. Most of this region formed an integral part of the feudal structure of Abyssinia. As is still the case, the area was also inhabited by the Saho-speaking agro-pastoralist Muslims, and the Jeberti, a population of Tigrinya-speaking Muslims.

The western lowlands of Barka (and present Gash-Setit) were dominated by various Tigre-speaking groups and Beni Amer clans, which, from time to time, were under the influence of the Funj Kingdom at Sennar (Sudan). These nomadic pastoral groups had little contact with the highlanders, except occasional reciprocal livestock raids. Smaller

---

[2] This section is adapted from Tronvoll 1998a and Mekonnen 2009: 18-59.

groups of hunters and gatherers, such as the Kunama and Nara, also inhabited these areas.

The Semhar region of Massawa and the coastal areas (including former provinces of Sahel and parts of Senhit) had, since the rise of Islam, been under Arabic/Muslim influence. Especially during the Ottoman Turk period this district created its own identity, distinguishing it from the neighbouring areas. The border areas of Keren sometimes fell under the influence of Islam, and at other times they paid tribute to the Funj Kingdom.

The Afar land of Dankalia is the coastal area extending southwards from the Gulf of Zula, south of Massawa, to the former French enclave of Djibouti. This area was part of the Sultanate of Assua, and the pastoral Afar clans who inhabited it had never been ruled by any outside power until the arrival of the Italians. The Afars have always been perceived by their surrounding neighbours as hostile and fierce people, with a strong clan and ethnic identity. After the colonial race for the Horn was over, the Afars found themselves fragmented between two new-born states – Eritrea and Djibouti – and the old, but expanding, Empire of Ethiopia.

Italian presence in Eritrea commenced in 1869 through a shipping company which purchased the Bay of Assab for strategic trading purposes (Negash 1987). In 1882, Assab was formally declared an Italian colony, and Italy started preparing for the colonial race for Africa. In 1885, Italy expanded its territory northwards and incorporated the port of Massawa into the colony, reaching out for the highlands as the next conquest. The first Italian attempt to enter the highlands in 1887 met with defeat at the hands of Emperor Yohannes of Ethiopia. However, troop reinforcements from Italy, the dire local situation caused by drought and famine in 1888-90, and the death of Emperor Yohannes in 1889, facilitated the Italian takeover of the Eritrean highlands. A treaty with the new Ethiopian Emperor Menelik II was signed at Wichale in May 1889, where Menelik was forced to accept the Italian colonisation of Eritrea (ibid.: 2). The Italian colony of Eritrea was subsequently proclaimed on New Year's Day 1890.

Colonial rule of Eritrea may be divided into six phases, comprising the period between the formal proclamation of Italian colonisation in 1890 and the defeat and the expulsion of the Derg army from Eritrean soil in 1991 and the subsequent formal proclamation of independence on 24 May 1993.

The first phase of this history ended with an Italian attempt to extend its expansionist policies and colonise Ethiopia. In the famous battle of Adwa (in Tigray) in 1896, the advancing Italian army was crushed by Emperor Menelik's troops. This humiliating defeat led to a reorganisation of Italian colonial politics.

The second phase of Italian colonialism in Eritrea lasted from 1907 to 1932. In this period, civilian Italian governors administered the colony as they consolidated the Italian presence in Africa. They sought neighbourly relations with Ethiopia and political stability within Eritrea. Initial Italian plans to make Eritrea a settler colony were not implemented, and Eritrea served instead as a reservoir, supplying colonial soldiers to consolidate Italian rule in Somalia (1908–1910) and later in Libya (1912–1932) (ibid.: 4).

The phase of colonial history in Eritrea marks the last phase of Italian influence, which began in 1932 with the preparations for the Italian invasion of Ethiopia, and ended in 1941 with the Italian defeat by the British/Allied forces as a consequence of World War II. In this short time, Eritrea experienced the most radical changes during its history as a colony. More than 300,000 Italian troops arrived in the mid-1930s. They followed another 50,000 Italian labourers, who had arrived earlier and had prepared the necessary infrastructure of transport and accommodation. In this period, the slumbering colony of Eritrea was turned into a commercial and industrial centre for the new empire and a traditional colonial economy gave way to a war economy. The growth of urban centres changed Eritrean society forever, and Italy transformed Eritrea into a real colony of settlement where Italians constituted up to 12 per cent of the entire population (ibid.) . The recruitment of Eritrean nationals to the colonial army created possibly the greatest impact on the general Eritrean society. Between 1935 and 1941 the colony produced 60,000 Eritrean men under arms, which constituted a large share of Eritrea's adult male population. Nearly all of these soldiers were used outside Eritrea, most of them in the Ethiopian occupation force.

During the final phase of Italian colonialism, Tekeste Negash (1997) argues that a combination of three factors contributed towards a development of what may rightly be called a separate and distinct 'Eritrean' identity and consciousness among major parts of the population; an identity which distinguished them from the old, 'greater Ethiopia' identity-sphere. The first was the growing racist ideology of the Italian colonial policy, which began to draw a distinction between 'Eritreans', as subjects under their civilising umbrella, and the rest of the inhabitants of the Ethiopian empire. This policy which was intended to enhance the Italian colonial ego appears to have been employed by the Eritrean literati in their shaping of 'Eritreaness'. A second factor, writes Tekeste Negash, was the economic boom created in Eritrea by Italian preparations for war against Ethiopia. A huge indigenous wage-labour market was created, whereby Eritrean citizens' inclusion in a modern money-economy distinguished them further from their Ethiopian neighbours. Finally, the third factor behind the emergence of an 'Eritrean' identity was the Italio-Ethiopian war itself and the vital role the Eritreans were made to play. With slightly more than 50,000 Eritrean troops fighting alongside the Italians in the occupation force – whose role was pivotal in the actual conquest of Ethiopia, and its later pacification – this broadened the division between the two peoples. Italian policy later cemented this division by passing a decree in 1937 which distinguished Eritreans from other subjects of the new colony. Eritreans were to be referred to as 'Eritreans' and were given special privileges in certain categories of jobs and professions, whereas the Ethiopians were termed 'natives' and were discriminated against vis-à-vis the Eritreans in certain fields (Negash 1997: 16-18; Negash and Tronvoll 2000). These three factors contributed to the creation of a nascent Eritrean identity, an identity whose main characteristic was based on the notion that the Eritreans and their land were more 'developed' than the rest of the Ethiopian empire.

The start of the Second World War marked the beginning of the end of Italy's influence in Africa. As a part of the overall war strategy, the British forces in East Africa captured enemy colonial territory, and by April 1941 all Eritrean territory was under British/Allied control and the fourth phase of the colonial history of Eritrea had begun. The British Military Administration (BMA) of Eritrea governed the territory according to international rules concerning the occupation of enemy territory in war time, and its authority was of a provisional character (Trevaskis 1960: 24). The British also dismantled large parts of the Eritrean infrastructure and factories and exported them to other British colonies during this period.

After a decision of the UN General Assembly, Eritrea was federated with Ethiopia in 1952, which marked the start of the fifth 'colonial' period in Eritrea. Even though the UN had drafted a particular Eritrean constitution in 1952, which explicitly mentioned the autonomous status of Eritrea under the Ethiopian Crown, these rights were infringed from the very start of the period of federation. The Eritrean police force was to take orders from Addis Ababa; Tigrinya and Arabic languages were substituted by Amharic as the official language; the Eritrean flag was abolished and so on. Finally, in November 1962, as a consequence of Ethiopian machinations, the Eritrean Parliament dissolved itself, a decision which, according to the UN-drafted constitution and the UN resolution on Eritrean/Ethiopian federation (390A, 1952), was illegal. From that date Eritrea was annexed as Ethiopia's fourteenth province.

With the Ethiopian annexation the sixth and last phase of the colonial history of the country commenced. The violation of the federal agreement triggered off armed Eritrean resistance in 1961, initiated by the Eritrean Liberation Front (ELF). The Ethiopian annexation and increasing oppression of the Eritrean people stimulated growing support for the liberation movements. In 1970 a faction of the ELF broke off and established its own movement, which, by 1975, took the name of the Eritrean People's Liberation Front (EPLF). During the 1970s the ELF and the EPLF engaged in civil war with each other, based on different strategies of liberation and views of ideology, in addition to an intensified war against the then Marxist-Leninist regime of Ethiopia. In 1981 the EPLF expelled the remains of the ELF from Eritrean soil, and thus could direct all its efforts against the Derg regime. With growing tension within Ethiopia, as a consequence of the liberation of Tigray by the Tigray People's Liberation Front (TPLF) in 1989, the EPLF prepared itself for the final push. On 24 May 1991 the EPLF marched into Asmara, and by the evening of 26 May, Assab was captured and the EPLF held control over all Eritrean territory.

It was during this last decade of the liberation war that one can say that traces of a true Eritrean national identity emerged and an all-encompassing form of nationalism was achieved, since the EPLF was uncontested in shaping the struggle to put an end to the Ethiopian hegemonic control of Eritrean society. 'Eritrea thus ceased to be a mere dream and became a reality,' writes Ruth Iyob, 'because those who shared in its construction attained the capabilities needed to counter those of its main opponent, Ethiopia' (Iyob 1995: 3).

After the fall of the Derg regime in May 1991, the Ethiopian People's Revolutionary Democratic Front (EPRDF) took power in Ethiopia, and the EPLF proclaimed a two-year transitional period which would end in a referendum on independence. In April 1993 the Eritrean people went to the polls and voted overwhelmingly in favour of independence and on 24 May 1993 the EPLF declared Eritrea an independent sovereign state. Immediately thereafter, the international community gave formal recognition to Eritrea as a sovereign state.

THE POLITICAL BACKDROP OF THE POST-INDEPENDENCE ERA

A 30-year-long liberation war led by the EPLF[3] against Ethiopian rule had, at the time of independence, moulded the Eritrean people into a determined and battle-hardened population. Although most of the country was in ruins in 1993, the Eritrean people strongly believed in a better and more prosperous future, as the liberation front established the first civilian government and appointed its much revered leader, Isaias Afwerki, as president of independent Eritrea. The absolute majority of the population looked on the EPLF with great esteem and admiration, as they had struggled and endured hardships and great sacrifices for the common good of the people. The leadership of the EPLF was at that time viewed as a 'new generation' of African leaders: they enjoyed popular support among their constituencies; they (rhetorically at least) endorsed liberal democracy, human rights and a free market economy, and they had a well-defined development policy based on their own priorities. As such, the EPLF heralded a clear breach with a long history of political violence the country has seen, at last since its modern political map was shaped by Italy.

The political history of Eritrea also gave hope for the development of a functioning multi-party democracy. During a short period of time in the 1940s and until the closure of the Eritrean parliament by Ethiopia in 1962, there were a number of organised political parties in Eritrea. Moreover, Eritrean society takes pride in being entrepreneurial, dedicated and hardworking. Hence, the former experiences with multi-party politics and democracy, a dedicated and conscientious political leadership, in combination with a hard-working and supportive population, were factors that boded well for the future development of a new Eritrean democracy.

The international community too was in need of an African success

---

[3] EPLF was renamed the People's Front for Democracy and Justice (PFDJ) in 1994. However, the government is sometimes known by its original name, EPLF. In this study, EPLF and PFDJ will be used interchangeably. EPLF is a splinter of another organisation known as Eritrean Liberation Front (ELF), which was militarily driven out of Eritrea by EPLF in 1981.

story, and Eritrea, with its tiny population and war-ridden history, came forward as a seemingly good candidate. The donor community, in particular, was positively surprised by the EPLF's will to reject donor-driven initiatives, instead emphasising its self-reliance and self-defined development objectives. The newly independent country, which had no foreign debt whatsoever in 1993, thus had the full backing of the international development community in its effort to deliver 'development' to its people.

CURRENT REALITIES AND INTERNATIONAL RANKING OF ERITREA

In assessing Eritrea today, however, the optimism displayed in the early 1990s has vanished, since the multiple promises given by the liberation leaders to the Eritrean people of a 'prosperous and peaceful development' have all failed to materialise. On the contrary, the Eritrean leaders have, during 23 years in power (counting from the *de facto* liberation of Eritrea in 1991), managed to ruin the country's reputation inasmuch as Eritrea today is perceived as a political pariah, a regional spoiler, and an unreliable and irresponsible regime.

During its term in power, the EPLF/PFDJ has, *inter alia*, managed to push Eritrea into armed clashes with three of its neighbours (Sudan, Djibouti and Yemen); waged the biggest and most devastating bilateral war on the African continent in recent decades, with Ethiopia (1998–2000); sustained a total militarisation of society; clamped down on and suspended all independent and privately-owned newspapers and magazines; closed down national and international NGOs; closed down the only university in the country and curtailed academic freedom; arrested thousands of dissenters; detained and tortured many thousands of ordinary Eritreans perceived as a threat to the regime's survival; pushed hundreds of thousands of Eritreans to flee their country as refugees; and devastated the state economy. These poor performances are also reflected in Eritrea's standing in the key international rankings and surveys on democratic governance and human rights:

- **United Nations Development Programme (UNDP):** Eritrea is ranked 181 of 187 countries on the 2013 Human Development Index (HDI), scoring an index of 0.351. This score places Eritrea not only in the category of 'low human development' but also below the regional average for sub-Saharan Africa, which is 0.475.[4]

- **Global Hunger Index:** In the 2013 Global Hunger Index, Eritrea is ranked 77 out of 78 countries assessed by the report.[5]

- **Freedom House:** In the 'Freedom in the World' survey for 2012, which provides an annual evaluation of the state of global freedom

[4] United Nations Development Programme (UNDP), 'Human Development Index 2013', available at http://hdr.undp.org/en/reports/global/hdr2013/, accessed 1 July 2013.
[5] Global Hunger Index 2013, available at http://www.ifpri.org/sites/default/files/publications/ghi13.pdf, accessed 21 October 2013.

as experienced by individuals, Eritrea is classified as being 'Not Free' and scored the lowest score possible, which is 7, in both political rights and civil liberties. Freedom House saw no improvement towards developing pluralist political institutions in Eritrea, and notes that Eritrea is an 'increasingly repressive police state'.[6] Freedom House also categorises Eritrea as the 'worst of the worst' and the country is included in the special report on the world's most repressive societies published in 2008.[7] Furthermore, in Freedom House's 'Freedom of the Press' 2012 ranking, Eritrea is designated the worst country in Africa in terms of press freedom (no. 49 out of 49), and is ranked as number 194 in the world (out of 197 countries in total), only worsted by Uzbekistan, Turkmenistan and North Korea.[8]

- *Parade:* In 2011, Eritrea's president was ranked the second worst dictator in the world, preceded only by that of North Korea, corresponding to the claim that the country has now become the North Korea of Africa.[9]

- *Mo Ibrahim Index:* The Mo Ibrahim Index of African Governance of 2011 is based on data from 2010. It shows that between 2006 and 2010 Eritrea's overall score declined to 35 out of 100, as the country ranked number 47 out of sub-Saharan Africa's 53 countries.[10] The most notable movement was in the 'Safety and the Rule of Law' category, in which Eritrea's score fell by nine points over the four-year period. Eritrea's scores fell in three out of four categories of the Ibrahim Index. In the 'Rule of Law' category, Eritrea is ranked as the second-worst performer, with a score of six out of 100, ahead of only Somalia, which scored 0. Additionally, in the 'Participation and Human Rights' category, Eritrea ranked last in both Participation and Rights.[11]

- *Reporters Without Borders:* On the Worldwide Press Freedom Index 2012, Eritrea occupied the last rank in the world (no. 179 out of 179 countries assessed) for the fifth year running.[12] Reporters

[6] Freedom House, 'Freedom in the World 2012', available at: http://www.freedomhouse.org/sites/default/files/FIW%202012%20Booklet_0.pdf, accessed 13 August 2012.
[7] Freedom House, 'The Worst of the Worst: The world's most repressive societies 2008', at: http://www.freedomhouse.org/uploads/special_report/62.pdf, accessed 7 May 2009.
[8] Freedom House, 'Freedom of the Press 2012: Global Press Freedom Rankings', http://www.freedomhouse.org/sites/default/files/Global%20and%20Regional%20Press%20Freedom%20Rankings.pdf.
[9] Parade, 'The World's Worst Dictators,' available at http://www.parade.com/dictators/index.html, accessed 6 July 2013.
[10] Mo Ibrahim Foundation: 'The Ibrahim Index of African Governance 2008', at: http://www.moibrahimfoundation.org/index-2008/index.asp, accessed 6 May 2009.
[11] Mo Ibrahim Foundation: '2011 Mo Ibrahim Index of African Governance, Summary', page 14, 16, 18 at: http://www.moibrahimfoundation.org/index-2008/pdf/press_release/Eritrea_english.pdf, accessed 6 May 2009.
[12] Reporters Without Borders: 'Worldwide Press Freedom Index 2012, at: http://en.rsf.org/IMG/CLASSEMENT_2012/C_GENERAL_ANG.pdf.

Without Borders has 'reacted to the scandalous situation within the country by campaigning for the Eritrean president and his ministers to be declared personae non grata in Europe'.[13]

- *International Press Institute (IPI):* In the World Press Freedom Review 2007, Eritrea was categorised as one of the world's most brutal suppressors of independent reporting.[14]

- *Committee to Protect Journalists (CPJ):* With at least 28 journalists behind bars, CPJ characterises Eritrea as Africa's leading suppressor of media freedom and the world's fourth worst jailer of journalists.[15] Additionally, the CPJ rated Eritrea the world's most censored country.[16]

- *Bertelsmann Foundation:* The Bertelsmann Foundation Transformation Index (BTI) of 2012 places Eritrea at a rank of 126 in its Political Transformation ranking and at a rank of 125 of its Economic Transformation Index out of 128 countries.[17]

- *Polity IV Index:* The Polity IV Project provides a coding of the authority characteristics of states in the world system.[18] Eritrea scores 12 in the State Fragility Index of 2011, placing it in the category of Moderately Fragile.[19]

- *Transparency International:* On Transparency International's Corruption Perceptions Index for 2008, Eritrea was ranked 134 out of 182 countries surveyed.[20]

- *Fund for Peace:* The Fund for Peace ranked Eritrea 27 of 177 countries on their Failed States Index in 2011, with 1st place representing the most failed state. Eritrea scored 93.6 out of a possible 120 points on this index.[21]

[13] Reporters Without Borders: 'Eritrea World Report – 2009', at: http://www.rsf.org/article.php3?id_article=31131, accessed 7 May 2009.

[14] International Press Institute: 'World Press Freedom Review 2007', at: http://www.freemedia.at/cms/ipi/freedom_detail.html?country=/KW0001/KW0006/KW0154/, accessed 5 May 2009.

[15] Committee to Protect Journalists: 'Journalists in Exile: 2012', at: http://cpj.org/reports/2012/06/journalists-in-exile-2012-crisis-in-east-africa.php#more, accessed 13 August 2012.

[16] Committee to Protect Journalists: '10 Most Censored Countries', at: http://cpj.org/reports/2012/05/10-most-censored-countries.php, accessed 13 August 2012.

[17] Bertelsmann Foundation Transformation Index (BTI) of 2012, available at http://www.bertelsmann-stiftung.de/cps/rde/xchg/bst_engl/hs.xsl/publikationen_111896.htm, accessed 1 July 2013.

[18] The Centre for Systematic Peace: 'Polity IV Project', 2010, at: http://www.systemicpeace.org/GlobalReport2011.pdf, accessed 13 August 2012.

[19] The Centre for Systematic Peace: 'Global Report on Conflict, Governance and State Fragility 2011, at: http://www.systemicpeace.org/GlobalReport2011.pdf.

[20] Transparency International: 'Corruption Perceptions Index 2011', at: http://cpi.transparency.org/cpi2011/results/, accessed 13 August 2012.

[21] Fund for Peace, 'Country Profile: Eritrea, December 2011, available at http://www.fundforpeace.org/global/?q=states-eritrea, accessed 16 August 2012.

PFDJ AND ITS CRISIS OF LEGITIMACY

When the PFJD came to power in 1991 as the EPLF, it was so popular that the conventional test of legitimacy, the ballot box, was considered irrelevant to verify the willingness of the people to be ruled by the EPLF, even for the initial two years during which the EPLF governed the country as a provisional government. No one could imagine that seven years later the EPLF would fight one of the most devastating wars in post-Cold War Africa, and ten years after it came to power it would become one of the worst totalitarian regimes in the world. Except for a few Eritreans, mostly associated with ELF-splinter organisations, almost the entire Eritrean society inside and outside the country was intoxicated for several years by the euphoria of a newly found independent nation. Thus, there was no need to care about legitimacy and its concomitant virtues, such as accountability and democratic representation.

Nowadays it is a matter of common knowledge that the Eritrean government is ruling the country with brute force. Due to PFDJ's utter failure in realising the post-independence aspirations of the Eritrean people, its popular appeal or legitimacy has suffered irreparable damage. What has transpired as a result of this has now produced a plethora of academic and non-academic literature ranging from political science to jurisprudence, to sociology and anthropology, and to ridicule in other popular media formats. The following remark, which comes from a former senior Eritrean government official, and one of the last in the list of individuals who have abandoned the regime since 2001, is illustrative:

> Independent Eritrea's experience to date evinces a marked deficit in democratic governance. Significant lapses have disconnected policy and practice in nation building, state construction and development. Nineteen years post liberation, the state in Eritrea, like the prototype postcolonial African state, is in deep crisis. It has failed to provide for the needs, promote the wellbeing, cater to the aspirations and safeguard the security of the people. It is characterised by a crisis of legitimacy, delivery and relevance. A dismal record has dashed hopes that Eritrea would avoid the continent's malaise and shine as the inspiring beacon of an African success story. (Welde Giorgis 2010: 1)[22]

Similarly, David Bozzini (2011) notes that the state in Eritrea is imagined by its society as authoritarian, unaccountable, volatile and violent; and the political leadership is all-powerful and capricious, ready to do whatever it can, at the cost of individual basic freedom, in order to hold state power intact and uncompromisingly. The political leadership continues in power despite its large delegitimisation and widespread popular disapproval of its policies (Bozzini 2011: 104, 110).

Another recent observation on this particular issue is that of Victoria Bernal (2013). Based on the analysis of Ahmed Raji's political parody, written in the hyperactive political landscape of 'cyberspace Eritrea', Bernal examines the level of dislike the Eritrea government suffered

---

[22] In a lecture he delivered at Drexel University in May 2013, Welde Giorgis describes Eritrea as a 'basket case of false hopes and thwarted expectations' (Whitworth 2013).

in comparison to the nearly universal popularity it enjoyed at the time of independence. The political parody examined by Bernal is entitled "Swedish TV Crew Defects to Eritrea", ironically denoting the bizarre political situation in Eritrea. In so doing, Bernal also shows how Eritreans have come to live in 'an ironic fate in that their achievement of national liberation has ultimately subjugated them to new forms of tyranny.' Taking the issue further from Raji's political parody, Bernal adds that 'some wits have parodied the name of the country's ruling party - the People's Front for Democracy and Justice (PFDJ) – as "Please Forget Democracy and Justice"' (Bernal 2013: 302).

There are remarkable similarities between the observations of Bernal (2013) and another political parody about Eritrea that was made in the 2012 Hollywood blockbuster comedy, *The Dictator*. Co-written and starred by the famous British comedian, Sacha Baron Cohen, *The Dictator* begins by showing the political map of a fictitious country called the Republic of Wadiya, whose leader is portrayed as an unpredictable dictator. The map shown in the movie as that of the State of Wadiya is that of Eritrea - with a metaphoric insinuation on the prevailing totalitarianism in Eritrea.

Not going far from Hollywood's dishonourable mentions of Eritrea, one also finds out in another illustration how the television show *Prison Break* is used as an example in epitomizing the deep political crisis in Eritrea. In the metaphoric observation of Nathaniel Meyers (who somehow travelled to Eritrea in mid-2010), *Prison Break* was the television series most Eritreans wanted to watch. This prominent American serial drama builds on the story of a man who was convicted of murder and sentenced to death wrongly, and the effort of a brother to help the prisoner escape. Beneath this penetrating metaphor is the tragedy of Eritrea becoming an giant open prison where every member of the population considers herself/himself a prisoner and relatives outside of the country are deemed rescuers. This has also given rise to the emergence of Eritrea as one of the major country sources for human trafficking, earning the lowest mark of a 'tier 3' in the annual *Trafficking in Persons Report* (2013).

In 2012 and 2013, Eritrea was also mentioned in different contexts by three prominent international personalities as an extremely sad example. In September 2012, American President Barack Obama picked Eritrea, along with North Korea, as examples, by saying: 'I recently renewed sanctions on some of the worst abusers, including North Korea and Eritrea.' Obama's remark was made in reference to his government's commitment to fighting human trafficking, which is often described as 'modern-day slavery' (Obama 2012). According to Google's Executive Director Eric Schmidt, North Korea was seen as 'the absolutely worst place' on Earth. In April 2013 Schmidt extended that dubious honour to Eritrea, by referring to the extreme situation of media freedom in the country (Schmidt 2013). In May 2013, Bill Gates mentions Eritrea, along with North Korea and Somalia, as an example where international cooperation and development is particularly difficult to pursue (Gates 2013).

On a lighter academic note, the prominent Eritrean cyber commentator, Berhan Hagos (2013), notes that, 'Today's Eritrea is a carbon copy of North Korea.' The comparable characteristics between Eritrea and North Korea, or the description of Eritrea as a giant prison, are confirmed by a diversity of non-Eritrean writers such as Nathaniel Meyers (*Foreign Policy* 2010), Shashank Bengali (*The Christian Science Monitor* 2009), François Soudan (*Jeune Afrique* 2010), *The Guardian* (2009), Media24. com (2009), Prunier (2010), Rickett (2013), BosNewsLife (2013), among others. On the other hand, a more nuanced observation is the following remark by a group of UN experts, who discern striking similarities between Eritrea and Somalia:

> It would be hard to conceive of two States that offer greater contrasts than Somalia and Eritrea: the former, a collapsed State for over two decades, with no functional national institutions; the latter, possessing the most highly centralized, militarized and authoritarian system of government on the African continent ... the two countries present very similar challenges: in both cases, *power is concentrated in the hands of individuals rather than institutions and is exercised through largely informal and often illicit networks of political and financial control...* And both countries – in very different ways – serve as platforms for foreign armed groups that represent a grave and increasingly urgent threat to peace and security in the Horn and East Africa region.
> (UN Monitoring Group 2011: 11; emphasis added)

There is no doubt that the PFDJ, as a political entity, has become rootless, free-floating, highly repressive and largely devoid of public support. However, we are cognizant of the counter argument that may be put forward in this regard by depicting the regime as some sort of political entity, like all other repressive regimes, with its own support base. As shown above, inside Eritrea the regime's nationalist ideology and populist appeal have been replaced by brute force, repression and structural surveillance. The gathering of more than seven people is absolutely forbidden in the country. Eritreans who have left the country in recent years note that even when people are holding marriages or funeral ceremonies, they are obliged to get permission from the local administration. The same applies to village communities in rural areas who want to hold even traditional meetings. All such meetings and social gatherings are thoroughly monitored by agents of the secret service to prevent such events from becoming forums for popular uprising (as a result of growing popular discontent). Private conversations in bars and cafés are closely monitored by the secret service. In a typical bar, restaurant or café in Asmara, the owner is much of the time obliged to act as an informant for national security, and among regular customers many also act as agents of both the military and the secret service. With the prevailing level of brute force, repression and structural surveillance, it is not difficult to imagine how fast the popular appeal and legitimacy of the regime has been eroded.

The only visible supporters of the Eritrean regime are those who are based in the diaspora communities and whose loyalty has been bought by a number of manipulative tactics or narrow interests (such as tribal loyalty with senior government officials or financial or economic ties with the regime). In particular, the PFDJ seems to have succeeded in establishing a seemingly robust support base by recruiting a new batch of diaspora youths known as Young PFDJ or YPFDJ. Most of these recruits are, however, inexperienced youngsters who are born from Eritrean parents and raised in the Western world, with little substantive knowledge about the political machinations of the PFDJ, and about what is really happening inside Eritrea. Many of these youngsters see YPFDJ as a source of solace after experiencing some degree of isolation or exclusion in their host communities for a variety of reasons. Most of all, the degree to which the PFDJ enjoys popular support from the Eritrean public (inside and outside the country) has never been put to the test, by being subjected to free and fair elections or referendums.[23]

CONCEPTUAL PARAMETERS

This book argues that it is possible to follow a conscious and deliberate pattern of political decision-making under the EPLF/PFDJ, as the national government gradually became more and more authoritarian. The climax of a societal clamp-down and the arrest of a number of key EPLF officials and cabinet ministers in September 2001 was just the last in a long line of decisions carefully taken in order to quell all opposition to the personal rule of Isaias Afwerki.

The authoritarian outlook of the government also impinges directly on the development and workings of wider civil society in Eritrea, both organisationally and economically. The extremely high military costs since the outbreak of the new war with Ethiopia in 1998 have led to a sharp decline in governmental investments in non-military sectors. Added to this is the partial cut, or sharp decline, in transfers of funds from the donor community, in addition to an alleged decline in the transfer of remittances from the Eritrean diaspora. The combination of these three factors has ruined the Eritrean economy, which survives on international development aid, forced labour of conscripts in the army, support from a few other 'like-minded' countries, and a growing revenue from gold mining production.

The consequences of the weak state economy are particularly observable in the rural areas. High inflation, drought, poor harvests, reduction of the traditional grain imports from Ethiopia, and reduction of donor relief aid, have led to increasing rural poverty. The high level of military mobilisation, where the able-bodied population is drained from the villages, has compounded this dire situation.

Due to the repressive and authoritarian context in Eritrea, the small and marginalised international community in Asmara – mostly diplomats – has opted for the same 'strategy of silence' as the majority of the population, in order not to be evicted from the country. International

---

[23] However, we note that the reader may at times grapple with a key question that looms very large: how does a brutally repressive regime like the PFDJ manage to survive? Our objective here is not to offer an answer to this enigmatic question but rather to explain why a once popular movement has become the brutal regime it is at the time of writing.

humanitarian NGOs have all been expelled or asked to leave the country.[24] Thus, the potential role of civil society, both domestic and international, as an agent of change is more or less non-existent.

The current situation in Eritrea regarding democratisation and human rights can only be described as an extremely totalitarian political order, given effect by the unchallenged personal rule of the state president, assisted by his close allies in the army. In this regard, we recognise the following essential elements as making the basic building blocks of a totalitarian political system, like the one which currently exists in Eritrea. Building on the 'classical' definition of totalitarianism articulated first by Carl Friedrich and Zbigniew Brzezinski (1956) and later expanded by Juan Linz (2000), we argue that the essential traits of a totalitarian political system are prevalent in Eritrea. First, there is a totalist political ideology that does not allow any other alternative than that of the sole and ruling political party, the PFDJ. Second, this single political party is led by one man, the state president, Isaias Afwerki. Accordingly, power is centred in the hands of the state president, who is assisted by his collaborators and a small group that is not accountable to any large constituency, and cannot be dislodged from power by institutionalised, peaceful means. Third, there is a fully developed secret police force, supported by a full monopoly over mass communication, operational weapons (military structure), and all organisations including economic ones, thus involving a centrally planned economy (Friedrich and Brzezinski 1956: 161-171; Friedrich, Curtis and Barber 1969: 126; Linz 2000: 67).

As argued in this book and also noted by Petros Ogbazghi (2011) among others, contemporary Eritrea lacks rudimentary principles of the rule of law and legitimate political institutions. In addition to characteristic features of totalitarianism, Eritrea also exemplifies personal rule as the main embodiment of the current politico-legal system. This, states Ogbazghi, is 'explained by the political strategy of unleashing sheer coercive force against citizens by the military whose loyalty is bought off by providing its top echelons with control over substantial state economic resources.' In this context, personal rule is defined as 'a distinctive type of political system in which the rivalries and struggles of powerful and wilful men, rather than impersonal institutions, ideologies, public policies, or class interest, are fundamental in shaping political life' (Ogbazghi 2011: 1-3). In concrete terms, Ogbazghi exemplifies the challenge as follows:

> Besides being the President of the State of Eritrea, Isaias Afwerki is head of government, chairman of the [now defunct] National Parliament, Commander in Chief of the army, and Chancellor of the now-closed University of Asmara, the only university in the whole country. He convenes at will and presides over all meetings of the party's central council, the National Assembly, the cabinet council, and regional administrator and military council meetings.
>
> (Ogbazghi 2011: 8)

[24] There were signs, when this was written in late 2013, that the Eritrean regime may open up and invite back some humanitarian agencies, in order to alleviate the dire and looming humanitarian disaster in the country. The tactic of expelling and inviting back humanitarian agencies when needed, is something the Eritrean regime has done regularly during its time in power.

With the help of a handful of men to control the security and military apparatus, the state president has effectively suppressed the entire Eritrean population. As this study is being written, there are no signs of change of mind or policies within the Eritrean government, and the extremely dire human rights situation is sustained with impunity. The following points sum up the overall political situation in the country:

- Although the Constitution has been ratified, it is not implemented, and the constitutional provisions regarding democracy, human rights and good governance are not observed;

- Only the government party (the PFDJ/EPLF) is allowed;

- The government controls all mass media; the independent press has been shut down since September 2001;

- The government directly interferes with and controls the judiciary;

- Extrajudicial sentencing and killings occur regularly;

- There is widespread detention without trial of individuals associated with any kind of activity not prescribed or sanctioned by the authorities;

- Detainees are routinely tortured, and prison conditions are in general inhumane;

- Freedom of expression and assembly are severely curtailed;

- The government restricts the development of an independent civil society. No independent human rights or civic rights organisations exist;

- Due to government priorities and mismanagement, there is escalating poverty and a sharp decline in economic activities;

- The government is nourishing a 'political culture of war' and enforces a continuous mobilisation of young men and women sustaining Africa's biggest army;

- The existence of an elaborate secret intelligence network, spying and informing on all sectors of society, prevails;

- Religious communities are restricted in the practice of their beliefs and 'new' religious groups (Christian and Muslim) are banned and their followers persecuted;

- The relevance of the international society is weakened, as the government becomes more and more totalitarian;

- The Eritrean government is seen as a regional 'spoiler' of peace, currently pursuing destabilising strategies in Somalia, militarily challenging Djibouti, and supporting the armed Ethiopian opposition.

Some of the characteristic features of the prevailing political system in Eritrea have closer resemblance with the perquisite factors that predict the emergence of a garrison state. Taking a cue from the theoretical framework of Harold Lasswell (1937; 1941), this angle will be exemplified throughout the book and further explored in detail in Chapter 10, along with a discussion of the alarming levels of militarisation in Eritrea.

We would, at this point like to mention that the extent to which the conceptual framework of the garrison state is directly linked to the discussion throughout this book differs from chapter to chapter. For instance, while the chapters on the judiciary, prison system, absence of civil society and militarisation portray closer links with the garrison state thesis, in other chapters, such as those on minority rights and cultural homogenisation, the link with the garrison state thesis may not appear as strong.

Before concluding the current chapter, we would like to explain the following cautionary methodological notes.

SCOPE AND METHODOLOGY

This book concentrates on presenting a comprehensive assessment of political and civil rights in Eritrea. Therefore, aspects of the socio-economic development of independent Eritrea are not fully covered, as this information is freely available from other open sources.

A number of academic contributions have examined the predicament of post-independence Eritrea, particularly the deep human rights crisis, using a diversity of theoretical frameworks. The following are a few examples: political economy and post-colonial history (Hedru 2003; Mengisteab and Yohannes 2005; Connell 2005; Reid 2009; Welde Giorgis 2010; Ogbazghi 2011); sociology (Kibreab 2008; Kibreab 2009a); forced migration (Kibreab 2009b; Hepner 2009; Bariagaber 2006); militarism (Hirt and Mohammad 2013; Hepner 2013); biopolitics (O'Kane and Hepner 2009); surveillance (Bozzini 2011); constitutionalism (Medhanie 2008; Habte Selassie 2002; Weldehaimanot 2011).

As a book written by a social anthropologist and a lawyer, our methodology is bound by the rules of socio-legal inquiry. We utilise analytical and descriptive approaches that combine traits of social anthropology, law, politics and history. By socio-legal inquiry, we mean an interdisciplinary approach which builds on the relationship between law and society, as compared to a strict doctrinal approach relying predominantly on self-informed analysis of legislation and judicial decisions. This approach perceives law as one of the fundamental institutions of the basic structure of society and examines the extent to which it serves as a source of coercion or social order (Cotterrell 2007). This approach enables the researcher to combine library-based theoretical work with empirical work that leads to the development of grounded theory, as we try to do throughout the chapters. This departs from the recognition of the study of legal phenomena as a multi- or inter-disciplinary affair (Banakar and Travers 2005; Travers 2009).

We would like the reader to take note of the following methodological

limitations. Current academic discourse on human rights and legal development in Eritrea must take into account the difficulty of obtaining
first-hand information using rigorous empirical research methods inside
the country. It is impossible today to undertake independent critical
research inside Eritrea. No official research permits are granted to independent researchers, and certainly not for the study of human rights
and political development. There is widespread academic consensus in
this regard (O'Kane and Hepner 2009: 170; Ogbazghi 2011; Bozzini 2011;
Müller 2012, 461). While preparing the manuscript for the initial report
this book builds on, Tronvoll sought permission to go to Asmara twice in a
written request conveyed directly to President Isaias Afwerki, in order to
formally interview representatives of the regime to hear their side of the
story. No response to these queries was offered in return.

There are also no organisations in Eritrea which undertake research
or monitoring of human rights in the country. The extensive security
and intelligence surveillance in the country prohibits and impedes any
clandestine gathering of information on human rights violations, which
would severely jeopardise the life and wellbeing of any informant. The
case of the UN Special Rapporteur on the Situation of Human Rights
in Eritrea is the best example in this regard. The mandate holder was
appointed in July 2012 by the UN Human Rights Council in Geneva to
investigate human rights violations perpetrated by the Eritrean government. The Special Rapporteur's request for permission to visit the
country was denied by the Eritrean government. In the past, the government has also denied permission to five other UN special procedures and
mandate holders, which are enumerated in the report of the Special Rapporteur on Eritrea (2013: 4, 7).

Lack of access to primary data on the human rights situation in
Eritrea is thus a key methodological constraint to any reporting on the
human rights situation in the country. In order to alleviate this situation, field trips have been mounted from January 2008 onwards, to the
Eritrean refugee camps in Kassala, Sudan, and in Tigray, northern Ethiopia. A number of interviews with recently arriving Eritrean refugees in
several camps were conducted. Newly arriving Eritrean asylum seekers
in other parts of the world, such as the Netherlands and Switzerland,
were also interviewed in 2010 and the years that followed. Interviews
were also undertaken with Eritreans who have lived in Khartoum and
Addis Ababa for several years, as well as exiled Eritrean civil society
representatives, academics, intellectuals, and representatives from the
political opposition.

A former security intelligence officer who defected to Ethiopia in
2008 was interviewed, particularly in relation to persecution suffered
by the Kunama ethnic group. Several other interviews with informants
knowledgeable about the situation in Eritrea—Eritreans in diaspora, international development aid workers, academics, and diplomats—have
also been undertaken at various locations during the course of the work
on this book. Additional analytical and desk research was conducted
up to July 2013. Information obtained from refugees is in general made

anonymous in the text due to possible repercussions against relatives and family remaining in Eritrea.

In addition to primary interviews, an extensive open-sources search has been undertaken to obtain information from all relevant UN agencies, other bilateral and multilateral agencies, non-governmental organisations, human rights agencies, newspapers, internet sites, and other reports on the situation in Eritrea. A large number of academic sources have also been consulted. As mentioned, for the purpose of this book two formal requests for interviews with government representatives were submitted to President Isaias Afwerki in 2008. No response to these requests was received. Official statements and the position of the government on various issues of concern have thus been taken from other government sources (such as official Eritrean websites, and the government newspaper *Eritrea Profile*), as well as interviews granted by government officials to international media organisations.

We would still like to emphasise that as a result of the methodological limitations highlighted above, some of the observations and conclusions we make in this work can only be taken as tentative hypotheses that could be improved in the future with the availability of new information, and unimpeded and free access for further independent research inside Eritrea.

A short note on the 1997 Eritrean Constitution is also in order at this point. Since the constitution is not formally implemented, fundamental rights and freedoms enshrined in the constitution are not enforceable by the courts. As a result, the relevance of the 1997 Constitution does not go beyond mere theoretical formulations and hypotheses. All arguments in this book referring to the 1997 Constitution are therefore premised on this general assumption. For instance, when a certain government conduct is described as illegal in terms of the 1997 Constitution, the argument is made based on a theoretical assumption of an enforceable or implemented constitution.

In order to trace the development trajectories of human rights in Eritrea, information obtained by the authors through previous long-term fieldwork, residential experience in the country, and human rights activism in exile has also been included in this work.[25] Apparently, some of the information and analysis used in this book was in gestation for some time in different forms. The observations draw on long-term academic and non-academic engagement on Eritrean politics. Some of them were reflected in the authors' previously published works as appearing in a diversity of mediums. Readers can easily discern, for example, that a considerable part of the analysis in the current work was previously contained in a report commissioned by the Oslo Centre for Peace and Human Rights, which was published in 2009. In that context, most of

[25] Kjetil Tronvoll carried out fieldwork in Eritrea from August 1991 to October 1992; and January-June 1993. Shorter periods of fieldwork were carried out in 1996, 1997 and 1998. Tronvoll conducted short fieldwork in Eritrean refugee camps in the Sudan and Ethiopia in 2008 and 2013. Daniel Mekonnen was born in Eritrea. He studied and worked in Eritrea until he left the country in 2001.

the material used in the previous report and the accompanying analysis were targeted for non-academic consumption. The book is now framed mainly with a focus on an academic audience, although it also portrays undiminished relevance to a non-academic audience. It is hoped that the re-exposition and expansion of the arguments and analysis that resurface in the current contribution will provide a wider platform for dissemination and discussion.

STRUCTURE

This book is divided into eleven chapters covering various aspects of human rights and political development in Eritrea. The present chapter (Chapter 1) provides a general introduction. In Chapter 2 our focus is on judicial development since Eritrea's *de facto* independence in 1991. This is done in the context of the distinctive characteristic feature of the Eritrean legal system, which is legal pluralism, and by way of outlining the sources of law and legal authority in a historical trajectory. In Chapter 3 we discuss the state of the rule of law. This entails critical analysis of the workings of the Eritrean judiciary, which is made up of civil courts, military courts, *Shari'a* courts and a Special Court. The focus in Chapter 4 is the absence of institutions of democracy that should have served as mechanisms of checks and balances to the unaccountable political power of the ruling party. In Chapter 5 the obliteration of civil society is discussed as one of the major challenges of democratisation efforts in Eritrea. The designation of Eritrea as an 'open-air prison' is explored in Chapter 6, which chronicles the dire situation of human rights taking place in the broad network of detention centres and prisons throughout the country. In Chapter 7 we discuss the most vulnerable segments of Eritrean society which are subjected to persecution of different sorts, political, religious and ethnic persecution being the most common features.

Chapter 8 deals with the policy and practice of the Eritrean government pertaining to ethnic diversity, particularly as manifested in two controversial areas: land and language rights. Taking this debate further, Chapter 9 analyses the persecution of the Kunama ethnic group as a specific case study highlighting the dire state of minority rights in Eritrea. In relation to this case study, we note that there are some other topical human rights issues that are currently articulated by other minority ethnic groups (such as the Afar ethnic group), whose academic merit grabbed our attention only at the very last stage of this book and are not covered in our study. These and other related issues should definitely make the focus of on-going academic and non-academic inquiry.

In Chapter 10 we expound in greater detail the core conceptual framework of our book, Eritrea as a garrison state. We do this by elaborating on the effect of militarisation on Eritrean society and by revisiting the arguments on totalitarianism and personal rule we have already clarified in the present chapter. In our last and concluding chapter (11), we point out some recommendations for improvement by reiterating the synthesis of our major findings.

Finally, there is another important feature of this book that we would like to highlight at the outset. A number of issues we discuss throughout the chapters overlap in a number of ways, thus creating a certain degree of reappearance of some issues in more than one chapter. This was unavoidable in order to present a coherent argument within each chapter, as one strand of information may be used to explain several other contexts in another chapter. Our Bibliography is strictly limited to standard academic works (books and journal articles).

2

Judicial Development in Independent Eritrea: Legal Pluralism and Political Containment

INTRODUCTION

The land of Eritrea has, over the centuries, been controlled by different powers, all of which have left an imprint on both official and informal sources of law and legal authority in the country. During the last century Eritrea has experienced five radical political transitions all involving shifts of judicial authority.[1] Consequently, in order to achieve a comprehensive understanding of the current workings of the judicial system and the rule of law in Eritrea, it is crucial to have knowledge about the historical trajectories of law in the country.

This chapter will thus first outline how the sources of law and legal authority in Eritrea have evolved historically. Thereafter the legal transition after military liberation in 1991 and *de jure* independence in 1993 and the constitution-drafting process will be discussed. Emphasis is put on how human rights issues have been handled in these processes.

SOURCES OF LAW AND LEGAL AUTHORITY

During pre-colonial times (prior to 1890), part of the Eritrean territory fell under the political realm of the Abyssinian state (Ethiopia). Eritrean highland society (*kebessa*) in particular was an integral part of Abyssinian feudal structures, as the governor paid tribute to the prince (*ras*) of Tigray, who was in turn subject to the authority of the king of kings (*neguse-nagast*), the emperor of Abyssinia. Hence, many of the customary sources of law still operating informally in Eritrea derive from, or are influenced by, an Abyssinian tradition. This is particularly relevant to customary forms of land tenure (Tronvoll 1998a). While this is the case with the Tigrinya-speaking Christian population of the highlands, this part of the country is also inhabited by the minority ethnic groups of Saho and Jeberti, both of which are Muslim communities. The major traditional settlements of Saho are in the former Akele Guzay region, mainly the towns and villages around Adi Keyh, Senafe, Hazemo,

[1] This chapter does not aim to give an elaborate outline of Eritrean history or the War of Liberation. For further discussion on this, refer to Kibreab 2008.

Quhaito, and the Soira and its surroundings. In those areas, the Saho ethnic group make up around 45 per cent of the population. In this society, the main sources of customary law feature strong influences of agro-pastoralist practices and *Shari'a* law (Mohammad 2013). The Jeberti live in the three traditional highland provinces of Akele Guzay, Hamasien and Seraye. They are governed by a combination of *Shari'a* law and Tigrinya customary laws of the respective communities where they traditionally reside (Hagos 2009). In many cases, the customary laws of the highland Christian population are discriminatory towards the Jeberti, as for instance restricting their access to usufruct rights in land.

The other Eritrean ethnic groups also have their own customary laws. According to Hagos (ibid.), there are at least seventeen written and four unwritten customary laws in Eritrea, from each of the nine officially recognised ethnic groups. Ten of the seventeen written customary laws belong to the dominant ethnic group, the Tigrinya of the highlands.[2] The remaining written customary codes are mainly from the Saho, the Tigre and/or the Beni Amer, the Afar and the Bilen ethnic groups.[3] In addition to the above seventeen written customary codes, Eritrea has a number of unwritten customary codes.[4]

The Italian colonial period (1890–1941) established Eritrea, within the borders existing today, as a definite territorial polity for the first time (Negash 1987). Italy constructed the modern institutions of statehood in Eritrea and developed the formal judiciary system. As in other colonies, a juridical distinction was made between Italian colonial officers and settlers, and the native population. In addition to laying the foundations of a modern Eritrean state, Italy also introduced a legal system with a robust bureaucracy and a relatively longer period of political stability in the country. For purposes of criminal law, all inhabitants of Eritrea, Italians and Eritreans alike, were subject to the Italian Penal Code. In civil matters, the Italian Civil Code applied only in situations where one of the parties was an Italian. The Italians recognised the application of *Shari'a* in certain matters involving Muslim litigants. Eritrean customary laws were also applicable in some disputes involving only Eritreans (Trevaskis 1960: 27). This period marked the beginning of modern litigation in Eritrea.

During the Second World War, in 1941 the Italian colony of Eritrea fell to British-led Allied forces. Eritrea was thus placed under the British Military Administration (BMA) pending an international decision on the future status of Italy's colonies (Eritrea, Libya and Somalia). The BMA

[2] These are: the Law of Logo Chiwa; the Law of Adkeme-Melga'e; the Law of Adgina-Tegeleba; the Law of Habtesilus, of Gebrekirstos from Dekiteshim; the Law of Shewate Anseba Zemat Tahtai; the Law of Siharti, Lamza, Wekerti, and Damba; the Law of Karneshim; the Law of Dembezan; the Law of Engan'a Atsmi Harmaz; and the Law of Enda Figrai Seleste Wa'ela Tsimaro (Timze'a Seraye).
[3] Described by Hagos as follows: the Law of Saho (Al-Qanun Al-Uruf Lil-Muslimin Akeleguzai Liqebail Saho); the Law of Sahil (Al-Qanun Al-Uruf Liqebail Sahil/Alam); the Law of Maria (Maria Tselim and Maria Keyh); the Law of Beniamir; the Law of Kil'e Mensa'e Fitih Mehari; the Law of Afar Bur Ali Med'a; and the Law of Bilen (Tarke, Tawke and the Twelve Tribes).
[4] The Law of Kunama (Buya); the Law of Nara (Buta); the Law of Bidawyet/ Hidareb (Oslif or Alsewalif); the Law of Rashaida (Med'a)

was only a caretaker administration for Eritrea as an occupied enemy territory following the principles of the Hague Convention of 1907. Basically, this mandated the BMA to 'govern humanely and maintain law and order' (Trevaskis 1960: 18-43).

After the war, the UN took upon itself the authority to decide the future of the former Italian colonies. In December 1950, the General Assembly voted to federate Eritrea with Ethiopia.[5] In accordance with the UN-controlled federation process, elections were conducted for an electoral college in 1952 which then again elected the new multi-party Eritrean National Assembly. The Assembly adopted the new UN-drafted Eritrean Constitution in July 1952, whilst Ethiopia ratified the federal act in September the same year (Iyob 1995: 87). The first Eritrean Constitution clearly stated that Eritrea should have internal autonomy, and the Eritrean Assembly passed laws applicable to the Eritrean citizens of the federation. Human rights were also incorporated into the Constitution, the 'idea of the citizen having any rights against the authorities being a startling innovation in Eritrea' (Smith 1955: 484). In the first years of the federation, several human rights cases were heard in Eritrean courts, and judgments were passed in support of the plaintiffs (Smith 1955). Soon, however, Ethiopia's expansionist ambitions led to the violation of the principles of self-administration, as the federal government – i.e. the emperor – intervened in internal Eritrean affairs. Finally, in November 1962, Ethiopia forced the Eritrean Assembly to annul the federation, and Eritrea was annexed as Ethiopia's fourteenth province (for various perspectives on Eritrea's annexation by Ethiopia, see Cliffe and Davidson 1988; Connell 1993; Gaim 1993; Iyob 1995; Negash 1997).

The Eritrean war of resistance against Ethiopian oppression commenced in the early 1960s, first spearheaded by the Eritrean Liberation Front (ELF). The current government party in the country, the Eritrean People's Liberation Front (EPLF), was a splinter group of the ELF and established itself as a separate organisation in the early 1970s. Due to a better military strategy and more popular political ideology, the EPLF quickly positioned itself as the dominant resistance front in the country. By 1981, the EPLF (with help from the Tigray People's Liberation Front (TPLF) in Ethiopia) crushed the ELF as a politico-military force within Eritrea and thus established a political hegemony defining the content and scope of Eritrean nationalism versus Ethiopia.

From the late 1970s, the EPLF functioned both as a liberation army and a government, as it built a parallel governance structure – with 'line ministries' controlling and administering the liberated areas (Iyob 1995; Pool 2001). The EPLF fighters, as well as civilians in the liberated areas, had to obey EPLF laws. Written codes and general norms were developed regulating life in the EPLF-controlled liberated areas of Sahel, and also a fighters' 'code of conduct' in relation to social relationships, gender equality, etc. The EPLF struggle was also conceived as a social revolution, where aspects of Marxist ideology emphasising equality were introduced to the highly segregated and hierarchical Eritrean society.

[5] UN General Assembly Resolution 390, 2 December 1950.

The EPLF entered Asmara on 24 May 1991, effectively liberating the country from Ethiopian control. A Provisional Government of Eritrea (PGE) was established, which immediately commenced the daunting task of establishing effective administration and rule of law through-out the territory. One of the first laws decreed by the PGE was the new Eritrean Nationality Proclamation (No. 21/1992), which clearly outlined the criteria of Eritrean citizenship as a prerequisite for participation in the upcoming referendum on independence (Iyob 1995). A UN-monitored referendum on independence was conducted in April 1993. The highly affirmative outcome of the vote (99.8 per cent voted 'yes' to independ-ence) paved the way for the formal declaration of independence on 24 May 1993 (Pausewang and Suhrke 1993; Tronvoll 1996). Just prior to the declaration of independence, the Central Committee of the EPLF discussed the formation of the first government of independent Eritrea, and decided to establish a four-year transitional government with the authority to run the country.[6]

The multiple politico-administrative and legal transitions in Eritrea's recent history have created a country with layers of overlapping legal traditions. As no full judicial revision has been carried out, laws from former regimes are still operative side by side with customary and religious legal traditions. Generally, however, Eritrea (like Ethiopia) follows in principle a civil law tradition, although some of its laws reflect a common law influence, as will be seen below. For instance, sections of the civil procedure incorporate practices from inquisitorial systems, and likewise for its criminal law procedure.[7]

LAW IN TRANSITION

At independence Eritrea adopted, with some amendments, the laws of the ousted Ethiopian regime.[8] This was done with the intention of maintaining law and order and avoiding an administrative-legal vacuum (Gebremedhin 2004: 5). A committee composed of senior liberation fighters was given the mandate to review the old Ethiopian law regime, in order to adapt the law to the 'current condition of the country' and to make it compatible with the 'values' and 'principles' of the EPLF

[6] Proclamation No. 37/1993 (see Iyob 1995).
[7] US Library of Congress: 'Introduction to Eritrea's Legal System', at: http://loc.gov/law//help/eritrea.html, accessed 12 June 2012.
[8] The majority of the Ethiopian laws were drafted by foreign experts during the 1950s, under Emperor Haile Selassie. The inherited Ethiopian Penal Code (of 1957), for instance, was originally drafted by a Swiss law professor, modelled on continental penal codes under a civil law doctrine. The inherited Ethiopian Criminal Procedure Code (of 1961) on the other hand, was influenced by a common law approach, since an English jurist had, upon Emperor Haile Selassie's request, revised and reworked the original draft presented by the same Swiss law professor. The new draft Criminal Procedure Code is based on an adversarial system of justice of common law, but without jury trial (Rosen 2001: 86). For a discussion of the implications of the effectiveness of inherited legal systems on the rule of law in common law and civil law countries in Africa, see Joireman (2001).

(ibid.: 85). Apparently, very few amendments were carried out (focusing mainly on personal law, family law, law of succession and criminal law), and the only major change was to make the laws gender neutral by stressing women's equality.

After independence, the EPLF put emphasis on 'social justice' as a concept going beyond mere legal principles, in order to transcend class and other social barriers in the strongly hierarchical and diverse Eritrean society. Social justice, as it was theoretically explained by the EPLF, was instrumental in 'narrowing the gap between the haves and have-nots, ensuring that all people have their fair share of the national wealth, and can participate in the political, social, and cultural life of the country, creating balanced development, respecting human rights, and advancing democracy'.[9]

The basic principles of human rights were not emphasised in the law review; neither were procedures of due process and models of judicial independence. Apparently the Ethiopian codes were considered adequate in this respect. Beyond gender rights, the only human rights concern to be revised was a stronger protection of the rights of the accused in criminal cases (ibid.: 91).[10] The fact that the committee entrusted with the task of revising the laws inherited from Ethiopia was composed solely of EPLF fighters, excluding members of the legal profession and civil society in Eritrea, clearly restricted the scope and substance of their work. International legal experts were not consulted or invited to participate in the process at this early stage, contrary to what is normal in transitional societies. The EPLF/PFDJ government assumed direct and exclusive control over the schedule and substance of legal development in independent Eritrea. The incremental legal reforms carried out since independence can thus be viewed as a response to the economic and political development of the new state, and as symbolic measures undertaken by a regime which considers 'law as one of the most important means for reconstructing the past and projecting a new future' (ibid.: 6). However, on this basis, there has been criticism of the lack of clarity of the new state legislation, as it is sometimes not clear which law pertains to any particular matter (Favali and Pateman 2003: 58).

During the first transitional period (1991–1993, after military liberation but before formal independence), the Central Committee of the EPLF was the supreme legislative body in Eritrea (ibid.: 135). In 1992, a new proclamation established the structure, power and functions of the Provisional Government (PGE),[11] and outlined a formal division of power

---

[9] *The National Charter of Eritrea*, adopted at EPLF's Third Congress, 1994.

[10] The new Article 1 of the Transitional Criminal Procedure Code (amended by proclamation no. 5, 1991) emphasises a new purpose of the law in order to create the necessary breach with the legal regime of the past: 'The purpose of criminal procedure is to provide a just and efficient investigation and judgement, to ascertain the proper application of the law, to save innocent persons from unnecessary criminal investigation or court proceedings, to punish criminals; [and] to cause persons to comply with the law and fight criminal acts consciously' (quoted from Gebremedhin 2004: 94-95).

[11] Proclamation No. 23/1992.

between the legislature, the executive, and the judiciary. However, the proclamation authorised the executive branch of the PGE with law-making powers as well, and in practice all new legislation was initiated by the President's Office alone, or in cooperation with the line ministry concerned (Gebremedhin 2004: 135; Weldehaimanot and Mekonnen 2009). During the interim period, there was apparently no tension between the executive and legislative bodies in relation to law-making. This was probably because top EPLF/PFDJ officials held dual membership in both sectors of governance (Iyob 1995: 141).

After formal independence and international sovereignty were achieved in May 1993, a new proclamation (No. 37/1993) reconfirmed the structure, function and powers of the government of independent Eritrea and *de jure* maintained the division of powers between the three branches of government.[12] However, as shown by Weldehaimanot and Mekonnen (2009), on paper (law in books) law-making powers are nebulously shared by the executive and legislative branches. In practice (law in action), the powers have been usurped by the main embodiment of the executive branch, that is the Office of the State President. Since February 2002, the time when the Eritrean National Assembly (legislative branch) convened for the last time, Eritrea does not have a functioning legislative branch. The National Assembly was tacitly replaced by a sort of tripartite joint body, comprising the Cabinet of Ministers, regional administrators and army commanders (ibid.191). This decision, which made Eritrea perhaps the only country in the world without a functioning parliament, was taken unilaterally by President Isaias (ibid.: 136).

In order to create a new judicial framework for independent Eritrea inspired by the EPLF's nationalistic ideology – and as a response to domestic and international pressure – a full-scale law reform programme was launched in 1997. This came as a follow-up to the new, although unimplemented, Eritrean Constitution which was ratified by the EPLF/PFDJ-appointed Constituent Assembly on 23 May 1997. Under the law reform programme, *inter alia*, a number of new codes were drafted: Penal Code, Criminal Procedure Code, Civil Code, Civil Procedure Code and Commercial Code (Gebremedhin 2004: 6-7).[13] The new draft codes built on the existing transitional codes inherited from Ethiopia, but were all updated and revised in accordance with international principles of law (Rosen 2001). Only the draft criminal procedure code, was completely revised, however, due to human rights concerns which were not reflected in the old Ethiopian criminal procedure code (Gebremedhin 2004: 119 ff.). Apparently, the other codes were deemed to be adequate in their protection of human rights standards.

The drafting process of the new codes, creating the potential for a solid legal foundation for the rule of law in the country, was seemingly

---

[12] Proclamation No. 37/1993 (which repealed Proclamation No. 23/1992).
[13] The new codes were initially drafted by foreign legal experts and subsequently revised by local law committees appointed by the government (Rosen 2001; Gebremedhin 2004).

a sound and dedicated endeavour (Rosen 2001). However, due to the EPLF's monopolisation of political power in the country, the law-making process – no matter its sound judicial objective – would inevitably be criticised by segments of the population who for one reason or another feel ostracised from the process. Criticism has in particular been raised by the banned and exiled political opposition. More important, though, is the fact that the laws under consideration are not even formally adopted. The government still uses the old laws inherited from Ethiopia. Furthermore, some laws which the National Assembly has enacted seem to undermine or restrict rights and liberties enshrined in the Eritrean Constitution and in international instruments ratified by the country.[14]

Frustrating any overview or analysis of effective Eritrean laws is the fact that even the validity of the transitional codes, as well as other proclamations issued by the transitional government, technically ceased with the ratification of the Constitution in May 1997, as this marked the end of the government's transition period. Since then, the Eritrean juridico-political system has been in a *de jure* legal limbo, since the Constitution is not yet in force (Favali and Pateman 2003: 58).[15] Thus, in practice, law-making in Eritrea today is not a formal and technical legislative process evolving in accordance with established and transparent procedures. The president, in the name of the government, issues most of the laws, more or less by personal decree. The National Assembly, which is formally vested with sole legislative powers, does not, according to Yohannes Gebremedhin, 'even have the luxury of "rubberstamping"' new laws' (2004: 136; Weldehaimanot and Mekonnen 2009). Thus, both the formal law-making process and – as we shall see below – the implementation and protection of the laws, are arbitrary and inconsistently applied.

Paradoxically, the post-independence history of the legal system in Eritrea appears to stand in sharp contrast to the political history of the period, as the legal system – two decades after liberation – remains principally grounded on legal traditions inherited from Ethiopia, the customary laws of different ethnic groups and norms and value systems of the EPLF (Gebremedhin 2004: 77-78; Hirt and Mohammad 2013).

Establishing a legal status of government

Immediately after assuming power over Eritrean territory and the capital Asmara on 24 May 1991, the EPLF established itself as a provisional government by a number of essential laws, which it promulgated

[14] According to Amnesty International, these include laws governing religion (adopted in 1994) and the Press Law (of 1996). In addition, there have been regulations promulgated on the registration of religions (March 2002) and censorship of publications, performances and artistic representations by a Censorship Committee (2003), which both apparently are in contradiction with the Constitution (AI 2004).

[15] Usually, a 'ratified' constitution means that it is operative; if not, a specific procedure of enactment is stated in its preamble or ratifying act. The Eritrean government has stated that the Constitution will be operational after the first general elections to the National Assembly. No such elections have been conducted in Eritrea and the constitution remains unimplemented.

unilaterally.[16] Before it formally established itself as the 'provisional government', the EPLF had already proclaimed several other laws which came into force on 15 September 1991, about four months after the liberation of Eritrea. These laws are Proclamation Nos. 1, 2, 3, 4, 5, 6, 7 and 8 of 1991. They set in motion Eritrea's major transitional codes (such as the Transitional Civil Code and the Transitional Penal Code), which were all inherited from Ethiopia with superficial amendments. The most important laws regarding the establishment and legitimacy of the newly formed provisional government were promulgated a year after the EPLF liberated Eritrea. The essential laws that provided for the establishment and 'legitimacy' of the provisional government are the following.

The first such law is Proclamation No. 23/1992, promulgated on 22 May 1992. The official name of Proclamation No. 23/1992 is *Proclamation to Provide for the Establishment, Powers and Functions of the Provisional Government of Eritrea*. Its main purpose was establishing the EPLF as the Provisional Government of Eritrea (PGE) and laying a roadmap for the envisaged provisional period. According to the Preamble of Proclamation No. 23/1992, these provisional measures were to serve until such time as the country would conduct a national referendum on the issue of independence from Ethiopia, draft and ratify its first post-independence constitution, conduct free and fair elections, and accordingly establish a democratically elected government. For all intents and purposes, and judging from its content, Proclamation No. 23/1992 can be rightly described as making 'the first interim constitution' or 'the interim constitutional framework' of Eritrea. The EPLF's motivation to establish itself as a provisional government, without popular consultation with the Eritrean people, is implicitly indicated in the last part of the Preamble of Proclamation No. 23/1992, which reads as follows:

> Recognising that in this transitional period, the Eritrean People's Liberation Front (EPLF) continues to shoulder the duty it assumed to achieve the liberation of Eritrea, and that having achieved the liberation, it is inevitable that the EPLF proclaims the establishment of a provisional government,

> The establishment of the Provisional Government of Eritrea (PGE) is hereby promulgated.
>
> (Translated from Tigrinya)

From the above, it is clear that the provisional government traced its legitimacy from its historic role and mandate in achieving the liberation of Eritrea from Ethiopia. At that time, pragmatically speaking, the EPLF was the only viable political force that could have led the nation to its envisaged transition to democracy on a provisional basis, as envisaged by the Preamble of Proclamation No. 23/199. In fact, the EPLF liberated Eritrea with unparalleled military success and glory, including with a virtually untainted national reputation as the foremost liberation front of the nation. At that time, the entire nation was literally intoxicated by

---

[16] The following paragraphs heavily reply on a pro bono legal opinion written by Daniel Mekonnen in March 2013 for a UN special mandate holder.

the ecstasy of national liberation that was made possible by the gallant freedom fighters of the EPLF.

Seen against this background, there may not have been any better option for testing the legitimacy of the EPLF to lead the nation to the envisaged transition to democracy. One thing is clear however. Whatever the source of the legitimacy at that time, a government cannot rule a nation indefinitely without confirming its access to power via democratic and popular consultation, which most of the time takes place in the form of free and fair general elections. Twenty-three years after Eritrea's independence, such elections are yet to take place. Moreover, the popularity about which the government prided itself in the early years of independence has diminished significantly with the government's increasing repression, particularly after September 2001. In reality, liberation struggle credentials (regardless of fame and glory) cannot serve as a source of legitimacy for an indefinite period of time.

The period of time the EPLF envisaged for its provisional governance was not clearly spelled out in Proclamation No. 23/1992. As will be seen below, the shortcoming was rectified a year later by Proclamation No. 37/1993, a law which also repealed Proclamation No. 23/1992. At the time of promulgation of Proclamation No. 37/1993, one of the major objectives envisaged in Proclamation No. 23/1992, namely the national referendum for independence, was already achieved in April 1993. Accordingly, the Eritrean people overwhelmingly voted for independence from Ethiopia, and Eritrea was immediately recognised by the international community as an independent state.

It seems that the main purpose of Proclamation No. 37/1993 was to adjust the status of the provisional government in line with the political realities that transpired with the achievement of the national referendum. However, the provisional/transitional status and nature of the government was not altered by the new law. Purpose-wise, there was no major difference between Proclamation No. 23/1992 and Proclamation No. 37/1993. The core building blocks of Proclamation No. 23/1992 were retained verbatim in Proclamation No. 37/1993 and in subsequent legal notices that were issued in furtherance of the broader objectives defined by Proclamation No. 37/1993. Even the very title of Proclamation No. 23/1992 was simply copy-and-pasted onto Proclamation No. 37/1993. In effect, the official title of the new law changed only 'Provisional Government of Eritrea' into 'Government of Eritrea,' dropping the term 'provisional'. In the body of the new law, however, the essential features of the government as 'transitional' remained intact.

The language of the new law, Proclamation No. 37/1993, seems to have preferred the term 'transitional' to 'provisional'. Aside from such superficial change of terminology, the government envisaged by Proclamation No. 37/1993 was undoubtedly transitional. This is particularly clear from the 5th preambular paragraph of Proclamation No. 37/1993. It says 'pending the establishment of a constitutional government, there is a need for a transitional government which respects fundamental rights and freedoms.' [17] This is further strengthened by article 3(1) of the same law, which says: 'The name of the *transitional government*[18] of Eritrea shall be "Government of Eritrea" ...'[19] Similar terminology is used in Article 10. The time for which the government is established is also defined as transitional in Article 4(4), in addition to what has been stated in the Preamble.

In spite of the confusing nature of the terminology, the government envisaged by Proclamation No. 37/1993 was transitional by nature and temporary by tenure. The last two paragraphs of the Preamble of Proclamation No. 37/1993 are specifically clear about the legitimacy and tenure of the transitional government. The language used in this part of the law is exactly the same as that of the old law (Preamble of Proclamation No. 23/1992). The new law says that by virtue of the duty it assumed in achieving Eritrea's independence, the EPLF inevitably becomes a major role player in the formation of the transitional government.

There is, however, one very important element in Proclamation No. 37/1993, which gives it a markedly different tone from Proclamation No. 23/1992. Article 3(2) of Proclamation No. 37/1993 placed a maximum limit of four years on the tenure of the transitional government. It literally states: 'The tenure of the Eritrean Government should be for a maximum of four years.'[20] Read in conjunction with the Preamble of Proclamation No. 37/1993, the law clearly obliged the transitional government to draft and ratify a constitution and conduct national elections pursuant to such a constitution, at the very latest by the end of the four-year period. Accordingly, the tenure of the transitional government effectively ended in May 1997, exactly four years after the promulgation of Proclamation No. 37/1993.

In May 1997, the transitional government finalised one of the core tasks envisaged by Proclamation No. 37/1993, namely drafting and ratification of the first post-independence constitution. For some obscure reason, the government did not put the constitution into effect immediately after its ratification. It also did not conduct free and fair general elections as envisaged by Proclamation No. 37/1993. Exactly a year after the ratification of the 1997 Constitution, the country was plunged into a two-year devastating border conflict with Ethiopia. Since the outbreak of the war, the government has been ruling the country under a *de facto* state of emergency. One clear point is that by the time the government went to war with Ethiopia it had never had a legitimate mandate to do so; neither did it have any legal authority to rule the country after 1997. On the contrary, it has been ruling the country for the last 17 years without any legal mandate. Almost for the entirety of this period (15 years out of the 17-year illegitimate hold on power) the government is ruling the country under a *de facto* state of emergency. What is important is that it

[17] The Tigrinya version reads: "ከሳብ ቅዋማዊ መንግስቲ ዝቆውም፤ መሰረታዊ መሰላትን ናጽነታትን ዘኽብር ናይ መስገገሪ እዋንን ናይ መሰገገሪ እዋን መንግስትን ስለዘድሊ...."
[18] Emphasis added.
[19] The Tigrinya version reads: "ናይ መስገገሪ እዋን መንግስቲ ኤርትራ ስም 'መንግስቲ ኤርትራ' ኮይኑ ..."
[20] The Tigrinya version reads: "ዕድመ መንግስቲ ኤርትራ እንተነውሐ አርባዕተ ዓመት ይኸውን።"

also did not hold its own party congress which was well overdue by the time Eritrea and Ethiopia went to war in 1998. The last organisational congress of the PFDJ was also held in 1994. By all measurements - legal and political—the government in power is an illegitimate political entity (in the period that runs since 1997). The government is simply forcing itself on the Eritrean people by brute force.

DOMESTIC SOURCES OF LAW

Based on its peculiar politico-historical development, legal pluralism prevails in Eritrea in the sense that there exist several socio-political bodies which produce laws or represent legal authority. The formal state authorities, ethnic groups, religious groups, the norm and value system of the EPLF, and international society all influence one way or another the formal legal regime in the country (Favali and Pateman 2003: 2). It is important to note, however, that this is basically a theoretical discussion aloof from the 'practice of law', which totally disregards the written or theoretical legal regime (as the next chapters will illustrate).

The official sources of law can formally be ranked in accordance with their stature.[21] The Eritrean Constitution ratified in 1997, but awaiting implementation, theoretically rests at the top of the hierarchy of Eritrean laws. The modified transitional codes inherited from Ethiopia together with new proclamations compiled by the National Assembly and signed by the government/president are next in the hierarchy. Thereafter follow legal notices issued by line ministries pursuant to powers delegated under the proclamations. Both proclamations and legal notices formally enter into force from the day of their publication in the official gazette, *Gazeta Awajat Eritra.*[22]

In a 2009 study, Weldehaimanot and Mekonnen (2009: 108-181) surveyed over 225 proclamations and legal notices promulgated since Eritrea's *de facto* independence in 1991. Of these laws, more than 62% were issued in the name of the Government of Eritrea, and around 29% in the name of ministers, government officials and departments, such as the National Bank of Eritrea. At the time of writing, the latest two proclamations issued by the Eritrean government are Proclamations No. 173/2013 and 174/2013. The former deals with foreign currency exchange and the latter deals with the establishment of a new government organ, called the Land Transport Authority. In the absence of a functioning legislative branch (the National Assembly), it remains enigmatic under whose authority these laws are promulgated, strengthening the claim we make elsewhere in this work that the country has indeed become a totalitarian state.

At the bottom of the law hierarchy sit administrative acts, directives

---

[21] This 'ranking' is adapted from US Library of Congress: 'Introduction to Eritrea's Legal System', at: http://loc.gov/law//help/eritrea.html, accessed 12 June 2012.
[22] *Gazeta Awajat Eritra* superseded the Ethiopian *Negarit Gazeta* in 1991 (Proclamation No. 9/1991).

and regulations issued by ministries and other public authorities. Of particular importance are regulations and directives issued by military authorities in the country, as the prominence of the army and security forces are increasing as a consequence of the profound militarisation of Eritrean society. However, since the president functions as the premier de facto law-making body in the country, official statements issued by his office are likely to overrule all other legislation. Additionally, the president's personal and informal intervention and statements regarding principles of law may also carry more weight than formally-adopted proclamations.[23] This overview of the sources of law in the country is thus more of a theoretical abstraction than an empirical reality.

Customary law

Beyond the official sources of law, both customary[24] and religious law play an important part in contemporary Eritrean society. Although customary or traditional law is not in itself recognised as an official source of law in Eritrea, it nevertheless plays an important complementary role in the formal legal system through incorporation. Furthermore, in the highly traditional and predominantly rural Eritrean society, customary law enjoys great importance in the everyday life of villagers (Tronvoll 1998a; Favali and Pateman 2003; Hagos 2009; Mohammad 2013). There are multiple sources of customary law in Eritrea, both written and oral, with variations along ethnic, clan and regional lines, anchored both in cultural and religious rationalities (for a schematic overview, see Favali and Pateman 2003: 20-38; Keika and Asmerom n.d.; Hagos 2009).

Tigrinya-speaking Eritreans usually refer to their customary laws as the 'law of the forefathera/ancestral home' (hiegi endabba). The laws are generally developed through a consensus-oriented process, where male inhabitants of an area agree to a certain set of procedures and rules to regulate their legal relations, such as marriage or vengeance, access to land, and property rights over houses and livestock. As such, the process is hardly 'democratic' as it excludes women, newcomers to the area, and certain despised groups (such as smiths and tanners), but nevertheless reflects and represents a broadly popular demotic consent.

The lack of uniformity of customary law in Eritrea makes the blanket application of customary law impossible. Due to a shortage of professional legal experts in the country, however, President Isaias Afwerki early on encouraged the use of customary law in order to ease the pressure on the formal judiciary by 'introducing the practice of solving legal cases out of court through the intervention of village elders, families or relatives'.[25] Reportedly, customary law maintains an important role in relation to the formal legal system through informal incorporation in new legislation. For instance, while the age of maturity according to

---

[23] Reportedly, President Isaias Afwerki has on several occasions intervened in court proceedings in favour of the accused in cases involving veterans of the war of independence or individuals close to the EPLF 'culture'.

[24] In the meaning of traditional 'cultural' codes and norms.

[25] Interview with President Isaias Afwerki published in the government daily, *Eritrea Profile*, 7 March 1998, p. 3.

the Civil Code is 18, the amended article 581[27] of the Civil Code tacitly acknowledges the permissibility of engagement (but not marriage) at the age of 15. This is a reflection of some aspects of Eritrean customary marriage practice.

Furthermore, the establishment of Community Courts in 2003 with the mandate to apply customary law as a supplement to other laws is further testimony to the importance of customary law in Eritrea. The establishment of the Community Courts may also be seen as a consequence of the political crack-down in the aftermath of the Ethiopian war (see Chapter 4), as new formal legislation has been put on hold for a considerable period of time and the government seems 'resigned and willing to allow more space for other legal actors to manoeuvre' (Favali and Pateman 2003: 8). In other words, the majority of Eritrean-trained lawyers have fled the country, are serving in the armed forces, or languishing in detention; consequently the formal judicial system is severely understaffed.

Religious law

Eritrean society is also deeply religious, and Christianity, Islam and traditional beliefs have co-existed for centuries. Religious institutions are also important in producing and overseeing law which regulates individual as well as collective behaviour. The Orthodox (Coptic) Church in Eritrea has a prominent role in the highland villagers' life, as this is the predominant faith of the Tigrinya speakers.[26] Traditionally, the Orthodox Christian society of Eritrea (and Ethiopia) was guided by the *Fewuse Menfessawi* ('Canonical Penance') and later *Fetha Negest*, the 'Law of the King' (Jembere 1998: 183-190). These laws were compiled during the reign of Emperor Zära Yaeqob (1434–1468 CE) in order to bridge the many customary law regimes existing in his realm. The emperor thus ordered the Ethiopian Orthodox Church to compile an authoritative written law (the 'Canonical Penance'), whose major sources were religious precepts advanced by the Church (Jembere 1998: 183-84). The emperor was not satisfied with the limited scope of the basically spiritual code, as it did not deal with the prevalent legal issues. A new code was thus suggested, the 'Law of Kings' used by the Coptic Church of Alexandria, which was translated from Arabic to Ge'ez.[27] The origin of this code is disputed (Jembere 1998: 185-189); however, some claim that it was originally compiled by an Egyptian scholar in the mid-thirteenth century, based on more ancient texts of Syrian/Roman origin (Favali and Pateman 2003: 33). It is plausible that the *Fetha Negest* has had an influence on the development of customary law in the Orthodox society in Eritrea, although in practical use its value was meagre. More than a legal code for everyday life, some argue that it was a quasi-religious text used

---

[26] The Catholic and Protestant Churches are also represented in the highlands, as well as new evangelical churches (Pentecostal). A small group of Tigrinya-speakers are Muslims (the Jeberti).

[27] Ge'ez is an ancient Ethiopian language (Semitic) which is still used as the liturgical language of the Orthodox Church.

to give legitimacy to the authority of the state and the emperor (Favali and Pateman 2003: 33).[28]

Whatever the case, the clergy of the Orthodox Church wield an important influence in village affairs in modern Eritrea, as they are held in high esteem due to their holy work. The village priests may also impose penalties on villagers who violate the law of the Church, as, for instance, ploughing the fields on religious non-working days.[29] This penalty may be in the form of a fee to the Church, in kind (i.e., grain) or in money, or that the violator has to offer a specific number of prayers in the Church. Beyond the village priest, it is also believed that God may punish any villager who disobeys his law, by destroying the harvest by 'hailstorms, locusts, army worms or things like that', as it was explained by a villager (Tronvoll 1998a: 169).

The Muslim groups in Eritrea also follow *Shari'a* law. *Shari'a* law is recognised in Muslim areas of the country to regulate certain civil and family law matters, which are enforced through separate *Shari'a* chambers in the civil court system.[30] Eritrean Muslims are Sunnis and overwhelmingly Sufis. Three out of the four Sunni schools are present in the country.[31] *Shari'a* law has also been influenced by customary law and traditions, and the adherence to the religious law varies considerably between the Eritrean groups. The Afar and Kunama, for example, allegedly have a slightly more esoteric perception of Islamic culture, influencing their interpretation of Quranic precepts such as fasting (Favali and Pateman 2003: 35). With the growth of *salafism* and political Islam in the Horn of Africa, it seems likely that *Shari'a* law will increase its importance among Eritrean Islamic communities (Østebø 2008).[32]

Finally, among some of the Eritrean ethnic groups, there are individuals believed to be endowed with special powers to communicate with the spirit worlds (shaman cults), or who possess some other specific quality which makes them ritual leaders. These individuals may prescribe rules that influence or regulate social behaviour, like, for instance, the traditional peacemakers among the Kunama group, the *Sanga-Na'ne*

[28] The *Fetha Negest* was formally incorporated into the legal system of Ethiopia in 1908 by Emperor Menelik II, and the criminal provisions of the law were applied in Ethiopia until they were replaced by the 1930 Penal Code (Jembere 1998). In order to make proper deference to this historical legacy, Emperor Haile-Selassie referred to the *Fetha Negest* in the Penal Code, 'in order to avoid the accusation that he wanted to change, through codification, established religious and traditional rules' (Favali and Pateman 2003).

[29] The Orthodox Church prescribes that saints' days should be revered as non-working days. There may be as many as three or four saints' days per week (for an overview of the Orthodox religious calendar and its implications on the peasantry, see Tronvoll 1998: 166-169).

[30] Cf. US Library of Congress: 'Introduction to Eritrea's Legal System', at: http://loc.gov/law//help/eritrea.html, accessed 12 June 2012

[31] The Maleki school is the largest (65 per cent), followed by Hanafi (26 per cent) and Shafi'i (9 per cent) (Favali and Pateman 2003: 34-35).

[32] Some Eritrean opposition movements are allegedly fighting for an Islamic state in Eritrea. However, their overall importance, and politico-military capacity, seems rather limited (Connell 2005). If President Isaias Afwerki remains in power, political Islam may be used as a mobilising factor against him.

(see Chapter 9). Traditional beliefs may thus also be sources of law and authority in the local community.

Judicial development in independent Eritrea seems to embody both political and legal contradictions. Apparently, legal pluralism is used deliberately to diffuse and dilute a coherent system of law which might effectively be used to establish a sound juridical foundation for legal accountability and proper mechanisms and procedures of the rule of law. In effect legal pluralism has been used as a tool for political containment by the regime, which is itself the worst violator of the country's laws.

THE MAKING OF THE ERITREAN CONSTITUTION

The Constitution of independent Eritrea was ratified on 23 May 1997 by the Constituent Assembly.[33] In principle, and as is conventional, it is thus a legally binding document, since the Constitution does not incorporate any specific date on which it should come into effect, nor is any specific procedure outlined in its preamble for its proper implementation. However, government officials have explained that the Constitution will come into effect once new elections for the National Assembly are conducted (Connell 2007). Initially scheduled for 1998, the elections have been repeatedly delayed by the government, first due to the outbreak of the new war and then subsequently due to the post-war dissent process (see Chapters 4 and 5 for elaboration). President Isaias Afwerki announced in May 2008 that elections would be postponed for 'three or four decades' or longer because they 'polarise society' vertically (Al Jazeera Interview 2008). The apparent formal implementation of the Eritrean Constitution is thus a distant event. Contradicting long-held views, government officials are lately claiming that certain aspects of the Constitution are actually implemented. A point in case is a speech delivered in May 2013 in Washington by Yemane Gebreab, the head of the political affairs department of the PFDJ and a presidential adviser.[34]

The constitution-drafting process aroused public debate, but the ratification event was not much celebrated, and was carried out more or less unnoticed by Eritreans and foreigners alike. Considering the fact that the Constitution – more than a decade after its ratification – is not yet implemented, the lack of fervent festivities surrounding its ratification was warranted.

A commission mandated to produce a draft constitution was established in 1994, composed of 50 individuals handpicked by the EPLF and supposedly 'representing a wide spectrum of the society, ethnically and

[33] The Constituent Assembly, composed of 550 members, consisted of the EPLF/PFDJ-appointed interim National Assembly (parliament), members of the six Regional Assemblies and 75 diaspora representatives (Article 2, 'Constituent Assembly Proclamation', No. 92/1996, (27 December 1996).

[34] Mr. Gebreab's account was given in a public briefing of regime supporters in Washington, DC. A copy of the audio is available on file with authors (http://www.wust1120.com/Audio/Voice%20of%20Eritrea.mp3).

politically' (Connell 1997: 140).[35] It was headed by Dr Bereket Habte Selassie, a respected legal scholar residing in the US, with a background as the former Attorney-General of Ethiopia, who turned EPLF member in the early 1970s.[36] Equally important was the secretary to the commission, Zemhret Yohannes, an obdurate senior EPLF cadre.

The constitution-making process was seen as an integral part of the overall process of nation-building in the incipient country (Yohannes 1996).[37] A broad-based civic consultation process was carried out, where constitutional commission members visited villages throughout Eritrea, and Eritrean communities in the diaspora, to present and discuss key principles of the new Constitution: the separation of powers; the type of government; the role of the military and political parties; and how human rights should be protected and enforced (Connell 1997: 140). Seminars were further conducted with key stakeholders and constituencies, and the first draft was presented for public consumption in 1996.

Apparently, the process leading up to the draft constitution was carried out in an open and inclusive manner, despite the fact that the organised, and exiled, political opposition was denied representation in the process (Rosen 1999). The absence of a free press and organised opposition in the country, however, 'limited popular influence in shaping the content of the constitution' (Mengisteab and Yohannes 2005: 139).[38] Many of the suggestions and important revisions recommended by the public and commission members were reportedly not reflected in the final draft version (Hedru 2003: 436). Apparently, the secretary to the commission personally oversaw that the final version was in line with the interests and ideology of the EPLF/PFDJ, and hence it did not necessarily reflect the opinions and interests advanced by the Eritrean public during the process.[39] Criticism has thus been made of the constitution-making process on the basis that it was 'designed to legitimise the exclusive role of the EPLF' in drafting a constitution fitting for its future role in Eritrea (Medhanie 1994: 65; Hedru 2003: 436).

[35] Pursuant to the 'Constitutional Commission (Establishment) Proclamation', No. 55/1994.

[36] For Bereket Habte Selassie's own account of the constitution-making process, see Selassie (1998; 2003).

[37] See, for instance, the speech by President Isaias Afwerki on the launching of the work of the Constitutional Commission, reproduced in full in the government daily, *Eritrea Profile* (1994) vol. 1, no. 6, pp. 2 and 7. *Eritrea Profile* carried a number of articles on the constitution-making process between 1994 and 1996; see, for instance, a Q&A article titled, 'Constitution-making: A people's project', in the issue of 4 November 1995, p. 3; and an interview with Zemhret Yohannes, 'A constitution from the people to the people', in the issue of 26 October 1996, p. 2.

[38] Some Eritrean scholars characterise the constitution-making process as 'undemocratic', since the organised political opposition was banned from participating, and on that ground they dismiss the legitimacy of the Constitution altogether (Medhanie 2008).

[39] Interviews by one of the authors with Taha Mohammed Nur, Constitutional Commission member in Asmara, October 1996. Taha Mohammed Nur was arrested by the government in November 2005, without any formal charges being made. He died in prison in early 2008 (see www.awate.com, 16 February 2008).

Human rights in the Constitution

The Eritrean Constitution does not explicitly make reference to the Universal Declaration of Human Rights, the Charter of the United Nations or the African Union's Charter. Neither does it incorporate any international human rights instruments. Its preamble, however, states:

> Convinced that the establishment of a democratic order, through the participation of and in response to the needs and interests of citizens, *which guarantees the recognition and protection of the rights of citizens*, human dignity, equality, balanced development and the satisfaction of the material and spiritual needs of citizens, is the foundation of economic growth, social harmony and progress. (Emphasis added)

In Chapter 3 of the Constitution, titled 'Fundamental Rights, Freedoms and Duties', explicit and prominent references are made to protection of fundamental human rights and freedoms and the rule of law. These human rights articles must be considered to be in force (as they also form part of international customary law) and are thus not dependent on the institution-building and democratisation measures not yet implemented, although the latter could be expected to provide fuller protection of human rights (AI 2004: 35).

Potentially curbing these articulated rights, however, and the main weaknesses of the Constitution, are the strong executive powers given to the president (Arts 42, 43, 46, 47, as well as Art. 27, the emergency clause). The executive power is constitutionally enshrined, seemingly without developing correspondingly proper institutions of checks-and-balances (Medhanie 2008). Furthermore, explicit constitutional limitations upon 'fundamental rights and freedoms' in cases of 'the interests of national security, public safety or the economic well-being of the country, health and morals, for the prevention of public disorder or crime or for the protection of the rights and freedoms of others' (Art. 26.1), may in effect constitute a clear breach of international standards.[40]

Constitutional rights related to the rule of law

The fundamental *rights to life and liberty* (Art. 15), as well as human dignity (Art. 16), are guaranteed as constitutional safeguards against torture or other inhumane treatment or punishment (Art. 16.2). Article 16.3 also prohibits slavery and forced labour. Likewise the right to privacy is protected (Art. 18.1) and 'no person shall be subjected to unlawful search' (Art. 18.2).

Important safeguards against *arbitrary detention* are provided, such as that no person shall 'be deprived of liberty without due process of law' (Art. 15.2) or 'be arrested or detained save pursuant to due process of law' (Art. 17.1). If detained, the detainee 'shall be brought before a court of law within 48 hours of his arrest [...] and no such person shall be held in custody beyond such period without the authority of the court'

---

[40] This clause was used by the government in its communication with the UN Working Group on Arbitrary Detention and the African Commission on Human and Peoples' Rights as a justification for detaining top-level government officials and journalists in the 2001 crack-down. See Chapter 5.

(Art. 17.4).[41] Furthermore, both *habeas corpus* and the entitlement to a 'fair and public trial by a court of law' are guaranteed (Art. 17.6), with the presumption of innocence (Art. 17.7) and the right of appeal (Art. 17.8).[42]

If any Eritrean feels that his/her rights are violated, the Constitution guarantees that their complaint shall be 'heard respectfully' and that they should 'receive appropriate and quick answers' from the relevant authority (Art. 24.1). If one's rights or interests are interfered with or threatened, one has the right to seek due administrative redress (Art. 24.2).

Constitutional rights related to democracy

Article 19 of the Constitution is titled 'Freedom of Conscience, Religion, Expression of Opinion, Movement, Assembly and Organisation', and guarantees all basic freedoms necessary for an open society and a functioning democracy. Every person's right to freedom of thought, conscience and belief (Art. 19.1) is articulated, as well as the freedom to practise any religion (Art. 19.4). Freedom of expression and of the media is guaranteed (Art. 19.2). All persons also have the right to assemble and demonstrate peacefully (Art. 19.5), as well as to form political, social, economic and cultural organisations (Art. 19.6). Furthermore, any citizen fulfilling the requirements of the electoral law has the right to vote and to stand for election if they so wish (Art. 20).

Why a non-implemented Constitution?

Despite its ratification in May 1997, the Eritrean Constitution has not yet been implemented. Furthermore, the institutions required to give the Constitution full effect are not yet established either. Various reasons may be cited to explain why the Eritrean government and its president have denied the citizens enjoyment of the realisation of the rights enshrined in the dormant Constitution. The US-based Eritrean scholars Kidane Mengisteab and Okbazghi Yohannes suggest four main reasons (Mengisteab and Yohannes 2005: 151-159). First, and the reason usually offered by the regime, is that the implementation of the Constitution and all other politically liberalising policies must await the final settlement of the border conflict with Ethiopia,[43] since the current state of affairs is too fragile and threatening for Eritrea's sovereignty. Second, the problems of internal stability caused by the post-war dissent process and

[41] Article 59 of the Eritrean Criminal Procedure Code also places a maximum limit of 28 days within which an arrested person brought to court should be charged or released, although this is not adhered to in practice (AI 2004: 35; Mekonnen 2006: 38). AI not in bibliog.?

[42] At a more detailed level, however, Amnesty International points out that the Constitution is deficient in not clearly specifying the right to legal defence representation and that the right of appeal should be to a higher court of law (AI 2004). However, this point may be considered subsumed under the guarantee of 'due process of law'.

[43] This means Ethiopia must first give Eritrea the control of Badme village and other territories granted to Eritrea by the Eritrean-Ethiopian Boundary Commission. On the border war and subsequent peace agreement, see Negash and Tronvoll (2000); Nystuen and Tronvoll (2008).

the call for democratic reforms by EPLF/PFDJ dissenters (the so-called G-15) and others (see Chapter 5), have forced the authorities to disregard constitutional principles in order to reconsolidate their power. Third, the displacement of a large number of people by the war, and the massive destruction of infrastructure, in combination with looming drought and famine, has pushed the government to take drastic measures in order to concentrate first and foremost on providing basic services to the population. Fourth and finally, the decision by the National Assembly in its fourteenth session to shelve the draft party and election laws condoned the suspension of the Constitution. The excuse given by the government for this action was that the 'overwhelming majority of Eritreans did not support the formation of political parties at the time', and that the country was not yet ready for democracy (Mengisteab and Yohannes 2005: 156) (see Chapter 4).

Presidential advisor and top-ranking cadre, Yemane Gebreab, elaborates on these issues in an interview:

> The war created obstacles and in some aspects did not enable us to move at the pace we would have wanted to move. Now there is relative peace and even in the last two years there has been a lot of progress in terms of elections for local government. This time round there will be elections for regional assemblies etc. So wherever there is an opportunity, the government embarks on this process. But at the end of the day, survival is paramount. It all depends on whether we'll be allowed to live in peace or not. And if we have to postpone certain issues, then they will be postponed. This is not like baking a cake, it's nation building and what do we care whether something happens today or next year as long as the process is right.[...] Frankly our preoccupation now is whether we will have peace or war. That is paramount. You cannot see these issues in isolation. The way the country reorganises itself in times of hostility is different to when there is normality. The situation now is mixed. The clouds of war are still hanging over us. It's a question of priorities for a young nation.[44]

Caution is due when speculating on the true motives behind the Eritrean government's suspension of its own Constitution; however, the reasons offered in various interviews by President Isaias Afwerki and his closest accomplices do not appear convincing. Kidane Mengisteab and Okbazghi Yohannes' explanations seem more plausible in that respect, as they point to the internal nature of the Front's leadership and its political culture, nourished through decades of war, as the direct cause for the development of totalitarianism in the country (Mengisteab and Yohannes 2005: 157) (see Chapter 4).

The widespread political crackdown in the autumn of 2001 and subsequent decisions by the regime suspended all legislative and political processes leading to the realisation of the rights enshrined in the Constitution and additional international human rights instruments ratified by the Eritrean government. The two sections below, on constitutional rights and the international human rights obligations of Eritrea, are thus a mere theoretical exercise in order to present the formal judicial context of human rights in the country, and should not be read as reflecting empirical reality.

[44] IRIN News: 'ERITREA: Interview with Yemane Gebremeskel, Director of the President's Office' Asmara, 1 April 2004, at: http://www.irinnews.org/Report. aspx?ReportId=49359, accessed 6 January 2009.

ERITREA'S INTERNATIONAL HUMAN RIGHTS OBLIGATIONS

Beyond the Constitution, Eritrea is obliged to comply with a number of key international conventions it has ratified protecting the rule of law; most notably the International Covenant on Civil and Political Rights (ICCPR, acceded 23 January 2002), and the regional African Union instrument, the African Charter on Human and Peoples' Rights (ratified in 1999). However, other conventions of importance to the rule of law have not yet been ratified by Eritrea, including the UN Convention against Torture and Other Cruel, Inhuman or Degrading Treatment or Punishment (1984).[45] The Eritrean government, which after independence did not show any great eagerness to ratify international human rights instruments, apparently changed its strategy as a consequence of the new war with Ethiopia (1998–2000), and started to accede to international instruments as part of the propaganda war against Ethiopia.[46] Such a blatantly pragmatic approach to acceding to international human rights instruments will, of course, influence the government's interest and willingness to comply with the obligations enshrined in the very same conventions. In this respect, Amnesty International observes that 'international and regional human rights treaty safeguards seem to mean nothing in Eritrea', as they are routinely ignored or contravened (AI 2004: 36).

Eritrea was represented for several years in the UN Commission on Human Rights (until 2006). However, with regard to its treaty obligations, Eritrea has only selectively submitted its state party reports under those UN conventions deemed not 'threatening' to its political order.[47] The state party report under the ICCPR was due in 2003, but no action has been taken about this in previous years. The country submitted its first Universal Periodic Report (UPR) in 2009 and its second UPR is due in 2014 (Special Rapporteur 2013: 7). Previously, Eritrea also submitted a report to the CEDAW Committee. As will be seen in Chapter 11, in relation to the government's hyperbolic 'achievement' in MDGs, the government's reports on human rights practices are submitted for purposes of lip

[45] Neither has it acceded to the Convention's optional protocol, the two Optional Protocols to the International Covenant on Civil and Political Rights, the Optional Protocol to the Convention on the Elimination of All Forms of Discrimination against Women, or the International Convention on the Protection of the Rights of All Migrant Workers and Members of Their Families.

[46] The Ethiopians tried to undermine Eritrea's legitimacy and political posture during the war by claiming that Eritrea was 'undemocratic' and 'denied human rights', as opposed to themselves who had implemented a democratic constitution and ratified all major human rights instruments. To counter these accusations, the Eritrean government rapidly acceded to various international conventions, portraying itself as a 'law-abiding' member of international society. See Tronvoll (2009b) for an elaboration on the Ethiopian discourse.

[47] Thus far, Eritrea has only submitted four state party reports to the UN treaty system: under the Conventions on the Elimination of All Forms of Discrimination Against Women (reported in 2004); under the Convention of the Rights of the Child (reported in 2007) and under the Universal Periodic Review of the UN Human Rights Council in 2009 and 2014.

service, while the political situation on the ground remains extremely hostile to the enjoyment of fundamental rights and freedoms.

In the past, Eritrean and non-Eritrean civil society organisations, such as Human Rights Concern–Eritrea, Christian Solidarity Worldwide, Human Rights Watch and others have submitted alternative UPR reports to the UN Human Rights Council. The very appointment of the UN Special Rapporteur on the Situation of Human Rights in Eritrea was also a result of a continued campaign by these civil society organisations and other stakeholders. Eritrea has never submitted any state party reports to the African Commission on Human and Peoples' Rights, as it is obliged to do. [48] At the time of writing, Eritrea is said to have submitted a report to African Committee of Experts on the Rights and Welfare of the Child (ACERWC). In response to this report, consultations are taking place among different civil society organisations on the idea of submitting an alternative report to ACERWC.

Formal complaints and/or communications on human rights violations pertaining to the rule of law in Eritrea have been made on several occasions to various international and regional human rights mechanisms. For instance, the UN treaty body system has dealt with several complaints against Eritrea within the field of torture,[49] arbitrary detention,[50] and enforced or involuntary disappearances.[51] Also, the African Commission on Human and Peoples' Rights has issued critical decisions ('communications') against Eritrea on violations of arbitrary arrest and detention and lack of fair trial (see Chapter 5).[52] Furthermore, in 2005, the African Commission issued a separate resolution condemning the human rights situation in Eritrea and calling for the country to 'guarantee, at all times, the right to a fair trial, freedom of opinion and expression as well as the right to peaceful assembly' and the release of political prisoners in the country.[53] As a party to the AU Charter, Eritrea is obliged to receive fact-finding missions from the African Commission on Human and Peoples' Rights to investigate accusations and claims of human rights violations in the country. Eritrea has, however, repeatedly barred the Commission access to the country, and as of yet – despite several requests – no fact-finding mission has been undertaken.[54] Another

[48] See http://www.achpr.org/states/eritrea/ , accessed 11 July 2013.
[49] See: A/HRC/7/10/Add.1, 2008; A/HRC/4/33/Add.1, 2007; A/HRC/4/21/Add.1, 2007; E/CN.4/2006/55/Add.1; E/CN.4/2005/60/Add.1; E/CN.4/2006/5/Add.1; E/CN.4/2006/95/Add.1; E/CN.4/2006/6/Add.1.
[50] See: A/HRC/7/10/Add.1, 2008; A/HRC/4/27/Add.1, 2007; A/HRC/4/21/Add.1, 2007; E/CN.4/2006/55/Add.1; E/CN.4/2005/60/Add.1; E/CN.4/2006/5/Add.1; E/CN.4/2006/95/Add.1;
[51] See: A/HRC/4/41, 2007; E/CN.4/2006/56; E/CN.4/2000/64.
[52] African Commission on Human and Peoples' Rights, Communication 275/2002 – Liesbeth Zegveld and Mussie Ephrem v Eritrea; and Communication 275/2003 – Article 19 v The State of Eritrea (EX.CL/364 (XI)).
[53] ACHPR/Res.91(XXXVIII)05: 'Resolution on the human rights situation in Eritrea', Banjul, 5 December 2005.
[54] Videotaped interview with Commissioner Bahame Tom Nyanduga, special rapporteur on Eritrea in the African Commission on Human and Peoples' Rights (Dar es Salaam, 6 August 2008, conducted by Anna Little).

request to visit made by the African Commission's Special Rapporteur on Prison Conditions was also denied (Mekonnen 2009: 101).

Ultimately, the human rights crisis in Eritrea attracted the attention of the UN Human Rights Council in Geneva. In July 2012, expressing deep concern at the ongoing reports of grave violations of human rights by the Eritrean authorities, the Human Rights Council decided to appoint a special rapporteur with the mandate of investigating the situation of human rights in Eritrea.[55] The outcome and the future of this process will be further explored in Chapter 11.

FINAL REMARKS: LAW IN THEORY AND PRACTICE

Judicial development in independent Eritrea gives mixed signals on how to interpret and understand the interests and genuine will of the Eritrean government. The constitution-making process was in general relatively participatory and various constitutional issues were debated throughout Eritrea. The end result, however, seems to be a constitution tailor-made for the EPLF which vests strong executive powers in the president, and has weak institutions of checks and balances. The human rights components in the Constitution are adequate, but leave room for local interpretation. During certain phases, the government has seemed interested in establishing a proper judicial framework, for example during the law revision programme carried out in the 1990s, and drawing on a number of foreign experts; however, at other times opportunistic tendencies undermine an accountable and transparent process of law making. Moreover, the ratification of several international human rights instruments – as part of the propaganda war against Ethiopia – gives evidence of the pragmatic and opportunistic approach the authorities have to law and its implications.

Despite the existence of a theoretically adequate judicial framework in Eritrea, the value of the Constitution and supporting laws are rendered more or less irrelevant as long as the authorities do not implement them or enforce them in practice. As this study illustrates, the blatant disregard for the legal regime the government itself has developed illustrates the moral, political and legal demise of the once popular liberation front. This position also manifests itself in the absurdity of a government without any legal foundation to its operations. By the laws the EPLF/PFDJ itself established the government is defunct and therefore illegitimate.

[55] UN Human Rights Council, Resolution 20/20, UN Doc. A/HRC/RES/20/20, 5 July 2012.

3

Rule of Law(lessness):
The Special Court and the Judiciary

Rights are not things that are given or denied at will.
We all should understand that rights are earned through struggle.
Ms. Fawzia Hashim[1]
Minister of Justice, Eritrean Government

You have no right to ask!
EPLF security officer,
responding to a group of mothers asking about the unlawful
detention of their children (AI 2004)

INTRODUCTION

The young Eritrean nation was established in 1991 with one great drawback: its freedom was secured from a dictatorship by a Marxist-Leninist-inspired liberation movement which was devoid of democratic experience and which abhorred dissent and divergent opinions. The political culture in the country at the time of independence was thus moulded by decades of war and driven by a government whose policies were anchored in ideological doctrines which lacked any regard for human rights. Consequently, as is illuminatingly described by an exiled Eritrean academic:

> Eritreans became prisoners of the warrior culture that brought them independence. By the end of the first decade of independence, values such as dialogue, compromise and consensus needed to build a democratic society came to be regarded as symbols of weakness, even treason. (Hedru 2003: 436)

In order to understand how the contemporary rule of law(lessness) in Eritrea developed, one needs to understand how the Eritrean People's Liberation Front (EPLF) handled such matters during their long struggle to liberate Eritrea from Ethiopian rule. For instance, it is plausible to argue, as Gaim Kibreab elaborates, that the 'seeds of dictatorship' in Eritrea were sown already at the incipient stage of the EPLF in 1973 when an internal dissent movement (called *Menqaé*) was brutally

---

[1] From the official website of PFDJ, www.shabeia.org: 'Public Dialogue: Human Rights in Eritrea', posted 6 June 2006 at: http://www.shaebia.org/cgi-bin/artman/exec/view.cgi?archive=14&num=4553, accessed 5 November 2008.

crushed. This paved the way for the current leadership of Isaias Afwerki of the EPLF, which subsequently 'adopted violence and arbitrary detention without due process as major means of dealing with internal dissent' (Kibreab 2008: 277).

A war of liberation is not won by democratic means and open deliberation of politico-military strategies, but through stern leadership willing to sacrifice its own supporters, and annihilate opponents of all kinds. The EPLF leadership under Isaias Afwerki embodied such characteristics, and internal dissent was ruthlessly crushed. No initiative or process was allowed to operate autonomously and the leadership centralised all power at the top of the organisation. The security apparatus constantly surveyed individuals or groups questioning decisions by the leadership and brutally eliminated perceived opponents both internal and external to the Front (Kibreab 2008: 277-291). When such operational rigorousness in pursuing political goals is matched with pragmatic and opportunistic qualities in relation to legal principles – and anchored in a society with a politico-historical tradition of authoritarianism and inequality – the resulting process of developing the rule of law in independent Eritrea was side-tracked at its start.

When the EPLF took power in May 1991, the same perceptions and the negative attitudes towards political pluralism, transparency and human rights held by the leadership, moved into the government offices. Although some alternative voices were heard, they did not manage to swat or modify the ingrained political culture wielded by President Isaias Afwerki and his loyal supporters. The informal legal culture of the EPLF defined 'rights' and 'duties' differently in relation to an individual's status (the main distinction being between fighters and civilians) (Gebremedhin 2004: 103).[2] 'Rule of law' was thus understood as defined by the EPLF and in relation to the so-called peculiar history of the Eritrean struggle, and not in accordance with universal principles and international human rights standards. In the view of the UN,[3] on the other hand, a country's national legislation constitutes the legal framework both for the realisation and enjoyment of human rights and for the activities of the promotion and protection of human rights. The duty-bearer in relation to respecting, promoting, and protecting human rights is the state. Individuals, groups and institutions of civil society all have a role to play in protecting and implementing human rights,[4] but the main responsibility rests with the government in power.

A lenient and perhaps naïve international society, content with the 'final' end of the troublesome Eritrean issue in international politics, applauded the stern principles of self- reliance and nationalism expressed

[2] Aspects of ethnicity and religion also influenced the 'ranking' of citizens in the post-independence period (see chapters 7, 8, and 9).
[3] See the Declaration on the Right and Responsibility of Individuals, Groups and Organs of Society to Promote and Protect Universally Recognized Human Rights and Fundamental Freedoms, UN General Assembly, A/RES/53/144, 8 March 1999.
[4] Cf. UN Commission on Human Rights, E/CN.4/2005/61/Add.1, 15 March 2005, Sixty-first session, Agenda item 11(e).

by the EPLF at independence, as it marked the dawn of a 'new gen-eration' of African leadership[5] hitherto considered to be donor-driven and corrupt. Hence, since the international community applauded the EPLF's 'model of development', no checks and balances on the omnipresent power of the top EPLF leadership existed. It was thus allowed to evolve into the current state of affairs – a one-man dictatorship antithetic to the rule of law. In Freedom House's index of the category of 'Rule of Law', Eritrea receives an extremely weak score of 0.71, out of a possible best performance score of 7.00.[6] In the 2011 *Worst of the Worst* report by Freedom House, Eritrea achieved a lower score than that of 2007, which was 0.27. According to this report, Eritrea is one of nine most repressive states in the world (Freedom House 2011).

This chapter will assess the workings of the judiciary in Eritrea, and critically examine the administration of the civil, military and the special court through the requirements of a rule of law-abiding system of gov-ernment. For purposes of clarity, we adopt the definition of 'rule of law' provided by the UN Secretary General, a definition which is aptly framed in the context of conflict and post-conflict societies. By 'rule of law' then, we mean the following:

> a principle of governance in which all persons, institutions and entities, public and private, including the State itself, are accountable to laws that are publicly promulgated, equally enforced and independently adjudicated, and which are consistent with international human rights norms and standards. It requires, as well, measures to ensure adherence to the principles of supremacy of law, equality before the law, accountability to the law, fairness in the application of the law, separation of powers, participation in decision-making, legal certainty, avoidance of arbitrariness and procedural and legal transparency. (UN Secretary General 2004)

THE ERITREAN JUDICIARY

The Eritrean Constitution (Article 48) and laws declare the Eritrean judiciary (*Ferdawi Akal*) independent from both the parliament (National Assembly) and the government.[7] In principle, the judiciary is mandated

---

[5] Isaias Afwerki of Eritrea, Meles Zenawi of Ethiopia, Yoweri Museveni of Uganda and Paul Kagame of Rwanda all came to power through violent means, but were – paradoxically – still considered by the international community to represent 'something new' in terms of political accountability and development in Africa.

[6] The score of the various indicators under the category 'Rule of law' are: 'primacy of rule of law in civil and criminal matters' scores 0.00; 'independent judiciary' scores 1.20; 'accountability of security forces and military to civilian authorities' scores 0.00; 'protection of property rights' scores 1.33; and 'equal treatment under the law' scores 1.00. See Freedom House 'Countries at a Crossroads' 2007 report, Eritrea chapter (at: http://www.freedomhouse.org/template.cfm?page=1 40&edition=8&ccrpage=37&ccrcountry=155, accessed 5 February 2009).

[7] Proclamation No. 23/1992 established the functions of the judiciary during the transitional period prior to formal independence. The judiciary was declared to be independent of the executive, but did not hold any powers to act as checks-and-balances to the non-elected executive or government (Gebremedhin 2004). After independence, proclamation No. 37/1993 established the structure, functions and

with 'protecting the rights (meselat), interests (rebhatat), and freedoms (natznetat) of the government, organizations, associations and individuals (Iyob 1995: 141). However, in its 2009 World Report, Human Rights Watch states that the Eritrean 'judiciary exists only as an instrument of control' (HRW 2009: 66), and Amnesty International reported in 2008 that 'there was no recognizable rule of law or justice system, civilian or military' in the country (AI 2008b).

International human rights reports on Eritrea all conclude that the judiciary is weak and subject to executive control (AI 2004; Connell 2011; AI 2008b; USSD 2008a; HRW 2009). Judicial corruption is widespread, and the EPLF 'fighter-culture' influences the outcome of court cases, as many of the judges are veteran fighters (USSD 2011). Further obscuring the role of the judiciary in Eritrea is the fact that the President's Office often serves as a clearinghouse for citizens' court petitions, where the president personally interferes in the court's jurisdiction, passing decisions based on personal favours or in accordance with EPLF 'fighter culture' and not the letter of the law (USSD 2011).

THE COURT SYSTEM

In principle, Eritrea has three types of courts, although their separate jurisdiction may at times be blurred; civil (three levels, including community and *Shari'a* courts), military (two levels), and the special court. Furthermore, there are indications that there exists a parallel secret system of extra-judicial sentencing of political prisoners that is not anchored in any laws or presidential decrees (AI 2004: 38).

The civil courts

The civil court structure in Eritrea has three levels of authority. The *Community Court* system was formally established by Proclamation No. 132/2003 to ease the pressure on the higher courts. It has a single-judge bench system filled by elected judges who hold jurisdiction over cases relating to minor infractions of the law, involving sums of less than approximately US$7300 (110,000 Nakfa) (USSD 2008a). The elected judges do not have any formal legal training, but base their decisions on traditions of customary law in the area in which they serve.[8] It is reported, however, that magistrates versed in criminal law also hear criminal cases at the level of the community courts (USSD 2011). All decisions made

---

(contd) powers of the Eritrean government, and ensures a division of powers between the executive, legislative and judicial bodies. However, the proclamation does not go beyond stating that the judiciary shall function independently of other bodies of the government, and it is not vested with the power to act as a proper independent check to other state or political organs (ibid.).

[8] The traditional village judge (*dagna*) was generally held in high esteem by the villagers, as he protected the 'inheritance from the forefathers' (i.e., the local cultural traditions), as well as trying to achieve decisions which restored peace in the village (Tronvoll 1998a).

by the community courts may be appealed to provincial (*zoba*) courts.[9] Most people's only contact with the legal system is with the traditional community courts (USSD 2008a). As the higher levels of the Eritrean judiciary are wholly inept and politically corrupt, the importance of the customary law-based village courts as providers of justice is increasing.

Before the establishment of community courts by Proclamation No. 132/2003, the courts in Eritrea were sub-regional. These were effectively replaced by the community courts, thus the latter have now become courts of first instance in several matters. In certain matters, the *Zoba Court* functions both as a court of first instance and as an appellate division for the appeals that ensue from the community courts. It has civil, criminal, and *Shari'a* benches. All first instance cases are heard by a single-judge bench system, but the *Zoba* Court has a three-judge appellate bench that hears cases appealed from determinations made by the Labour Office on employer-employee relations. The *Shari'a* bench adjudicates matters of personal status of followers of Islam only. Decisions rendered by any of the benches at the *Zoba* Court can be appealed to the appropriate benches at the High Court.

The *High Court*, although primarily an appellate court, is the court of first instance for a significant proportion of cases involving murder, rape, and other serious felonies (USSD 2011). It has a three-judge bench system with jurisdiction in civil, criminal and commercial cases, and *Shari'a* benches. Eritrea also has a five-judge bench that hears final appeals in lieu of a Supreme Court.[10] Although at the same level as all other benches in the High Court, the final appeals panel functions much as a Supreme Court does and it is the bench of last resort. The president of this bench is the president of the High Court and includes four other judges from the other benches at the High Court. In theory, the president of the High Court is envisioned as the equivalent of a chief justice in other jurisdictions (AI 2004: 37).

Professor Abdulkader S. Mohammad, a distinguished Eritrean sociologist and an insider into the *modus operandi* of *Shari'a* courts, notes that the independence of these courts (like that of ordinary courts) is gravely compromised by undue government interference ranging from political appointment of judges to interpretation of *Shari'a* law. This kind of political meddling has been a continuous challenge experienced by the *Shari'a* courts even before Eritrea's independence. Government interference is also seen in the appointment of Awqaf community members, Qadis and Sheikhs or Mo'azzin (Mohammad 2013: 316; Miran 2007: 111-112; Venosa 2007: 68-72). Moreover, at the appellate level of *Shari'a* courts, cases were heard for long time by the same judges who presided over the same cases at the *zoba* level, rendering the appeal a sham (Mohammad 2013: 316).

Although serving the civilian community, civil courts judges include former senior military officers with inadequate legal training (USSD 2011: 8). Judges are routinely appointed and dismissed at the will of the govern-

---

[9] '*Zoba*' is Tigrinya for province.
[10] Eritrea does not yet have a Supreme Court although the Eritrean Constitution (Article 49) envisages one.

ment, despite the constitutional requirement that such actions are based on the recommendations of an independent Judicial Service Commission (Articles 52 and 53 of the Constitution; AI 2004; Connell 2011; Mekonnen 2006). Such a commission has yet to be established in the country.

The Military Court[11]
The Military Court has jurisdiction over penal cases brought against members of the armed forces in addition to crimes committed by and against the members of the armed forces. The presiding judges in the Military Court are all senior military officers. The Court is structured in two levels (higher and lower); the jurisdiction of these two levels depends on the seriousness of the offences in question. Neither level, however, affords the right of appeal to the accused. The higher level of the Military Court is part of the Eritrean High Court.

The Military Court also functions as a political court in certain circumstances, as it also passes sentence on military personnel expressing criticism of the regime. For instance, after the so-called fighter rebellion on the eve of independence in May 1993 – when groups of EPLF fighters took control of certain venues in Asmara protesting against the unilateral decision of the government to prolong their unpaid service for another two years – 130 ringleaders of the rebellion were sentenced by the Military Court.[12]

The Military Courts embody an enormous – and unchecked – judicial importance in the country, considering the high level of militarisation of society in Eritrea, where about 600, 000 people are reportedly enlisted in the armed forces (regular and reserve army) (Bertelsmann Stiftung 2010: 2, 13; Connell 2011: 6). As a result, there might also be a blurred distinction in jurisdiction between the military courts and the Special Court.

The Special Court
The Special Court was established in 1996 by Proclamation No. 85/1996, in the aftermath of Eritrea's first publicly known corruption scandal in the mid-1990s, involving officials in the EPLF-owned Red Sea Trading Corporation. No published records of its procedures or cases are available, as the court generally operates in secrecy (AI 2002: 19). The rationale for the establishment of the Special Court was reportedly the impression that the 'moral values' of EPLF cadres were in decline after independence, as corruption increased when EPLF members assumed formal positions of power. An additional concern was the President's

---

[11] This section builds on US Library of Congress: 'Introduction to Eritrea's Legal System', at: http://loc.gov/law//help/eritrea.html, accessed 12 November 2008.
[12] This was confirmed by President Isaias Afwerki in an interview he gave to the government daily, *Eritrea Profile*. According to the President, as quoted in the interview, one of the fighters was set free and four were warned. A further 19 were dishonourably discharged from the army. The remainder were sent to prison; 21 were sentenced to a year and a half, 33 were sentenced to between one and a half and three years in prison, 36 to between four and six years, eight to six to ten years, and the remaining eight were sentenced to more than ten years (*Eritrea Profile*, 17 September 1994, p. 4).

wish for more stern measures against corruption than the 'lenient deci-sions' – in the eyes of the battle-hardened president – of the civil courts.

The judges of the Special Court are predominantly senior military offic-ers and EPLF commanders hand-picked by the president and accountable to his office only (Hedru 2003: 437; Connell 2011: 8). Their recruitment to the court is likely to be based on personal affiliations and loyalty to the president, and their proven 'toughness' in disciplining their troops. There are no formal requirements of judicial training or competence, and many of the judges have little or no legal training whatsoever (AI 2002: 19; USSD 2003). According to Hirt and Mohammad, the Special Court has three benches divided by themes: 1) general criminal cases; 2) corruption; and 3) illegal foreign currency exchange and smuggling (Hirt and Mohammad 2013).

The Special Court is an executive-controlled separate jurisdiction, not under the authority of the President of the High Court (AI 2002: 18). The Office of the Attorney-General decides which cases are to be tried by a Special Court (USSD 2008a). The Court primarily has jurisdiction over criminal cases involving capital offences, theft, embezzlement, and cor-ruption (USSD 2011: 9), and other unspecified abuses by government and party officials (Connell 2011: 8). The Special Court also issues directives to other courts regarding administrative matters (USSD 2011: 9). Allegedly, the Special Court has also tried cases of a political nature (AI 2004: 39), and reportedly supporters of the Islamist movement, Eritrean Islamic Jihad, and other opposition activists abducted by Eritrean security services from the Sudan and Ethiopia have been tried by the Court (Hedru 2003: 437).

The Special Court is bound neither by the Code of Criminal Procedure or the Penal Code, nor by precedents set by earlier court decisions. Judges generally base their decisions on 'conscience' – in relation to the particu-lar history of the Eritrean struggle and EPLF fighter culture – without reference to the law (USSD 2011: 8). The Special Court also has the power to re-open and adjudicate cases that have already been processed through the civil courts (USSD 2003). The Special Court can also over-rule existing court decisions and increase without limit the penalties for existing relevant offences the government regards as being inadequately prosecuted and punished (AI 2002: 18), thereby subjecting defendants to double jeopardy (USSD 2011: 8).

A number of formal and operational elements put the Special Court in stark contradiction with the Eritrean Constitution and laws, and inter-national standards of fair trial. Of particular concern is the fact that the trials are conducted in secret and do not allow for any legal representa-tion for the defendants. The judges serve as the prosecutors and may request the individuals involved in the cases to represent themselves in person (USSD 2011: 9). Individuals arrested under the Special Court are kept in detention incommunicado, usually in a secret location, and there is no time limit on pre-trial detention (AI 2002). After the court has de-cided upon a case, the detainee is transferred to an official prison or one of the many detention camps scattered throughout Eritrea (see Chapter 6). All decisions passed by the court are final and binding, as there is no appellate court. However, reportedly, in rare instances, appeals made to the Office of the President have resulted in Special Courts rehearing certain cases (USSD 2011: 8).

A few Special Court cases have come to public knowledge. One involved the senior EPLF cadre Ermias Debessai, a former EPLF representative to the United Kingdom, and, at the time of his arrest in 1997, Eritrea's Ambassador to China. Amnesty International reports that he was held for three years in pre-trial detention before he was brought before the court in 2000. The Special Court convicted him of embezzling government funds and sentenced him to seven years imprisonment. Amnesty International received allegations that he was prevented from presenting his own case properly and was unfairly convicted, possibly for political reasons (AI 2002: 19).

In 1997, the government daily, *Eritrea Profile*, carried a front-page story reporting on the cases heard by the Special Court. Up to the middle of February 1997, the Special Court had passed decisions on 1331 cases involving corruption, embezzlement and fraud. Out of these, 34 people were accused of abuse of power and 78 charged with 'drug dealing'. The court acquitted 360 persons, and set free 237 others with a stern warning. Furthermore, the court ruled that among 1279 individuals, some would pay a fine only, while others were sentenced to both fine and imprisonment. Reportedly, the highest penalty given at that time was 12 years imprisonment.[13]

In 1999, the Attorney-General of Eritrea informed Amnesty International that the Special Court was a 'temporary measure'; and the Minister of Justice reported that there were 450 people in detention awaiting trial at that time (AI 2002: 18). However, there are still no signs that the government is rescinding the Special Court, and the 2001 political reform protest has possibly convinced the President of the Court's continued importance. In August 2001, just prior to the mass arrest of EPLF reformists and civil society leaders, the chief judge (or President) of the High Court, Teame Beyene, was dismissed from his position after calling for the dismantling of the Special Court and complaining in general about executive interference in judicial proceedings (see Chapter 5).[14] He criticised the Special Court in particular for its 'illegality or unconstitutionality', saying 'No legal mind can condone and be comfortable with such a disturbing legislation' (AI 2002: 18; Beyene 2001: 10). While the Special Court was initiated with the objective of combating corruption, Hirt and Mohammad (2013) note that after 2005 cases which are regarded as 'politically sensitive' are directed to the Special Court.

---

[13] 'Special Court decides on more than 1,300 cases', *Eritrea Profile*, 12 April 1997, p.1.
[14] Cf. US State Department Country Reports on Human Rights Practices 2001; Human Rights Watch: 'Escalating crackdown in Eritrea: Reformists, journalists, students at risk', 21 September 2001; and Amnesty International 'Eritrea: Arbitrary detention of government critics and journalists,' pp.. 22. London: Amnesty International, 2002. See also Connell (2007).

Extrajudicial sentencing

Since it is impossible for outsiders to gain independent access to case information from the Eritrean court system, it is difficult to obtain a full overview of the structure and workings of sentencing in the country. Amnesty International has, however, been informed by released prisoners and other sources that some detainees have been sentenced to prison terms extra-judicially (AI 2004: 39). Allegedly, secret committees of security, police and military officers have passed judgment and delivered sentences after reviewing statements taken from prisoners after interrogation (and possible torture), and on advice from the interrogators. In these cases, according to Amnesty International, there was no hearing or opportunity for the detainee to present a defence or submit an appeal.[15]

Extra-judicial sentencing was put into practice immediately after the EPLF took power in 1991. According to Amnesty International, about 150 Eritrean officials and collaborators of the former Ethiopian military regime (Derg) were detained when Asmara was liberated in May 1991.[16] Apparently, the EPLF did not want to stage open trials of the former collaborators; instead they were administratively sentenced to imprisonment mostly for 10-15 years (AI 2004: 39). The Eritrean government admitted later that various people were being 'punished' after the EPLF takeover, for working too closely with the Ethiopians and because of their 'ossified [political] attitudes'.[17] Due to the secretive and arbitrary nature of extra-judicial sentencing, it is difficult to obtain verified information on the nature of such processes in Eritrea. Obviously, the practice of secret administrative sentencing contravenes the Eritrean Constitution and laws, and international human rights law.

One very common aspect of extrajudicial sentencing is a variant of detention without trial, which is manifest in the form of 'imprisonment by delegation'. This practice is commonly known by its Tigrinya rendition, *nay hadera*. The term means literally 'that of pledge' . In its ordinary usage, *nay hadera* denotes the act of entrusting someone with some responsibility on behalf of others; for example, entrusting others to look after one's belongings (personal items, valuable material, etc.) until such time as the owner comes back and retrieves the material or object from the entrusted attendant. In the context of detention without trial, the phrase denotes the practice of imprisoning individuals on the basis of verbal request made by others. In English, the closest that comes to this concept is 'imprisonment by delegation'. Individuals imprisoned under such circumstances are most of the time entrusted to the police by military or intelligence officers on the basis of a 'temporary storage

---

[15] These cases might also refer to the workings of the Special Court.

[16] The most prominent being Isaac Tseggai, former Chief Administrator of Eritrea, and Tesfuney Ma'asho, his deputy. Tens of thousands of other so-called collaborators, i.e. Eritrean women who married or had children with Ethiopian administrators/soldiers, were forcibly expelled from Eritrea in June/July 1991 and ended up as refugees in Ethiopia (the estimated numbers are 80,000–90,000).

[17] President Isaias Afwerki gave this explanation to Robert M. Press, an American journalist working for *Christian Science Monitor* in the article "Prisons of Free Eritrea Still Cage 'Collaborators'" May 6, 1993.

agreement', as if the police officer is taking charge of a commodity or a non-human object.

In many cases, individuals handed over to the police under the *nay hadera* scheme are kept in detention for an indefinite period of time until the person who handed over the individual to the police comes back and 'takes' or 'frees' the prisoner. The chances are high that the person who surrenders the victim to the police may not come back 'as promised' or with the lapse of time may completely forget about the victim, in which case the victim is condemned to remain in detention without trial indefinitely. In such cases, relatives of victims have to make use of their social networks in order to get information about the whereabouts of their missing family members and only if they are lucky can they eventually get hold of their loved ones. This practice often takes place when individuals fall out of favour with some high-ranking government, military or intelligence officials and are accordingly wanted to be punished for whatever acts, even when such acts are not criminally punishable. As in many other cases of abuse, there is no official control mechanism on this practice as well, highlighting the fact that the practice is tacitly tolerated by the state president and his close aides.

THE ADMINISTRATION OF (IN)JUSTICE

The unimplemented Eritrean Constitution states that the 'justice system of Eritrea shall be independent, competent and accountable' (Article 10.1); sadly the reality is far from this, as the 'administration of justice in Eritrea provides no protection for the rule of law' according to Amnesty International (AI 2004: 37). No doubt, the Eritrean court system is seriously inept, not only due to political interference as mentioned above, but also for the lack of resources and skilled personnel. The EPLF has never been dedicated to strengthening juridical academic knowledge and capacity-building *per se*;[18] 'fighter-skills' obtained through the war of independence usually out-rank scholarly expertise obtained through university education. Hence, the posts of judges and other formal positions in the judiciary are often filled by uneducated individuals drawn from the military forces.

Compounding this initial lack of legal expertise in the Eritrean judiciary is the drastic effect of the full military mobilisation in the country since the start of the Eritrean-Ethiopian war in 1998. The drafting into the army (through the compulsory national service programme) of court administrators, defendants, judges, lawyers, and others involved in the legal system, continues to have a significant negative impact on the judi-

[18] As a case in point, it can be mentioned that prior to the outbreak of war in 1998, the Norwegian Centre for Human Rights at the University of Oslo offered several MA scholarships in human rights law to students at Asmara University, with an expression of interest to enter into an institutional cooperation agreement with the university in order to strengthen its legal education programme and library. The offer, however, was rejected by Asmara University as it was not in accordance with 'their priorities'.

ciary (USSD 2002; AI 2004; UNHCR 2004; USSD 2011: 8). Consequently, in 2001, the High Court was reduced from seven benches to three, and the personnel of the *zoba* and community courts were reduced by 40 per cent (USSD 2002). Thus, beyond the political infringements, the lack of trained personnel, inadequate funding, and poor legal infrastructure in the country restrict the Eritrean judiciary's ability to grant accused persons a fair trial (AI 2004; USSD 2011). Public trials are held, but virtually no cases involving individuals detained for alleged national security or political reasons have been brought to public trial since the political crack-down in 2001.

Trial procedures
As described earlier, Eritrean law and the unimplemented Constitution provide safeguards and specific rights to defendants in the regular court system. Among other things, the law prohibits indefinite and arbitrary detention, requires arrested persons to be brought before a court within 48 hours, and sets a limit of 28 days in which an arrested person may be held without being charged with a criminal offence. However, this legal limit is routinely violated in regard to political and other arrests (AI 2004: 37; Mekonnen 2006).

Defendants also have the right in principle to be present during the trial and to consult with an attorney; however, many defendants lack the resources to retain a lawyer, and government legal aid is limited to defendants accused of serious crimes punishable by more than 10 years in prison (USSD 2008a; USSD 2010: 10; USSD 2011). Moreover, Eritrea is seriously lacking in qualified lawyers who can serve as defence attorneys in court; and since 2000 the government has refused to issue licences to lawyers wishing to enter private practice (USSD 2008a). Contrary to the Special Court, the High Court trial procedures formally grant defendants the right to confront and question witnesses, present evidence, gain access to government-held evidence, and to appeal against a decision. The US State Department claims that these rights were upheld in practice (USSD 2008a; USSD 2011: 10), an assertion disputed by other observers of the judiciary (AI 2004; Connell 2007). Nonetheless, the lack of juridical accountability among judges lacking formal training in law has undermined these safeguards, as court decisions are often based on the particular judge's 'conscience' without reference to the law (USSD 2011: 8).

There are no civil judicial procedures established for individuals claiming human rights violations by the government despite the fact that the unimplemented Constitution enshrines the principle of administrative redress for citizens whose rights are violated (Article 24). According to Amnesty International, there has not been any legal challenge or redress through the courts for violations of human rights (AI 2004). In the aftermath of the political crack-down in 2001, however, the High Court granted a *habeas corpus* application against the Prisons Commissioner in respect of the detained student leader Semere Kesete, who was allegedly not produced in court (AI 2004: 37). The president of the High Court was subsequently dismissed; and since then 'the *habeas corpus* safeguard against arbitrary detention has been defunct, with no lawyer daring to make an application and no court challenging any detention as unconstitutional or unlawful or contrary to Eritrea's treaty obligations' (AI 2004: 37) (see Chapter 5 for elaboration). In July 2011, for example, Esayas Isaac, the brother of jailed Eritrea-Swedish journalist Dawit Isaac, filed a writ of *habeas corpus* with the help of three lawyers, Jesús Akcalá, Prisca Orsonneau, and Percy Bratt, but there has never been any positive outcome (USSD 2011: 14). Thus, for the majority of the Eritrean population there are few remedies available for enforcing court orders or their rights. Persons affiliated with high-ranking party or government officials, former EPLF fighters and the rich, however, can use their influence with the court to secure civil remedies before the law (USSD 2011: 11).

FINAL REMARKS

It seems clear that the political ideology of the regime in Eritrea, both prior to and after the political crackdown of 2001, has inhibited the development of the rule of law in the country. In particular the workings of the judiciary have suffered, as executive interference and lack of resources have seriously undermined its operational independence. The workings of the Special Court are particularly worrying in this regard. The 2001 crackdown augmented this negative trend and basically rendered the Eritrean judiciary meaningless in fulfilling its stated and formal objectives. The concept of the rule of law is in fact antithetical to the reality in Eritrea today.

The idea of accountable government and leaders as enshrined in the doctrine of rule of law are alien to the prevailing Eritrean political culture. The challenge has been exacerbated by the total emasculation of the Eritrean judiciary. The Eritrean judiciary is the most enfeebled state institution in the country. With the arbitrary dismissal of the highest judicial officer of the country in 2001 – the then president of the High Court of Eritrea – the Eritrean judiciary has suffered an ever-deepening crisis of irrelevance. In the area of human rights and fundamental freedoms, the Eritrean judiciary has no meaningful role or power. The erosion of the rule of law is one of the primary reasons for the continued arbitrary practice of the government. As noted by the UN Special Rapporteur on the Situation of Human Rights in Eritrea, the utter disregard of the rule of law has deprived Eritrean citizens of their fundamental right to 'a transparent legal system to protect them from the arbitrary use of power by the State, other institutions and individuals' (Special Rapporteur 2013: 18).

4

Democratic Curtailment:
'Never Democracy, Always Control!'

Just as the People's Front [EPLF] had a clear vision during the liberation struggle that enabled it to realize the dream of establishing a free and peaceful Eritrea, likewise in the new post-independence period it had a clear vision for the future development of Eritrea. This vision aims at establishing a country where justice, democracy and prosperity prevail.
Eritrean Government, Ministry of Information, 19 April 2005[1]

What kind of country is that which everyday throws its sons and daughters to the furnaces of war? Whoever is spared from that is thrown in jail because they pronounced truth and demanded justice. Whoever escapes that fate is stranded in the diaspora, always suffering the distance, missing his country and living in hope of returning.
Mohammed Nur Ahmed, *former Eritrean Ambassador to China,*
Extracts from a letter sent to the Eritrean Ministry of Foreign Affairs[2]

INTRODUCTION

Eritrea today is a country under siege by its own government, the Eritrean People's Liberation Front (EPLF). The pretext of external enemies is used as an excuse to deny people their basic rights and freedoms of opinion and expression, to organise and assemble, and to practise their religious beliefs (Connell 2007; AI 2008b; RWB 2008; USSD 2008a, 2008b; HRW 2009; USSD 2009). The Eritrean government does not allow any alternative voice or opinion to be heard; all resources and people are mobilised and channelled into maintaining the country's totalitarian and militaristic structure. No private or independent press or media houses exist. Not *one* non-governmental organisation (NGO) is allowed to operate outside the direct control of the government party, the EPLF/PFDJ. The government even sanctions and controls all religious communities, and dismisses at will religious leaders who become outspoken or try to defend the rights of their fellow believers. Churches – and other civil society organisations – which the government cannot control are prohibited. Institutions and organisations associated with the sphere of 'civil society' plainly do not exist in Eritrea today. The government aims to

---

[1] Taken from an editorial at the Ministry of Information's webpage: 'Reaffirming our values', at: http://www.shabait.com/staging/publish/article_003357.html, accessed 26 March 2009.

[2] Cited from Hedru (2003).

control all sectors and actors of society through a total mobilisation and harnessing of the country's human resources in favour of its policies, or if that is not possible, incarceration and elimination.

The current context of human rights abuse in Eritrea did not come about all of a sudden, but originates in praxes and ideologies adopted by the EPLF during the war of liberation, and evolved progressively since liberation in 1991, culminating in the widespread national political crackdown in September 2001. The lack of democratic development and respect for human rights in post-independence Eritrea is as such not a unique case, it has developed in a similar way to many other Marxist-Leninist liberation movements coming to power by violence.

Comparative politics has taught us that the establishment and endurance of any armed liberation movement necessary to win the struggle against a suppressive regime has to involve extraordinary measures and stern strategies. In its formative years, the EPLF had to develop its armed capability and a strict politico-military hierarchy where no disobedience or alternative opinions were allowed to come to the fore (Kibreab 2008). A highly centralised and authoritarian organisational model evolved, where discipline, loyalty and political indoctrination managed to foster one of the most efficient and capable liberation armies in the world (Pool 2001). It must be remembered that the EPLF and its leadership not only fought the Ethiopian regime; they fought other Eritrean and Ethiopian resistance movements too, as well as internal dissent and competing leadership figures, in order to establish hegemony – internally as well as externally – within their political realm. The organisational 'purity' and monolithic ideology of EPLF was enforced from the top by a handful of dedicated men, led by the former liberation leader and current president, Isaias Afwerki.

The organisational supremacy of the EPLF, however, came at a cost. Individual autonomy, leadership accountability and organisational transparency were qualities which were deliberately ignored in order to concentrate solely on one goal: the liberation of Eritrea from Ethiopian domination. The civilian government established in independent Eritrea in 1993 was thus far from 'civilian'; it was a direct continuation of the political culture fostered during the liberation war. In the words of the Eritrean scholar Gaim Kibreab: 'the seeds of tyrannical rule and control-freakery were sown in the process of building a monolithic military organisation' during the war of liberation (Kibreab 2008: 214).[3]

This chapter will outline the gradual 'de-democratisation' of Eritrean society, as the EPLF constructed its structures of totalitarianism which denies democracy and the right to assembly in the country.

[3] Professor Gaim Kibreab's magisterial book of 450 pages, *Critical Reflections on the Eritrean War of Independence* (2008) is a ground-breaking critique of EPLF's development and the machinations of the Eritrean political elite. It provides a massive amount of information on the formative years of the EPLF and its internal conflicts and ideological positions. It should be noted, however, that it has been written in a context where the liberation front had already developed into a one-man dictatorship, i.e., current realities may have been projected back to interpret historical data. Although the book presents a plausible interpretation of the development of EPLF, it does not properly include and reflect upon alternative models and explanations.

'NEVER DEMOCRACY, ALWAYS CONTROL': DENYING POLITICAL RIGHTS

'Never democracy, always control' was a phrase used by a veteran EPLF liberation fighter to illustrate the enduring core interests and mentality of the EPLF leadership in the post-independence period.[4] 'The EPLF's political culture has long been predicated on secrecy and the exercise of absolute power, often by violent means', explains the American journalist Dan Connell, a long-term observer and supporter of the EPLF cause (Connell 2007: 3). Illustrative of this point is the fact that throughout the war of independence, the broad-based liberation movement was led by a clandestine inner party, called the Eritrean People's Revolutionary Party (EPRP).[5] This structure was established in the early 1970s and headed by Isaias Afwerki. Strongly influenced by Maoist ideology[6] and principles of 'democratic centralism', it worked as an inner decision-making unit, providing ideological guidance to the struggle and defining the premises for EPLF's operational policies (Connell 2001; Pool 2001: 91; Mengisteab and Yohannes 2005: 52-53).

In its formative years, the leadership of the EPRP also formed the leadership of the EPLF. The EPRP secretively conferred ahead of every important EPLF congress or gathering, deciding on the formulation of the EPLF programme and slotting the 'correct' individuals in place for so-called 'elected' positions in the EPLF (Connell 2007: 3). The EPRP was instrumental in the propagandisation and indoctrination of EPLF cadres. Through ideological training courses offered by a special cadre school to a selected group of particularly loyal individuals it maintained political control of all activities of the EPLF and its mass movements.[7] Disobedience or questioning of the decisions passed by EPRP was ruthlessly punished with long-term imprisonment and rehabilitation, or summary execution (Connell 2007: 3). The establishment of EPRP thus 'guaranteed the ubiquity of internal repression of dissent, unmistakably putting the trajectory of the liberation struggle on the classic road to dictatorship', observe the Eritrean scholars Mengisteab and Yohannes (2005: 53).

The clandestine workings of the EPRP were supposedly suspended in 1989, but the inner party was not officially abandoned until after independence in February 1994.[8] Its 'secretive pattern of rule' – possibly even sustained to this day – thus remained during the design of

---

[4] Interviewed in Asmara, 3 February 1997.

[5] Some translate it as the Eritrean People's Socialist Party.

[6] Isaias Afwerki underwent political training in China in 1968-69, at the height of the Cultural Revolution.

[7] The head of the political department of the party and the cadre school, the former Minister of Foreign Affairs, Haile Weldensae, was instrumental in organising this indoctrination culture of EPLF (Pool 2001). Ironically, he was still languishing in jail at the time of going to press, arrested by Isaias Afwerki in the 2001 crackdown.

[8] Isaias Afwerki disclosed this information during the Third Congress of the EPLF in 1994, when the military front EPLF was officially transformed into the 'civilian party', the PFDJ (Connell 2001).

post-independent governance policies in Eritrea, and the construction of state institutions (Connell 2007: 3). It should therefore come as no surprise that when the Eritrean government drafted its first post-liberation policy paper on 'State, Government and Party' in 1992 – discussing various models and theories of democracy and governance applicable to the Eritrean case – it concluded its deliberations with the following assertion:

> As has been seen in the experience of Third World countries, when political parties are influenced by religion or ethnicity, or when they serve the interests of foreigners, let alone to serve for democracy, they lead the country into chaos and destruction. Therefore, the question of democracy should not be seen in relation to the number of political parties established.[9]

The position paper was unnoticed by most local and international observers of Eritrean liberation; however, it should have been read as a clear warning of what was to come in the country.[10]

The first practical 'test' for pluralism through voting was the Eritrean referendum on independence, conducted in April 1993.[11] There was never any doubt that the overwhelming majority of Eritreans would vote 'yes' to independence; they had clearly articulated such a wish through the 30-year-long war of liberation. Thus, the EPLF could have opened the way for true and realistic alternatives (as they argued prior to 1991), i.e., to have ballots reflecting the three alternatives of 'independence', 'federation with Ethiopia', or 'integral part of Ethiopia'. However, when they organised the referendum process, the alternatives were only 'yes' or 'no' to independence, without defining the content of the 'no' alternative. Through an elaborate information campaign, the meaning of a possible 'no' vote became clear for the electorate: a 'no' vote implied a recommencement of the war and a prolongation of the people's sufferings (for elaboration see Tronvoll 1993b, 1996).[12] Furthermore, groups who were believed to be critical of the referendum process were actively suppressed, for instance, the Jehovah's Witnesses who were persecuted, arrested and stripped of their citizenship when they expressed that they would not register to vote due to their faith which prohibits them from actively engaging in politics (see Chapter 7). Other parts of the Eritrean

---

[9] Provisional Government of Eritrea: *State, Government and Party*, issued by Department of Information and Culture, Asmara, 1992, p. 56 in original. Unofficial translation from the original version in Tigrinya.

[10] Tronvoll obtained a copy of the position paper during fieldwork in 1992. When showing it to rank-and-file EPLF members, none had seen or heard of it.

[11] Eritrea carried out its first local (village and district) elections during 1992. Political parties were prohibited and the individual candidates were not allowed to communicate any political programme or platform to their 'constituency'. Furthermore, there were no secret ballots and the EPLF changed the 'electoral procedures' during the process due to a lot of confusion on the registration/ nomination of candidates. Thus, the 1992 local elections cannot be characterised as a formal electoral exercise.

[12] One of the current authors, Tronvoll, carried out fieldwork in Eritrea from August 1991 to June 1993, and actively researched the referendum process during *all* of its phases (as opposed to the UN observers or international journalists who arrived some few months, or even days, prior to voting day).

population believed to be ambivalent in their support for the EPLF – namely the Afar and Kunama ethnic groups straddling the Eritrean-Ethiopian border – were kept under surveillance and a noticeable military presence was mobilised in Afar region as a preparation for possible unrest instigated by the Afar resistance movement or other factions not supportive of the EPLF (Tronvoll 1994).

At this incipient stage of Eritrean development, civil society initiatives were also suppressed. A case in point is the closure and prohibition of the dissemination of independent information during the referendum process, as the only 'independent' NGO established in the country after the EPLF takeover was suddenly closed down when it wanted to publish a newspaper debating the referendum and Eritrea's future development plans.[13] Later initiatives to establish independent newspapers were also repressed.[14]

No doubt the Eritrean people wanted independence in 1993; but the reality behind the 99.8 per cent 'yes' vote may be questioned.[15] Segments of certain ethnic constituencies (the Afar and Kunama) had previously displayed support for Ethiopia during the war of liberation; segments of the merchant and trading class would favour a stronger affiliation to Ethiopia as a safeguard for market access; and the Orthodox Christian Church and highland society had historically expressed interest in remaining within Ethiopia (Negash 1997); these are all factors which presumably ought to be reflected in a vote on independence or continued affiliation with a 'friendly' TPLF/EPRDF government in power in Ethiopia. However, this did not manifest itself in the outcome of a 99.8 per cent 'yes' to independence; and should again raise some questions on how the medium of 'elections' and 'free opinions' were communicated by the EPLF during the transitional period (see also Pausewang 1993; Tronvoll 1993a). The referendum process – in the eyes of the rural electorate – appeared to be a well-orchestrated exercise without any meaningful choice of alternatives; but it is worthy of note that the absolute majority of the electorate had no interest in a meaningful choice. The referendum was merely a symbolic act manifesting what the Eritrean people had achieved on the battlefield.

[13] The Regional Centre for Human Rights and Development was established in April 1992 by Paulos Tesfagiorgis, founding chairman of EPLF's humanitarian wing, the Eritrean Relief Association (ERA). It was closed down by the Eritrean security service upon Presidential orders at the beginning of 1993, and Paulos was confined to house arrest for three months. The first shoot of an independent civil society was thus crushed before it had taken root.

[14] The respected elder and Eritrean nationalist, Taha Mohammed Nur, asked for permission to establish a newspaper in the mid-1990s in accordance with the press law, but was then ordered by the Minister of Information to let 'them read everything before it was printed'. Taha rejected this type of censorship and had to give up the initiative of establishing an independent paper. (Information given in interview conducted on 26 February 1997 in Asmara).

[15] The outcome of the Eritrean referendum is one of the most affirmative in the history of elections, with a turnout of 98.5 per cent of registered voters of which 99.8 per cent voted 'yes'.

IDEAS AND POLICIES ON 'DEMOCRACY'

In its National Democratic Programmes formulated during the war of liberation, the EPLF officially endorsed 'people's democratic rights – freedom of speech, the press, assembly, worship and peaceful demonstration'.[16] Also the EPLF's 'National Charter for Eritrea: For a Democratic, Just and Prosperous Future', adopted at the third congress in 1994, safeguards democratic rights and the formation of political organisations is even encouraged.[17] It must be remembered, though, that the vocabulary of 'democracy' as used by the EPLF during the struggle and after independence implied a Marxist-Leninist understanding of the term, and not 'liberal democracy' as it is often understood or interpreted by diplomats, development aid workers and other foreign observers.

The National Charter establishes the ideological guidelines for structuring politics and institutions in independent Eritrea. In the Charter, the PFDJ summarises its vision of Eritrea's future in terms of six basic goals: national harmony, political democracy, economic and social development, social justice (termed 'economic and social democracy'), cultural revival, and regional and international cooperation. These goals are meant to be pursued through the means of six principal guidelines, based on experiences from the liberation struggle. *National unity* is declared to be the paramount guideline, to which all work and policies will be aligned, thus rejecting 'all divisive attitudes and activities, [and] places national interest above everything else'.[18] It is further stated that the national development policies will be implemented through the means of *broad-based participation* by the people, combined with *individual dedication of self-sacrifice* – as guidelines two and three respectively – and based on the philosophy of *social justice* as the fourth guideline. *Self-reliance* in all fields – political as well as economic and cultural – is another basic principle of the PFDJ, experienced and learned through the solitary struggle for independence. The last guideline is the *strong relationship between the people and the leadership* of the organisation, a leadership which, according to the Charter, is mature and just in its role as decision-maker.[19]

The National Charter seems to coalesce several thoughts, ideas and inspirations articulated by the EPLF leadership over time, and hastily put together into a symbolic manifestation of their political 'uniqueness' and 'maturity'. There is, however, not much intellectual maturity or political uniqueness found in the Charter, and, as observed by Mengisteab and Yohannes, 'The document is fraught with contradictions, clichés, redundancies and platitudes' (Mengisteab and Yohannes 2005: 58). The

---

[16] Article 1.D of The National Democratic Programme, endorsed at the First EPLF Congress, 31 January 1977. In the programme adopted at the second congress in March 1987, a more or less similar phrase is included, but also adding the 'rights' of 'nationalist political parties'.
[17] EPLF, *A National Charter for Eritrea, For a Democratic, Just and Prosperous Future*, Nacfa, February, 1994.
[18] EPLF (1994: 13).
[19] EPLF (1994: 18).

National Charter must of course be read within the historical context in which it was drafted, just a couple of years after the end of the liberation war. However, the Leninist doctrines of political control and Albanian-inspired policies of self-reliance articulated in the Charter ought to have flagged several warning signs among donor countries flocking to Eritrea to assist the EPLF in rebuilding the war-torn country.

In particular, the Charter's notion on democracy should be seen as a worrying sign by the international community. 'Political democracy' in the Charter is defined as consisting of 'patriotism, national unity, secularism and social justice', not multipartyism, regular elections and the division of power. The Charter elaborates further on the understanding of democracy: 'In the context of our society, democracy is dependent not on the number of political parties and on regular elections but on the actual participation of people in the decision making process at community and national level'. Apparently, the EPLF tries to distinguish procedure from substance in relation to democratic values and principles (see also Yohannes 1996: 163), a distinction often favoured by authoritarian regimes claiming to represent the 'masses'. The Charter is thus silent on mechanisms to operationalise and institutionalise the values and principles of democracy (Mengisteab and Yohannes 2005: 81). President Isaias Afwerki has on several occasions expressed reservations about multiparty democracy as an appropriate system of governance for Eritrea, and explained that 'the time is not yet right'. Instead, he has speculated on models of 'traditional African democracy' without specifying the procedural and structural arrangement of such a model (Hedru 2003: 437).

It thus seems clear that the idea of the EPLF all along was that the Eritrean people – the masses – should participate in the running of the state through clearly defined structures, processes and roles provided for them by the EPLF – the vanguard needed to guide the population to development (Tronvoll 1998b; Mengisteab and Yohannes 2005: 87). This political culture also influenced the discourse on democracy during the Constitutional Commission, where the ambiguity of the EPLF concept of democracy came to the fore.

CONSTITUTIONAL DEBATES AND RIGHTS OF DEMOCRACY AND BASIC FREEDOMS

The discussion paper, *Constitutional Proposals for Public Debate*, which was widely disseminated for public consumption prior to the formal drafting of the Constitution, emphasised the need for a firm and strong government in order to create the necessary conditions for the growth of democracy, which 'has to develop gradually, taking root through a process of struggle and change' (cited from Pool 2001: 168). However, the idea of a multi-party system and free competitive elections was apparently viewed negatively by the EPLF and described as a 'procedural as opposed to an essential' aspect of democracy (ibid.).

The unimplemented Eritrean Constitution partly reflects this hesitation, as the democratic principles enshrined are somewhat vague on committing to full freedom of organisation and assembly in the country (see also Chapter 2 for elaboration on constitutional rights). On the one side, Article 19 of the Constitution enshrines 'Freedom of Conscience, Religion, Expression of Opinion, Movement, Assembly and Organisation'. The article reads in full:

1. Every person shall have the right to freedom of thought, conscience and belief.
2. Every person shall have the freedom of speech and expression, including freedom of the press and other media.
3. Every citizen shall have the right of access to information.
4. Every person shall have the freedom to practise any religion and to manifest such practice.
5. All persons shall have the right to assemble and to demonstrate peaceably together with others.
6. Every citizen shall have the right to form organisations for political, social, economic and cultural ends.
7. Every citizen shall have the right to practise any lawful profession, or to engage in any occupation or trade.
8. Every citizen shall have the right to move freely throughout Eritrea or reside and settle in any part thereof.
9. Every citizen shall have the right to leave and return to Eritrea and to be provided with a passport or any other travel documents.

Leaving aside the fact that all these basic freedoms are purely theoretical in Eritrea today, since they are violated on a massive, systematic and consistent basis every day, another constitutional article puts restrictions on these presumably basic freedoms. In Article 7, titled 'Democratic Principles', it is made clear that: 'The organisation and operation of all political, public associations and movements shall be guided by the principles of national unity and democracy' (7.5). Furthermore, in Article 7.6 it is articulated that: 'The State shall create conditions necessary for developing a democratic political culture defined by free and critical thinking, tolerance and national consensus'. Such provisions clearly indicate that the government defines the criteria for public participation in the country's 'democratisation process'. It presages government-defined restrictions and control of the political context wherein 'parties' are supposed to be established (see also Pool 2001). Democratic rights and freedoms are thus not freely given in Eritrea, but need to be compliant with the overall political directions offered by the EPLF/PFDJ regime.

Criticism of the lack of full guarantees for democratic *multipartyism* in the Constitution was raised during the drafting process. For instance, Constitution Commission member Taha Mohammed Nur, a distinguished elder and prominent Eritrean fighter for independence, was openly dismissive towards the new Constitution and claimed that many commission members, including its chairman, voted against their own belief on the issue due to the 'political reality of EPLF' in power and the fact that 'no one dares to oppose the party stand'.[20] Taha was critical of the EPLF's reasoning on this matter and explained:

> If our people 50 years ago in 1946[21] could form political parties of varying ideologies and policies and manage to hold a dialogue with each other, and then after 50 years of fighting the EPLF says that we are not matured politically to do the same today! This is nonsense. The reason is that the EPLF wants to dominate everything in Eritrea: politics, economy, society – everything.

Taha Mohammed Nur was arrested by the EPLF in November 2005 and was never released or tried in court before he reportedly died in prison in early 2008 (see Chapters 6 and 7).

The draft Constitution was made ready prior to the first Eritrean elections conducted in March 1997 for regional assemblies, the Constituent Assembly and, by indirect vote, the National Parliament. Thus, the democratic 'principles' agreed upon by the EPLF/PFDJ in the Constitution were put to the test immediately through the 1997 elections.

DE-DEMOCRATISING ERITREA:
THE 1997 'ELECTIONS' AND LOCAL GOVERNMENT REFORM[22]

As mentioned above, the totalitarian structure of Eritrea originates in political ideologies and practices developed during the war of liberation and manifested through new policies, legislation and state institutions established after independence. The most radical event in this regard was the local government reform and subsequent elections of 1997. The reform was anchored in a resolution passed by the Third Congress of the EPLF in 1994, where it was decided to re-draw the internal administrative boundaries of the country. This political decision by the EPLF was implemented by the government through the *Proclamation for the Establishment of Regional Administrations* (No. 86/1996), gazetted on 15 April 1996. The proclamation abolished the historical nine provinces (*awraja*) of Eritrea and established six new administrative zones (*zoba*)[23] instead; with a corresponding new system of local administration and governance.

After liberation, the *awraja*-system had elected people's assemblies (*baito*) functioning as administrative bodies in the villages (*baito adi*) and at the level of the district (*baito woreda*). Significantly, the *baito* members, who were individually elected, were all accountable to their

---

[20] Interview with the author, 26 February 1997 in Asmara.
[21] After the Second World War, Eritrea was temporarily administered by the United Kingdom (since Italy was defeated and lost all its colonial possessions). During this transition period, and until the annexation of Eritrea by Ethiopia in 1962, several political parties existed in Eritrea and candidates ran for election to the Eritrean national assembly.
[22] This section builds on material previously presented in Tronvoll (1997, 1998b).
[23] Gash Barka, Anseba, Maakel (Central), Debub (Southern), Semienawi Keyih Bahri (Northern Red Sea), and Debubawi Keyih Bahri (Southern Red Sea).

constituencies for their decisions and actions.[24] At the level of the sub-province (*neus-awraja*), appointed EPLF cadres worked as administrators, who also had the responsibility to guide and assist the *baitos* at district and village level in their decision-making. People's assemblies (*baito awraja*) – with the majority of the representatives elected from the districts and a minority appointed by the EPLF – were also found in the nine provinces, operating as quasi-legislative bodies, whereas the executive branch of provincial administration was staffed by appointed EPLF fighter-administrators. This system of local government was introduced throughout the country after liberation, effectuated by the local and regional elections which started early in 1992 and ended with elections in Dankalia in the beginning of 1993.[25] It is important to note that the *baito* system is a customary and familiar system of local governance in many parts of Eritrea (Tronvoll 1998a), and that the EPLF/PFDJ no more than formalised this institution by passing official proclamations and by nationally conducted local and regional *baito* elections in 1992.

The 1997 elections
Since the 1997 election was the first, and so far the only, election conducted under the EPLF, it is worthwhile presenting it in more detail.[26] The elections for the new *zoba* assemblies were held in the first two months of 1997, ending with the capital region, Maekel, on 1 March.[27] To elect the representatives for the regional assemblies was, however, not the only function of this ballot. The 399 elected *baito* representatives in the six regions, together with 75 representatives appointed by the EPLF/PFDJ and 75 representatives elected by Eritreans in the diaspora, would constitute the Constituent Assembly which later ratified the new Eritrean Constitution. And, in addition to this, the 399 *baito* representatives subsequently elected among themselves 75 representatives who, together with 75 EPLF/PFDJ appointed representatives, formed the new National Assembly.

The triple mandate of the ballot – first, to elect candidates for the *zoba* assemblies; second, to elect candidates for the Constituent Assembly; and third, by indirect vote, to elect members of parliament – was not properly communicated to the electorate, who generally believed that the vote was for the regional assemblies only. Adding more confusion to

[24] See the pamphlet, *Short Exposition on Local Government in Eritrea*, by the Ministry of Local Government, Asmara, September 1993.
[25] See also an unpublished paper by the Ministry of Local Government, 'Experiences on the Introduction of Decentralization in Eritrea' (1993); and see Tronvoll (1998a) for further comments on the workings of the *baito* system during the transitional period.
[26] Local 'elections' were reportedly conducted in May 2003, less than two years after the widespread political crackdown and arrests. No independent assessment or reporting are available from these elections, however, reportedly all candidates were hand-picked loyal EPLF/PFDJ cadres (Hedru 2003).
[27] No international observers were invited to follow the 1997 elections. Only the Norwegian government was privileged to send a small team of election observers (headed by the author), since the Norwegian development agency (Norad) had helped to finance the local government reform programme.

the vote was the system with reserved seats for female representation. In order to safeguard female representation, a parallel election with a separate ballot of female candidates was conducted.[28] Thus, a double ballot was used; one for the reserved seats with a pink ballot paper, and another for the open seats, with a blue ballot paper.

Since the country did not yet have an electoral law, the legislative basis of the *zoba* elections was therefore to be found in the *Proclamation for the Establishment of Regional Administrations* and subsidiary in the *Proclamation Issued to Establish the Constituent Assembly*. In addition to these legal instruments, the Ministry of Local Government issued an *Electoral Guidelines* document which described the mode of the elections, formation of the election committees, and procedural electoral aspects.[29]

The electoral system adopted was a multiple-member constituency system with majority vote.[30] The range of representation was determined on the basis of population concentration and size. However, there was a different ratio of voters to representatives from a rural electorate to an urban one, in order to safeguard rural interests.[31] The election for the reserved seats was delineated in different, more encompassing constituencies, which entailed that the female representatives in the reserved seats had an electorate of between 8000 and 10,000 people, whereas in the open election each representative was backed by approximately 4000 to 5000 people (in the Maekel *zoba*). This difference between the open and reserved constituencies was not mentioned in either the Proclamation or the Election Regulations. According to interviews with presiding officers, they had just been orally informed about this system. That such an important aspect of an electoral system was not specified in either the law or the regulations was of course unfortunate, but rather typical of the EPLF way of orchestrating political processes.

Individual 'election campaigning' was only allowed to be carried out over five days. The campaign activities conducted were also very limited, based almost entirely on displaying campaign posters with a picture of the candidate and a listing of his/her experience. Some posters had also a few sentences on what the candidate recognised as his/her major political issues, which were practically always in accordance with the official development policy of the government of Eritrea. One or two joint meetings, where all the candidates were allocated two minutes to

[28] Almost one-third (30 per cent) of the seats in the assembly had been reserved for female representation. Cf. Article 10.3.A in the *Proclamation for the Establishment of Regional Administrations*.

[29] *Electoral Guidelines for Assembly Elections*, issued by the Ministry of Local Government, October 1996, Asmara (our version is an unofficial translation from the Arabic/Tigrinya original). The 'guidelines' had not been discussed or ratified by the existing National Parliament, nor gazetted, and its formal status as a legal instrument was thus unclear, even though it was formalised by Articles 11 and 41 in the *Proclamation for the Establishment of the Regional Administrations* which stated that such regulations shall be issued.

[30] As prescribed in the *Proclamation for the Establishment of Regional Administrations*.

[31] Article 10 of *Proclamation for the Establishment of Regional Administrations*.

present themselves, were arranged by the Election Committee. A well-known EPLF member and female candidate interviewed admitted that it was not necessary to do much campaigning since the candidates were all known to their constituencies and that the voters were not particularly preoccupied with political issues. In this candidate's constituency, the government had, just prior to the election, announced that it would nationalise several residential houses, which had raised a lot of concern and criticism from the local inhabitants. When asked if this issue had been raised in her campaign, she was dismissive:

> We cannot advocate the cases of our constituency if it goes against the national politics and government decisions. Concerning the nationalisation of housing some of the voters have asked me to take their case to the assembly, but that is a decision of the government. The assembly assesses and gives recommendations only which the administrator passes on to the Minister of Local Government who confirms and decides. This has to be done so we do not decide anything that will go against the government development policies.[32]

This explanation offered by a prominent candidate illustrates the shallowness of the election and the concept of 'democracy' as introduced by the EPLF/PFDJ (note that this was four years prior to the crackdown and before the start of the new Eritrean-Ethiopian war). No political substance was allowed to be communicated in the electoral process, and all candidates were aware of this restriction. The candidates and the voters had to conform to procedural technicalities only, without raising or discussing any local political grievances or issues of national concern. That was the solitary prerogative of the EPLF to handle — an ironic and paradoxical parallel to how the EPLF itself had characterised liberal democracy as 'procedural as opposed to an essential' democracy (see below).

Since the elections were only about symbolic procedures and not substance politics, there were no 'official' EPLF or fighter candidates. A female candidate explained that:

> The fighters do not want to mingle so much with civilian life. They keep closely together and do not interact with the civilian population, and in a way they are a community within a community.[33]

Yemane Gebreab, head of the Department of Political Affairs in the EPLF/PFDJ, confirmed in an interview that there was no need for party-endorsed candidates in the elections, since, as he claimed, the Front would take all the seats due to its popularity.[34] He added that it did not really matter, since 90 per cent of the candidates were party members anyway. The purpose of the election, as explained by Yemane Gebreab, was threefold: first, to secure people's participation along the lines of government priorities and to let them know the importance of elections; second, to make sure that the people did not look at ethnicity, kinship,

---

[32] Interview by Tronvoll with *zoba* candidate Sara Solomon (the sister of the imprisoned former Foreign Affairs minister Petros Solomon), 27 February 1997, Asmara.
[33] Interviewed by Tronvoll 25 February 1997, Asmara.
[34] Interviewed by Tronvoll, 26 February 1997, Asmara.

village candidates, or narrow regionalism, but at the national issues; and lastly to enhance the role of women, youth and 'minorities' in national processes. All of these are priorities which fit well with the ideological doctrines established during the war of liberation.[35] Since the elections were intended to have an 'educational' effect, and to mobilise the masses according to the priorities dictated by the government, pressure was applied to compel people to register and vote.[36]

Although minor discrepancies and breaches of the electoral guidelines were observed during the 1997 elections, the overall impression was that the process was, technically, carried out in a commendable manner (Tronvoll 1997). However, the purpose of the elections was a sham, as the *Proclamation for the Establishment of Regional Administrations* outlines a system of local governance which seems not to hold any decentralisation of power and authority, but rather the contrary. The elected *baitos* were not vested with any powers or implementing mandate, but recognised only as a symbolic rubber-stamping body which had to offer praise of the national policies of development drafted and decided by the national government and the President. The Eritrean electorate was not allowed to voice its true opinion on these matters, and foreigners too were warned not to do so. In the interview with Yemane Gebreab during the elections, he gave the following blunt warning: 'I hope you have not come here to verify that the elections are free and fair. It is not up to the foreigners to verify the elections, but to the people of Eritrea.'[37]

National elections, but notably without political parties, were again scheduled for 1998, but were postponed due to the outbreak of war with Ethiopia.[38] After signing the ceasefire agreement in the summer of 2000, new plans for elections were made and a draft *Proclamation on the Formation of Political Parties and Organisations* was developed. A committee led by the then Minister of Local Government, Mahmoud Ahmed (also known as Sherifo or Mahmoud Sherifo), was appointed to oversee the electoral process. However, being part of the growing post-war dissent against the President, Mahmoud Sherifo was summarily dismissed from his position in February 2001 and subsequently imprisoned during the September 2001 crackdown (see Chapter 5). Being one of the key architects of the system of control and surveillance in Eritrea, and a government strong man, his dismissal was received with shock by the

[35] However, the fact that the Jehovah Witnesses, due to their dis-engagement in the referendum process, were stripped of their right to vote or to stand as a candidate in the local elections, if they so wished, indicated that the formal purpose of the elections as explained by Yemane Gebreab was not intended to be converted into practical realities.

[36] Confirmed by several voters and a foreign lecturer at Asmara University, who had witnessed a government propaganda vehicle driving in the streets of Asmara and announcing that people who did not register to vote would be punished.

[37] Interviewed by Tronvoll, 26 February 1997, Asmara.

[38] See IRIN interview with Yemane Gebremeskel, Director of the President's Office, 1 April 2004, Asmara, at: http://www.irinnews.org/Report. aspx?ReportId=49359, accessed 6 January 2009.

public at large. Subsequently, Mahmoud Sherifo claimed that he was dismissed because President Isaias Afwerki wanted to suspend the democratisation process and the formation of political parties in the country.[39] The draft legislation on political parties was subsequently annulled, and general elections were postponed indefinitely. On 1 January 2003, an official declaration was made claiming that: 'In accordance with the prevailing wish of the people it is not the time to establish political parties, and discussion of their establishment has been postponed'.[40] While carrying out tightly controlled, non-party,[41] local elections, party-based national elections are not on the agenda in the foreseeable future.[42] In an interview with Al Jazeera, President Isaias Afwerki announced in May 2008 that elections would be postponed for 'three or four decades' or longer because they 'polarize society' (Al Jazeera Interview 2008).

Local government reform: formalising totalitarian structures

The new system of local government introduced in 1996 builds on the aforementioned *Proclamation for the Establishment of Regional Administrations* (No. 86/1996) The most radical change introduced by the reform was the discontinuation of elected people's assemblies at the lower levels of the administration, leaving the *baito* institution intact – although with a severely restricted mandate and authority – only at the level of the *zoba*. The traditional district (*woreda*) entity is obliterated, and the three new levels of local government administration are the village/area (*adi/kebabi*), sub-region (*nues zoba*) and region (*zoba*) (Art. 6

---

[39] BBC News, 'Eritrean minister speaks out', 17 April 2001, at: http://news.bbc.co.uk/2/hi/africa/1281386.stm, accessed 17 March 2009.

[40] Posted in the government daily, *Hadas Ertra*, 1 January 2003, cited from Hedru (2003).

[41] Local elections were carried out between 2003 and 2005. In this regard, President Isaias Afwerki explained that 'the foundation of the regional elections of administrators, work managers and village magistrates that we are now celebrating has its roots in the political culture we developed during our national liberation struggle. These elections have also proved the popular participation of the people along the path of development of free Eritrea.' Explaining the conduct of the elections, the party EPLF/PFDJ website asserts that: 'The basic beliefs of the country's peoples and its martyrs who fell heroically for the people is that no step forward can be obtained without the participation of its citizens. "There is no victory without its people, no development without its people," were the words of wisdom articulated by the President' (Shaebia: 'Elections for Regional Assemblies to be held soon', ERNA News, 24 September 2003, at: http://www.shaebia.org/artman/publish/article_1881.shtml, accessed 26 March 2009). Furthermore, according to the government, the local 'elections aimed at fostering active popular participation in public administration and strengthening the existing administration network in the country.' Cf. Ministry of Information's webpage: 'Elections to take place in 46 administrative areas in the Central region', 7 April 2005, at: http://www.shabait.com/staging/publish/article_003302.html, accessed 26 March 2009.

[42] See interview IRIN: 'ERITREA: Interview with Yemane Gebremeskel, Director of the President's Office' 1 April 2004, Asmara (IRIN), at: http://www.irinnews.org/Report.aspx?ReportId=49359, accessed 6 January 2009.

in the proclamation).[43] The establishment of an executive line of command from the President's Office all the way down to the village/area level – through the Minister of Local Government, and the chief administrators of the region, sub-region and village/area, who are all personally and permanently appointed by the president or his representative – is also a new arrangement within the field of local government. The administrators at each level are accountable for the conduct of their office to their immediate superior – and not to their constituencies – ending with the regional administrators who are accountable directly to the Minister of Local Government, and, notably, not to their elected regional people's assemblies (*baito zoba*) (Art. 20.3).

Whereas the former elected *baito* representatives were accountable to the village inhabitants for the conduct of their office – and thus were replaceable by vote – the new position of village/area 'chief' is only accountable to the government-appointed chief administrator of the sub-region (Art. 30.B.1).[44] Within the given context, this appears natural, since the village/area administrator's duties are to 'execute and implement the directives and programmes' given to him by the sub-region administrator (Art. 30.B.4). The village/area administrator also holds the responsibility within his/her domain to 'control compliance with and the implementation of the central government's policies, plans, programmes as well as regional directives and programs' (Art. 30.B.1). The village/area is thus explicitly not mandated to represent/administer the interests of the village, but to enforce the authority of the president at the village level.

According to the deputy Minister of Local Government, the reason for abolishing the elected village council (*baito adi*)[45] as the responsible administrative body of the village, was that the councils 'promoted prestige projects which did not benefit the community' (Pool 1997: 25).

[43] Eritrea is divided into six regions, 54 sub regions and 2000 village districts (interview with Vice-Minister for Local Government published in *Eritrea Profile*, 17 February 1996, p. 2).

[44] As a substitute for the grassroots democracy of people's councils (*baito adi*), a meeting of the whole village community is introduced, named after a customary institution of justice called *megaba'aya*. According to the Proclamation, the *megaba'aya* comprises all village inhabitants within the administrative area who are above the age of 18 (Art. 3). The powers and duties of the *megaba'aya* will be to 'discuss programmes to be carried out in the village/area, make comments and recommendations and approve programmes requiring its participation' (Art. 30.A.2). It will also 'generally hear, investigate and comment on performance reports presented by the administrator and pass on to the regional administration its objections and reservations thereon' (Art. 30.A.3). Finally, the *megaba'aya* will 'provide the necessary cooperation in electing committee members who would participate in the implementation of different programmes' (Art. 30.A.4). Meetings of the *megaba'aya* will be conducted regularly every two or three months (Art. 30.A.5), and will be chaired by the permanently appointed village/area administrator, who is the highest administrative authority of the village/area (Art. 30.B.1).

[45] The *baito adi* is the village assembly, a gathering of all the villagers. They elect a council or administration, called *memhedar*, which consists of a chairman, and his/her secretary (deputy), a cashier and two additional administrators.

The government has a responsibility to plan and implement the overall development strategies of the country, and must prioritise according to various national needs and factors which might not be seen or comprehended from a local perspective. Consequently it ends in a difficult balance between genuine grassroots participation and peasant decision-making related to their own development process, on the one hand, and state responsibility and guidance vis-a-vis national priorities on the other. The government of Eritrea solved this quandary by purging all decision-making authority from the people's assemblies and vesting the authority in permanently appointed executive administrators in the local government structure. The only remaining people's assembly, the *baito zoba*, is left without any authority or mandate to decide on or implement development policies of its own choice, and with only the mandate of recommendation. The proclamation states that the regional *baito* is to have the powers and duties to: 'prepare regional development programmes relating to economic and social services and pass resolutions and issue directives pertaining to its particular conditions in harmony with central government policies, proclamations and regulations and to implement the same when approved by the Minister of Local Government' (Art. 13.1, emphasis added).

The *baito* may recommend solutions based on the people's wishes (Art. 13.4), and 'hear, investigate and comment on the performance reports and evaluations of the executive body and submit its objections and reservations thereon to the minister of local government' (Art. 13.7), but it does not hold decisive authority within any field, and must submit to any national priority defined by the government. It has no independent fiscal authority, but is required to 'collect local revenues, based on the central government's local duty and taxation directives' (Art. 13.6).

To safeguard against any possibility that the *baito zoba* might recommend or suggest anything which goes against national priorities and planned strategies, the government appoints regional administrators vested with 'the power to suspend the *Baito*'s resolutions and recommendations until the Minister of Local Government decides on them, if he thinks the policies and regulations of the central government are violated' (Art. 20.B.2). To avoid utilising such radical measures, however, the regional administrator attends all meetings of the *baito* where he/she 'gives recommendations and advises the *baito* on matters related to the central government's policies and regulations and programmes before the *baito* passes resolutions and recommendations' (Art. 20.B.1).

It appears that the structure of local government introduced in 1997 in Eritrea reflected the idea that only a few individuals at the top of society should be entrusted with the power and duty to decide what is the optimal strategy of development for Eritrea and all its citizens. The small group of dedicated men, and a few women, who are trusted by the president thus have an enormous influence on issues of local governance, a power seemingly without any checks and balances. No counterpoised power which emanates from, and is accountable to, a demotic constituency exists as an integral part of the new system of local government. In this manner, the decisions of the village/area administrator – which are based on directives from above – appear incontestable (according to the proclamation). Long before the 2001 crackdown, the authoritarian traits of the EPLF/PFDJ were clearly understood by the Eritrean peasants. An elderly and much respected villager explained after the 1997 regional elections:

> We have seen this system of governance before during the Italian period. We resisted the authority imposed on us by the colonial administrators at that time; this time it is our own kinsmen who do it; and we do not know what to do.[46]

The ubiquitous one-party structure

Since coming to power in 1991, the EPLF/PFDJ has not allowed any organised political opposition to emerge within Eritrea. The spectrum of Eritrean opposition movements are forced to operate in exile, disconnected from the domestic constituency.[47] In the immediate post-liberation phase, individuals with opposition sympathies or membership were allowed to return to the country, but were prohibited from articulating opposition politics or organising into political alternatives.

The third EPLF Congress conducted in 1994 aimed to transform the EPLF military front into a broad-based civilian movement, called the People's Front for Democracy and Justice (PFDJ). Although the PFDJ formally became separate from the government of Eritrea, there was a direct overlap between its central council of 75 members and the National Assembly and government ministers. The PFDJ also inherited all assets of the EPLF, and continued to establish new businesses in independent Eritrea, as part of securing control over the 'free' economic sector as well as safeguarding a future direct source of income to the party independent of state finances (Pool 2001).

The 1994 Congress also designed strategies to revitalise the party and to extend its party structure in order to, in its term, 'reinforce' its ties with the Eritrean population at large. By 1996, the party had established over 1000 branches throughout the country, with a membership base of around 600,000, a figure embracing a large share of the adult Eritrean population (Pool 2001: 177). The enlargement of the party membership base was conducted in such a way – with implicit and explicit coercion – that few people dared to decline membership if they were asked to register.[48] Furthermore, anybody aspiring to employment and a career in the civil service or EPLF/PFDJ-controlled companies was better off being a member of the party. The expansion of the party structure continued until the outbreak of the 1998-2000 war, which temporarily put a stop to

[46] Interviewed by Tronvoll February 1997, highland village outside of Asmara.
[47] For a comprehensive overview of historical and contemporary Eritrean political movements and organisations in opposition to EPLF/PFDJ, see Günther Schröder, *Directory of past and present Eritrean political organisations in opposition to EPLF/PFDJ*, unpublished report, created March 2000, last updated October 2010, 91 pages.
[48] Information given to authors by Eritreans in exile. For example, one of the current authors (Mekonnen), was compelled to become a party member in 1999 while he was serving as Judge of the Senafe Sub-Regional Court.

the recruitment campaign. After this, the recruitment campaign scaled down considerably, seemingly because the upper PFDJ stratum feared the wrath of the displeased segment of 'masses' even within its own organisation. The base of the PFDJ party has since been significantly weakened.

Clearly, the objective of the EPLF/PFDJ was to develop a mass party organisation which through its structure was able to mobilise and control all citizens and societal activity in the country. Additionally, the party structure also aims to control the government structures, as party organs are organised in parallel to the new local government structure outlined above. Furthermore, in order to create an in-built structure of control within the party, two party branches were established in all villages/local level communities. When villagers were asked why the EPLF/PFDJ established such an elaborate party structure throughout Eritrea in 1997, the usual answer given was the need for control and surveillance. As explained by a village militia member in a highland village outside Asmara:

> The new party organisation in my village is established to look after the village administrator and to check that the government policies are followed and implemented. But, since the top leaders cannot be sure that the party organisation in the village is reliable, they have decided to establish two branches in each village. In this way the party will check on and control the village administrator, and each party branch will check and control each other.[49]

The structure of government and party governance established in Eritrea in 1997 thus gives a clear line of command from the President of the State and Chairman of the Party, Isaias Afwerki, at the pinnacle all the way down to the smallest village. Accountability is one-directional, always to the upper level of command and not to the constituency supposed to be served.

However, with the arrest of the former of Minister of Local Government, Mahmoud Sherifo in 2001, the Ministry of Local Government is no longer in existence. The functions of the now defunct Ministry of Local Government are now abrogated by the Office of the President. In the aftermath of the 2001 political crisis, the president has also unilaterally introduced a new military administrative structure, which runs in parallel with the pre-2001 civilian administration structure of *zoba, neus zoba* and *adi/kebabi* (regional, sub-regional and village/local level). In effect, however, the military administrators, known as the zonal commanders, are the most powerful next to the state president. At the upper level of both structures, the president still retains the strongest strings of political power. The new military administrative structure is headed by five high ranking army commanders at the rank of generals, namely: Tekle Kiflay 'Manjus', Filipos Weldeyohannes, Umer Tewil, Haile 'China' Samuel, and Gerezghier 'Wuchu' Andemariam. Each of them is the commander of the five military administrative zones named numerically from one to five.

---

[49] Interviewed by Tronvoll 25 February 1997.

With its senior members, including Central Council and Executive Committee members in prison or in exile, the PFDJ has also been considerably weakened since 2001. The ultimate result is excessive concentration of power in the hands of President Isaias Afwerki at the helm of the state structure with a few loyalists under his control. In the face of the new military administrative structure, the old civilian administrative system has become meaningless. It appears that one major reason why the old civil administration system has not been formally abolished is to serve as a diverting tactic in the face of the prevailing military administrative structure. This has rendered the country a mixed model of military dictatorship and totalitarianism, thus befittingly becoming an African garrison state.

FINAL REMARKS

Comparative politics and history have taught us that the establishment of mass political movements or parties does not bode well for the development of liberalism, democracy and the plurality of choice and opinion. Mass parties are convenient instruments of control by a small clique at the top of society rather than mediums of broad-based participation. The mass membership is generally unable to do more than obey the policies set by the leadership, and is forced into quiescence.

At an incipient stage, it became clear that the EPLF/PFDJ had a different notion and understanding of 'democracy' from what Western liberal political theory implies. The local government reform and the 'democratic institution building' which were put into effect from the mid-1990s, actually entailed a de-democratisation of Eritrean society. Traditional democratic village and regional assemblies were replaced with an authoritarian command structure controlled by the President at the top and branching out to all villages in the country. The evolution of this structure, and the parallel transformation of the EPLF/PDFJ into a mass party, combined with the new military administrative structure, gave evidence that the political leadership had no interest whatsoever in relinquishing the political power they had fought so bitterly to obtain.

5

Obliterating Civil Society:
Denying Freedom of Organisation and Expression

INTRODUCTION

When Eritrea achieved independence, *de facto* 1991 and *de jure* 1993, many national and international observers expressed a strong degree of optimism towards a positive development of democracy, civil society and a culture of human rights in the country. President Isaias Afwerki was characterised as belonging to the 'new breed' of African leaders who apparently enjoyed popular support among their constituencies, rhetorically endorsed liberal democracy, human rights and a free market economy, and had a well-defined development policy based on their own priorities. As such, Isaias Afwerki, and the rest of his generation of leaders,[1] heralded a clear breach with the ancien regime of Mengistu Haile-Mariam.

Today, however, Eritrea is characterised as one of the world's worst dictatorships, where human rights are violated on a massive and systematic scale. Institutions of democracy and civil society – which ought to function as checks and balances to unaccountable political power – plainly do not exist in the country. As this study illustrates, the seeds of dictatorship were sown early in Eritrea (Kibreab 2008); whereas the final blow to democratic development was experienced in the aftermath of the 1998-2000 Eritrean-Ethiopian war.

OPPOSING THE EMERGING ONE-MAN DICTATORSHIP:
POST-WAR REFORM MOVEMENT

Eritrean-Ethiopian relations gradually deteriorated after Eritrean independence, as the two formerly friendly resistance movements held different perceptions about how to organise state and governance, and opted for varying strategies of 'development' (Negash and Tronvoll 2000). The 1998-2000 war shattered Eritrean-Ethiopian relations, and the UN/AU negotiated peace process failed to provide a sustainable settlement to the dispute (Nystuen and Tronvoll 2008). With the

[1] The group of new-breed African leaders included; Meles Zenawi (Ethiopia), Yoweri Museveni (Uganda), Paul Kagame (Rwanda), and to some extent also Thabo Mbeki (South Africa).

withdrawal of the UN peacekeeping force (UNMEE) in 2008, the two countries were once again on the brink of war.

The 1998-2000 war had dramatic implications for domestic politics in both countries, as it inspired dissent movements within the two government parties, the EPLF in Eritrea and the TPLF/EPRDF in Ethiopia, questioning the decisions made which led to the outbreak of war and the conduct of the fighting itself (Plaut 2002; Tadesse and Young 2003; Vaughan and Tronvoll 2003; Tronvoll 2009b). In the subsequent 2005 election in Ethiopia, for instance, the opposition made great electoral advances and challenged the EPRDF's grip on power, partly as an effect of the war (Tronvoll 2009a).

In Eritrea, the war was used as an excuse by the EPLF to postpone the scheduled 1998 elections. Many Eritreans, however, saw the war as an illustration of the EPLF's failure to build an accountable system of governance which would prevent the outbreak of war in the first place. In October 2000, a group of thirteen prominent Eritrean intellectuals (later called G-13),[2] wrote a confidential letter to President Isaias Afwerki, questioning the outbreak of war and raising a wide range of critical issues on the EPLF's dominant role in the country's politics and economy and on the matter of the unimplemented Constitution. The group, some of whom held high-level civilian and symbolic positions within the EPLF (like the Constitutional Commission Chairman, Bereket Habte-Selassie, and the former head of the Eritrean Relief Association, Paulos Tesfagiorgis), admitted that they had kept quiet for too long due to self-censorship, as they became aware of the negative development trends in Eritrea at an early stage after independence. However, the outbreak of the new war and the continued negative political developments within the country compelled them at this late stage to raise a direct criticism of President Isaias Afwerki's rule:

> We must now say that, in our considered opinion, the government has lagged behind in the development of democratic institutions, including mechanisms for ensuring accountability and transparency. The advent of one-man dominance has had the effect of suffocating a variety of ideas from blossoming and denied meaningful popular participation. It has inevitably prevented the growth of democratic institutions. A new nation with very limited and under-developed resources facing enormous challenges in all fields – political, security, economic, social – cannot afford to have a government that depends only on one person. In fairness, the blame must also be shared by other members of the leadership to the extent that they did not object to the negative practices. They may have put up some feeble complaints, but we have heard of no such protests. So, they too have failed the nation along with you in allowing power to be concentrated in the hands of one man.[3]

This confidential letter was soon leaked and created an uproar of interest among Eritreans in the country and the diaspora. A delegation

---

[2] All but two were living outside Eritrea: Araya Debessay, USA; Assefaw Tekeste, USA; Bereket Habte Selassie, USA; Dawit Mesfin, UK; Haile Debas, USA; Kassahun Checole, USA; Khaled A. Beshir, USA; Lula Ghebreyesus, South Africa; Miriam M. Omar, UK; Mohamed Kheir Omar, Eritrea; Mussie Misghina, Sweden; Paulos Tesfagiorgis, Eritrea; and Reesom Haile, Belgium.

[3] Letter to the President of Eritrea from G-13, 1 October 2000.

from the G-13 travelled to Asmara to meet with President Isaias personally in order to discuss the letter and a way forward to handle the criticism. They managed to secure a brief meeting with the president, who did not enter into the substance of their criticism but was more preoccupied with trying to identify who leaked the letter to the press.[4] Thus, no concrete follow-up strategy to the letter was agreed upon, and the G-13 group as a collective did not follow up on their initial criticism, although many of the individual signatories to the letter have continued their peaceful struggle for change in Eritrea from exile through various means.

Protest against President Isaias Afwerki's monolithic power was also brewing within the top echelons of the Front towards the end of the war. The political and military leadership of EPLF/PFDJ was particularly concerned with the fact that Isaias Afwerki, as both President and party chairman, had neglected the routine of convening regular meetings in the party's Central Council (the top legislative committee of EPLF /PFDJ) and the National Assembly during the war, as well as failing to organise a fourth party Congress and national elections. After the active warring ceased in the summer of 2000, the pressure from top-level military and party leaders increased on President Isaias to open the way to re-introducing a collective leadership model of the EPLF/PFDJ and the government.[5] An initial group of 15 top-level government officials coordinated their critique of the president (thus called the G-15). The opponents of the president were formidable in their own right, as both founding members of the EPLF and liberation war heroes, as well as being incumbent government ministers and generals. They included two former Foreign Affairs Ministers, Petros Solomon and Haile Weldensae, the Minister of Local Government, Mahmoud Sherifo, the former Minister of Defence (and the person second only to Isaias in the most recent party elections), Mesfin Hagos, as well as the serving generals, Ogbe Abraha and Estifanos Seyoum.[6]

[4] See Saleh Younis, 'Dawit vs. Goliath. An interview with Dawit Mesfin, member of G-13', published on www.awate.com, 2 December 2000.
[5] According to information disseminated by the EPLF/PFDJ dissenters (G-15) (see 'open letter' to all PFDJ/EPLF members of May 2001 from the G-15), criticism was directed at President Isaias Afwerki at a EPLF/PFDJ Central Council meeting which was convened from 31 August to 2 September 2000 and to some extent at the 13th session of the National Council, which was held from 29 September to 2 October 2000. The substance of the criticism was, *inter alia*, to undertake genuine reviews of policies and to establish deadlines for conducting the party congress and national elections. Furthermore, since military and diplomatic efforts had to be strengthened, it was also decided by the National Council to form a military committee to do an appraisal of the war in order to advise the president in the future. According to the dissenters, however, none of the decisions taken at these two important meetings were implemented due to obstruction from President Isaias Afwerki.
[6] The G-15 originally consisted of (alphabetically): Adhanom Gebremariam, Astier Feshatsion, Beraki Ghebreselassie, Berhane Ghebreghzabiher, Estifanos Seyoum, Germano Nati, Haile Menkerios, Haile Weldensae, Hamid Himid, Mahmud Ahmed Sheriffo, Mesfin Hagos, Mohammed Berhan Blata, Ogbe Abraha, Petros Solomon and Saleh Kekya.

The growing dissent within the leadership's own ranks, in combination with pressure from the diaspora and civil society representatives in Eritrea, warned the president of his waning power. The regime thus started to plot against the dissenters and in January 2001 a presidential commission of inquiry to investigate the political crimes of 'sub-nationalism' and 'defeatism' was established (Hedru 2003: 441). Its objective was to undermine the accusations and criticism raised by the dissenters by launching a smear campaign accusing them of regionalism and treason – a deadly sin within the nationalistic and militaristic ideology of the EPLF/PFDJ. Loyal cadres in the party arranged seminars hinting at the existence of a 'fifth column' inside the country which was aiding the Ethiopian government in its aggression against Eritrea. In late January, the Minister of Local Government, Mahmoud Sherifo, was dismissed from his post, as the internal battle within the EPLF/PFDJ hardened. The dissenters tried to counter the government's accusations by giving interviews and statements to the press, and newspaper sales skyrocketed in the spring and summer of 2001 (Hedru 2003: 441).

The dissenters thrice requested in writing (in February and March 2000) that the president convene meetings of the Central Council of the PFDJ and the National Assembly. Their intention was to use the formal rules and procedures of the EPLF/PFDJ and the National Assembly to push through a vote of no-confidence in the president, and thus open the way for general elections in the country (Hedru 2003: 442). The president, however, responded with a blunt warning: 'Again today you have sent me another letter. I have seen it. I repeat, you are making a mistake.'[7] Not satisfied with the rebuff, the G-15 gave the president until the end of March to convene meetings in order to address the critical issues of governance in the country, but to no avail. The president rejected the fact that there were any problems as indicated by the group, and again asked them to refrain from 'this mistaken path and come to your senses'.[8]

As a last measure to increase the pressure on the president, the G-15 signed an open letter to all EPLF/PFDJ members and to Eritrea at large in May, outlining in detail the development of authoritarianism under President Isaias, the basis of their criticism, and possible solutions to the problems Eritrea was facing. The justification for this move, as seen by the G-15, was to 'pave the road for peaceful, legal and democratic transition to a truly constitutional government, and to establish guarantees for Eritrea to become a peaceful and stable nation where democracy, justice and prosperity shall prevail'. The open criticism of the president by top-level EPLF/PFDJ cadres was unprecedented and shocking, within the usually cloaked and secretive leadership. The letter spelt out the core of the criticism in the following way:

> Because of the weaknesses of the legislative and executive bodies, the President has been acting without restraint, even illegally. While the judiciary lacks

[7] Letter from the Office of the President addressed to Mahmoud Sherifo, 13 March 2000.
[8] Letter from the President dated 29 March 2000 to Mahmoud Sherifo (reference: N.I.: A290301.RTF).

adequate human and institutional capacity, instead of providing resources to build up its capacity, the President has created a competing Special Court reporting directly to him. People are being jailed for years without the knowledge and agreement of the judiciary, and independence of the judiciary and rule of law are being violated. The problem is that the President is conducting himself in an illegal and unconstitutional manner, is refusing to consult, and the legislative and executive bodies have not performed their oversight functions properly.

By appealing to the Eritrean public at large and EPLF/PFDJ members in particular, the G-15 seemed to have aimed to remove President Isaias Afwerki from power by popular pressure. Considering the personal knowledge and experiences of the G-15 individuals, their naïveté in this regard is puzzling. Instead of succumbing to pressure, President Isaias went about doing what he knows best: plotting the elimination of an enemy threatening his power.

THE REGIME HITS BACK: THE 2001 CRACKDOWN AND THE CLOSURE OF THE PROCESS OF 'DEMOCRATISATION'

The nascent private Eritrean press started to write about the emerging criticism of President Isaias Afwerki in the spring of 2001. By publishing the views of the EPLF/PFDJ reformists and other civil society voices, the Eritrean public at large became aware for the first time of the internal power struggle within the EPLF/PFDJ, and their lingering doubt was confirmed that even their much revered liberation leader and president was not a person without flaws.

The dissemination of news on the internal EPLF/PFDJ power struggle was seen as an advantage for the reformists; thus the regime tried to stifle the press on this issue. In April 2001, Paulos Zaid, an assistant editor of the government weekly *Eritrean Profile*, was picked up at his home by security agents and detained at an unknown location.[9] This followed the suspected arrests and conscription to the armed forces of other journalists. In June 2001, the Committee to Protect Journalists, a US-based organisation dedicated to freedom of expression, sent a letter to the Eritrean Minister of Justice questioning the whereabouts of 15 Eritrean journalists who were believed to have been arrested or forcibly conscripted into the army since the end of the war in order to silence them.[10] On 25 July, Mattewos Habteab, editor-in-chief of the private

[9] Committee to Protect Journalists (CPJ), 'CPJ asks Justice Minister to clarify whereabouts of 15 journalists', 7 June 2001, New York, at: http://cpj.org/2001/06/cpj-asks-justice-minister-to-clarify-whereabouts-o.php#more, accessed 17 March 2009.

[10] In a subsequent response, Eritrea's Minister of Justice claimed that five of the 15 journalists mentioned in the CPJ letter were employed with local publications or NGOs, and that 'the remaining journalists are performing their obligations in the National Service Program'. The CPJ was not able to independently verify this claim ('CPJ Delegation meets with Eritrean Ambassador. Expresses continued concern about whereabouts of 15 journalists', 13 June 2001, Washington DC, at: http://cpj.org/2001/06/cpj-delegation-meets-with-eritrean-ambassadorexpre.php, accessed 17 March 2009).

Tigrinya-language *Meqaleh* newspaper, was allegedly kidnapped by security forces and forced to enlist in the army.[11] His newspaper had published a critical editorial the day before, calling on the Eritrean government to improve its treatment of independent journalists. It seems clear that forcible conscription to the armed forces was being used in reprisal against journalists writing on the reform movement and criticising the regime of President Isaias Afwerki (AI 2002: 6-7).

As the private media started to question the sanctity of the president, it opened the way for a broader demand for democratic reforms, particularly spearheaded by the students at Asmara University. The university students demanded greater academic freedom, social liberties, and the right to be consulted on matters of interest to them. Of particular concern for the students was the infamous and mandatory 'summer work programme', which required all students to undergo intensive military training (as their regular military service is deferred until after graduation) and to carry out what amounts to forced labour on behalf of the regime (on forced labour in Eritrea, see Kibreab 2009). The living conditions in the military/work camps, and the abuse and harsh treatment of the students, made the student leader Semere Kesete publicly announce that students would not enrol in the summer programme unless specific reforms were carried out.[12] To question publicly a military operation like the summer programme was tantamount to treason in the highly militaristic Eritrea. The day after his statement, 31 July 2001, Semere Kesete was arrested without charge by the security forces.

A *habeas corpus* application was made to the High Court on 11 August, for the authorities to bring Semere Kesete to court in order to justify his detention. Semere was represented by the prominent lawyer, Kesete Haile. He was accordingly brought before a bench of the High Court but only once. After this, the police requested more time and Semere was never brought back to the court (AI 2002: 7). The regime supported the police in their handling of the matter, effectively suspending the court's decision. Parallel to this, the President of the High Court, Teame Beyene, had the previous month presented a paper at the International Eritrean Studies Association conference in Asmara where he severely criticised the government's interference in the judiciary and the operations of the Special Court (see Chapter 3). After this, he was summarily dismissed as President of the High Court, effectively the equivalent role of a Chief Justice (USSD 2001; AI 2002; Connell 2007).[13]

During the High Court's deliberation of the *habeas corpus* plea, hundreds of students gathered outside the courthouse in support of their student union leader. The police seized the opportunity and 400 students

[11] CPJ, 'Journalist abducted by security forces, many others still missing', 6 August 2001, New York, at: http://cpj.org/2001/08/journalist-abducted-by-security-forces-many-others.php#more, accessed 17 March 2009.

[12] Human Rights Watch, 'Escalating crackdown in Eritrea', 20 September 2001, at: http://www.hrw.org/en/news/2001/09/20/escalating-crackdown-eritrea, accessed 17 March 2009.

[13] See also Human Rights Watch: 'Escalating crackdown in Eritrea: reformists, journalists, students at risk', 21 September 2001.

were rounded up and sent to the summer work programme in Wia, a reputed military/detention camp located in the inhospitable and scorching desert south of Massawa.[14] Parents of the students and elders who protested over the arrest and tried to negotiate their release were also detained (Hedru 2003: 443). According to Human Rights Watch, the government accused the students of 'unruly behaviour' and 'unlawful acts', but no formal charges were made. Immediately following the forcible transfer of the arrested students to Wia, 1700 others 'voluntarily' joined them there, according to the government, as the regime moved in to quell the growing public protest among the youth of the country.

Amnesty International reports that many of the students were severely beaten and not given any food for the first three days in detention (AI 2002: 7). As additional punishment in Wia, the students were forced to work in harsh conditions and extreme heat, building roads and crushing stones. Two of the students died from dehydration and heat stroke during their ordeal (ibid.: 8),[15] something the government attributed to 'lack of adequate logistical support' at the camp.[16] The student leader Semere Kesete languished in solitary confinement in a dark cell in Asmara, until he managed to escape in August 2002 (AI 2002: 8). He is now in exile in Europe.

When the regime began to round up and detain critical voices in the country, officials of the party and government started to defect. The first to leave was the Eritrean Ambassador to Scandinavia, Ms Hebret Berhe, who resigned from her post and said that she could no longer serve a government that was trying to block the Eritrean people's aspirations for democracy and the rule of law.[17] Her resignation sent shock waves through Eritrean society – as the first high-profile EPLF defector – and she was soon followed by the Eritrean Ambassadors to Nigeria and the European Union, as well as other diplomats and officials at the Ministry of Foreign Affairs in Asmara (Plaut 2002: 122).

The combined pressure from the G-15 top EPLF/PFDJ leaders, the private media, students and other civil society voices came to bear on President Isaias Afwerki and his regime. With events spiralling out of the regime's control, the loyal PFDJ party secretary, Alamin Mohammed Seid, publicly accused the dissidents and reformists of treason in assisting the enemy, Ethiopia (Plaut 2002: 122). In August 2001, in a desperate attempt to swing the EPLF/PFDJ support in their favour, the reformists issued a public document, 'An Open Letter to the Eritrean People: Important and Urgent Issues'. It summarised earlier statements

[14] Human Rights Watch, 'Escalating crackdown in Eritrea', 20 September 2001, at: http://www.hrw.org/en/news/2001/09/20/escalating-crackdown-eritrea, accessed 17 March 2009.
[15] See also BBC News, 'Students die in Eritrea detention camp', 20 August 2001, at: http://news.bbc.co.uk/2/hi/africa/1501092.stm, accessed 17 March 2009.
[16] Human Rights Watch, 'Escalating crackdown in Eritrea', 20 September 2001, at: http://www.hrw.org/en/news/2001/09/20/escalating-crackdown-eritrea, accessed 17 March 2009.
[17] BBC News, 'Attack on president "no big deal"', 20 July 2001, at: http://news.bbc.co.uk/2/hi/africa/1448575.stm, accessed 17 March 2009.

and rebutted the regime's accusations of treason, as well as warning that Eritrea would descend into tyranny if they did not receive the support of the party and its cadres (Hedru 2003: 443).

Understandably, though many Eritreans were passive bystanders in the power-struggle among the EPLF/PFDJ party echelons, they found it hard to believe the newly-found 'democratic' commitment by the so-called reformists, as they had been part and parcel of the regime which had developed the system of control and surveillance and abused human rights during the post-independence period. Hedru concludes: 'Unaccustomed to public airing of differences among the elite, and uncomfortable with the promises of the regime's critics, most Eritreans reserved judgement' (2003: 443).

In the mindset of President Isaias Afwerki, a threat from an enemy is not supposed to be negotiated, but eliminated. In the shadow of 9/11, when the world's attention was focused on the tragic events in the US, the President mobilised the coercive instruments of the state. In dawn raids on 18 and 19 September 2001, loyal security forces struck against and arrested the G-15 EPLF/PFDJ leaders opposing the president. Three members of the group, Mesfin Hagos, Adhanom Gebremariam and Haile Menkerios, were abroad and escaped arrest. The rest[18] were thrown in jail without any formal charges. The government spokesperson and senior EPLF/PFDJ cadre, Yemane Gebremeskel, claimed that those arrested had been involved in illegal activities, such as organising clandestine cells inside the country and within the armed forces, that had endangered the sovereignty of the country. The reformists were thus accused of treachery which included cooperating with opposition groups that were supported by Ethiopia.[19]

Following these two initial raids, the regime commenced a nationwide crackdown and mopping up operation, arresting hundreds of people. All private newspapers and magazines, eight in number, were closed down, and their journalists either arrested or forced into exile. Dozens of senior civil servants, diplomats, military commanders, journalists, business people and other professionals were detained, nearly all of whom were EPLF/PFDJ members and ex-fighters (AI 2004: 8). Many of them had not expressed public criticism of the president, but they were nevertheless associated with the reformers and considered a threat to the regime.[20] For instance, Edris Abaare, the director-general of the Ministry of Labour and a veteran liberation war hero, was arrested in the first week of October. His only public criticism of the government was in a debate some months prior to his arrest on the use of minority languages in primary education. A prominent elder businessman, Abdu Ahmed Yonus, was arrested for

---

[18] One of the original signatories to the G-15 letter, Mohammed Berhan Blata, had taken fright and disassociated himself from the group, and was thus not arrested.
[19] BBC News, 'Eritrea defends political crackdown', 10 October 2001, at: http://news.bbc.co.uk/2/hi/africa/1591835.stm, accessed 18 March 2009.
[20] As of 2004, only four of these had been released from detention, according to Amnesty International (AI 2004).

signing a letter written by Eritrean elders to the president urging reconciliation with the dissidents.[21]

The dire political repercussions and the massive human rights abuses following the September crackdown compelled the diplomatic community in Asmara to protest the government's handling of the matter. As a consequence, the dean of the diplomatic community, Italy's ambassador to Eritrea, was singled out and expelled from the country.[22] This subsequently led all the EU countries to remove their envoys from Asmara in protest.[23] The Eritrean Ministry of Foreign Affairs later expressed 'puzzlement' over the many 'negative' statements from diplomats and foreign ministries on the measures they had taken and perceived as justifiable: 'The Government of Eritrea particularly finds inexplicable the attempts to "whitewash" crimes against the nation's security and sovereignty and present it as advocacy for democratic reform.'[24]

On 26 November, a *habeas corpus* request for the G-15 was made to the Minister of Justice, pursuant to the Eritrean Constitution (Article 17), asking him, *inter alia*, to reveal their place of detention; to either charge the G-15 members and bring them to court, or release them; and to guarantee their adequate treatment in prison and to grant them access to lawyers, their families and adequate medical care. No response to the *habeas corpus* petition was received from the government.[25] However, in early February 2002, President Isaias Afwerki delivered a speech to the National Assembly, based on the government's investigation into the events of 2001,[26] indicting the reformists for 'committing treason by abandoning the very values and principles the Eritrean people fought for'. The Assembly responded by condemning them 'for the crimes they committed against the people and their country' (Hedru 2003: 444; Mekonnen 2006).

By the end of 2001, all dissenting voices demanding democratic reform in Eritrea were quelled. All had been arrested, driven into exile, or cowed into silence. The nascent Eritrean civil society and independent press were shut down, their spokespersons and journalists and editors arrested. Thenceforth, no opposition or alternative voices have been

---

[21] BBC News, 'Eritrea defends political crackdown', 10 October 2001, at: http://news.bbc.co.uk/2/hi/africa/1591835.stm, accessed 18 March 2009.

[22] BBC News, 'Eritrea expels Italian ambassador', 1 October 2001, at: http://news.bbc.co.uk/2/hi/africa/1572517.stm, accessed 18 March 2009.

[23] BBC News, 'European envoys pull out of Asmara', 10 October 2001, at: http://news.bbc.co.uk/2/hi/africa/1589148.stm, accessed 18 March 2009.

[24] Human Rights Watch, *World Report 2002*, at: http://www.hrw.org/legacy/wr2k2/africa4.html, accessed 18 March 2009.

[25] UN Working Group on Arbitrary Detention, Opinion No. 23/2007 (Eritrea), paragraph 6. Subsequently a new request of *habeas corpus* was filed in the Eritrean High Court on 26 June 2002 to which there was no reply either (African Commission on Human and Peoples' Rights, *Communication 250/2002 – Liesbeth Zegveld and Mussie Ephrem v. The Government of Eritrea*, 34th Ordinary Session, 6-20 November 2003, Banjul, The Gambia).

[26] See reference to the report in the Eritrean Government's response (of 29 August 2007, ref.: MO/145/07) to the UN Working Group for Arbitrary Detention, paragraph 2.

allowed to be heard inside the country. Today, it is forbidden in Eritrea for any group of more than seven people to assemble without approval by the government.[27]

Since September 2001, the G-15 detainees and civil society representatives have been kept incommunicado in secret detention camps and prisons. Little is known about their situation and physical and mental health, though unconfirmed information suggests that several of the reformists and journalists have died in prison due to lack of medical care, torture and inhumane treatment. The UN, the AU, and other agencies have requested the release of the prisoners and information on their whereabouts and status, but with meagre results. The African Commission on Human and Peoples' Rights has on two occasions sent written appeals to President Isaias Afwerki to intervene in the matter to ensure that the G-15 detainees are removed from secret detention and brought before the courts of law, all in vain.[28] Furthermore, the UN Special Rapporteur on the right to freedom of opinion and expression sent an inquiry to the Eritrean government concerning the alleged deaths of three of the journalists imprisoned in the 2001 crackdown.[29] The Eritrean government did not bother to reply to the UN on the question.[30] Most recently, the UN Special Rapporteur on the Situation of Human Rights in Eritrea requested to visit Eritrea for consultations with government authorities. The request was not heeded.[31]

THE 2001 CRACKDOWN: A CLEAR VIOLATION OF BASIC HUMAN RIGHTS

The international system of justice has through four separate opinions – two by the African Commission on Human and Peoples' Rights and two by the UN Working Group on Arbitrary Detention – made clear that the Eritrean government's 2001 crackdown on the EPLF/PFDJ reformists and civil society activists constituted a clear and grave violation of basic human rights, and continues to be so as long as the detainees are not brought before a court of law or released.

---

[27] UN Commission on Human Rights, Report submitted by the Special Representative of the Secretary-General on human rights defenders, E/CN.4/2006/95/Add.5, 6 March 2006, paragraph 558.

[28] See paragraph 54 of African Commission on Human and Peoples' Rights, *Communication 250/2002 – Liesbeth Zegveld and Mussie Ephrem v The Government of Eritrea*, 34th Ordinary Session, 6-20 November 2003, Banjul, The Gambia.

[29] On 29 November 2006, in regard to Seyoum Tsehaye, freelance, Dawit Habtemichael, deputy editor and co-founder of *Meqaleh*, and Yusuf Mohamed Ali, a journalist who is thought to be the editor of *Tsigenay*; all of whom were detained in Ira'iro prison.

[30] UN Human Rights Council, A/HRC/4/27/Add.1, 26 March 2007, paragraph 224 and 226.

[31] Report of the Special Rapporteur on the Situation of Human Rights in Eritrea, Sheila B. Keetharuth, UN.Doc.A/HRC/23/53, 28 May 2013, para 8.

The case of the G-15

Just a few months after the detention of the eleven top government officials (G-15), the UN Working Group on Arbitrary Detention received a plea concerning their situation.[32] Eritrea was at that time not a party to the International Covenant on Civil and Political Rights, but nevertheless upon request provided information on the case to the Working Group. The undisclosed source of the complaint argued that the G-15 members had been unlawfully detained 'solely for the peaceful expression of their political concerns' and that their detention violated their rights and freedoms as guaranteed by the Universal Declaration of Human Rights (Art. 9, 10, 14, 19 and 20).[33]

In its reply to the accusations, the Eritrean government maintained that the detention of the G-15 was made in consonance with the Transitional Penal Code of the country and other relevant national and international legal instruments, as they were detained, *inter alia*, for:

> conspiring to overthrow the legitimate Government of the country in violation of the relevant resolutions of the Organization of African Unity (OAU), colluding with hostile foreign powers with a view to compromising the sovereignty of the State, undermining Eritrean national security and endangering Eritrean society and the general welfare of the people.[34]

This argument was opposed by the complainant, referring to the Penal Code (Art. 29) and the Constitution (Art. 17) which states that any person accused of a crime has the right to due process of law and to be brought before a court of law within 48 hours. In considering the contradictory statements of the complainant and the Eritrean government, the Working Group on Arbitrary Detention was not convinced by the Eritrean Government's position on the subject matter due to lack of concrete evidence:

> Therefore, the Working Group concludes that the political leaders in question were arrested and are being detained for having expressed their political opinions and convictions and that they are victims of having exercised their right to freedom of opinion and expression guaranteed under article 19 of the Universal Declaration of Human Rights.[35]

Moreover, the Working Group concluded that the continued detention of the eleven former top officials in 'isolation in one or more secret locations where they have had no contact whatsoever with lawyers or their families', and the absence of a 'court ruling on the legality of their

[32] UN Commission on Human Rights, E/CN.4/2003/8/Add.1, 24 January 2003; Working Group on Arbitrary Detention, *Opinion No. 3/2002 (Eritrea)*, Adopted 17 June 2002.

[33] Paragraph 7 in UN Commission on Human Rights, E/CN.4/2003/8/Add.1, 24 January 2003; Working Group on Arbitrary Detention, *Opinion No. 3/2002 (Eritrea)*, Adopted 17 June 2002.

[34] Paragraph 8 in UN Commission on Human Rights, E/CN.4/2003/8/Add.1, 24 January 2003; Working Group on Arbitrary Detention, *Opinion No. 3/2002 (Eritrea)*, Adopted 17 June 2002.

[35] Paragraph 14 in UN Commission on Human Rights, E/CN.4/2003/8/Add.1, 24 January 2003; Working Group on Arbitrary Detention, *Opinion No. 3/2002 (Eritrea)*, Adopted 17 June 2002.

detention', all 'constitutes a series of violations of such gravity' that the deprivation of their liberty is *arbitrary* and thus a violation of Articles 9 and 10 of the UDHR.[36] The UN Working Group on Arbitrary Detention consequently requested the Eritrean government to 'take the necessary steps to remedy the situation of those individuals by bringing it into conformity with the standards and principles' in the UDHR.[37] Needless to say, the Eritrean Government neglected to take action on the Working Group's concluding request.

Subsequently, the African Commission on Human and Peoples' Rights (ACHPR) followed up on the G-15 case and in November 2003 delivered a landmark judgment against the Eritrean government.[38] The ruling was motivated by a complaint submitted by a Dutch lawyer (Liesbeth Zegveld) and an Eritrean living in Sweden (Mussie Ephrem), on behalf of the eleven former top-level government officials detained by the regime in September 2001.[39] Despite the Eritrean government's objection, the Commission found the case admissible. Since the government had ignored the detainees' previous *habeas corpus* requests to be brought before a court, the requirement to exhaust local judicial remedies could no longer apply in Eritrea.[40] After the Commission accepted the complaint's admissibility, the Eritrean government declined to forward its written statements on the merits of the case, and the African Commission was left with no alternative but to proceed to deliver a decision on the case based on the statements of the complainants only.[41]

The African Commission accepted in full the deposition submitted by the complainants and thus found the State of Eritrea responsible for violation of Articles 2, 6, 7(1) and 9(2) of the African Charter on Human and People's Rights, involving respectively the violation of individual rights and freedoms of liberty and security, the right to fair trial and due process of law, and the right to freedom of opinion and expression. The Commission hence urged the Eritrean government to release the eleven prominent prisoners immediately and to grant them compensation for their illegal detention.

[36] Paragraph 15 and 16 in UN Commission on Human Rights, E/CN.4/2003/8/Add.1, 24 January 2003; Working Group on Arbitrary Detention, *Opinion No. 3/2002 (Eritrea)*, Adopted 17 June 2002.
[37] Paragraph 17 in UN Commission on Human Rights, E/CN.4/2003/8/Add.1, 24 January 2003; Working Group on Arbitrary Detention, *Opinion No. 3/2002 (Eritrea)*, Adopted 17 June 2002.
[38] African Commission on Human and Peoples' Rights, *Communication 250/2002 – Liesbeth Zegveld and Mussie Ephrem v. The Government of Eritrea*, 34th Ordinary Session, 6-20 November 2003, Banjul, The Gambia.
[39] These were: Mahmoud Sherifo, Haile Weldensae, Ogbe Abraha, Hamid Himid, Saleh Kekya, Estifanos Seyoum, Berhane Ghebreghzabiher, Astier Feshatsion, Petros Solomon, Germano Nati, and Beraki Ghebreselassie.
[40] The Eritrean government tried to explain that it had been unable to bring the detainees before a court of law because of 'the nature of the criminal justice system in Eritrea [... as it was] inherited from Ethiopia and is therefore lacking' and as such it is 'highly congested and difficult to manage' (paragraph 33 in the ruling). This reason was not considered relevant by the Commission.
[41] Paragraph 46 in the ruling.

The lack of compliance by the Eritrean government with the unambiguous ruling by the African Commission motivated Dawit Mesfin (an Eritrean with German citizenship) and Habtom Yohannes (an Eritrean with Dutch citizenship) to ask Liesebeth Zegveld to continue to pursue the case within the international system of justice. On 1 February 2007 she opened a new case with the UN Working Group on Arbitrary Detention on the continued detention of the eleven former top-level government officials. The Eritrean government tried once again to justify the detention by citing the war-like situation in Eritrea, and that the detainees had attempted to undermine and topple the government. More intriguing, though, is the Eritrean government's justification of not yet having taken the detainees to court, due to the fact that 'there are co-offenders who are not yet apprehended'.[42] Obviously, such arguments were rejected by the UN Working Group on Arbitrary Detention.[43] It appears that the government of Eritrea tries to justify incommunicado detention without trial and formal charges being pressed over eight years, since they will continue to arrest people suspected of being opposed to the regime.

The Working Group observed that no new element (but the ruling of the African Commission on the case) had been brought to light that would change their previous ruling on the arbitrariness of the detention of the eleven former government officials. In 2002, the Working Group requested that the government take 'the necessary steps to remedy the situation', but the government's communication to the Working Group indicated that they had done nothing in this regard. The Working Group thus restated their opinion that the continued detention without trial of the G-15 'seriously contravenes' the principles of due process of law (as enshrined in Article 9 of the International Covenant on Civil and Political Rights, to which Eritrea in the meantime had become a state party).[44] Furthermore, the Working Group reiterated their decision that keeping the G-15 in detention solely for expressing dissent against the authoritarian policies of the regime 'constitutes a clear violation of the rights of these 11 persons to exercise their right of freedom of opinion and expression' (Art. 19 ICCPR).[45] Thus, the deprivation of liberty of the eleven former leaders was considered to be arbitrary and the Working Group requested once more that the Eritrean government 'remedy the situation' and suggested that an adequate remedy would be the immediate release of the detainees.[46] However, considering their previous ruling five years earlier, the Working Group took note of the 'obvious unwillingness of the Government to comply with the Working Group's Opinion' as

---

[42] See the Eritrean Government's response of 29 August 2007 to the Working Group's communication (Eritrean government reference: MO/145/07).
[43] UN Working Group on Arbitrary Detention, *Opinion 23/2007 (Eritrea)*, adopted on 27 November 2007.
[44] Paragraph 26 in UN Working Group on Arbitrary Detention, *Opinion 23/2007 (Eritrea)*, adopted on 27 November 2007.
[45] Paragraph 27 in UN Working Group on Arbitrary Detention, *Opinion 23/2007 (Eritrea)*, adopted on 27 November 2007.
[46] Paragraph 29 and 30 in UN Working Group on Arbitrary Detention, *Opinion 23/2007 (Eritrea)*, adopted on 27 November 2007.

'particularly worrying'.[47] The Eritrean government continues to ignore the Working Group's decision and recommendation and at the time of going to press in 2013 the prisoners had still not been freed.

The case of the journalists and the closure of the private press

Prior to the African Commission's final ruling on the detention of the G-15 in November 2003, another complaint was submitted to the Commission in April of that year on the continued incommunicado detention of 18 journalists arrested in the 2001 crackdown while working for the private media, and the banning of the private press in the country.[48] Article 19, an international organisation dedicated to freedom of expression that had taken up the case on behalf of the detained journalists, submitted the complaint.[49] Despite the Eritrean government's repeated attempts to convince the African Commission of the complaint's inadmissibility – principally due to failure to exhaust domestic judicial remedies in Eritrea – the Commission finally accepted the admissibility of the case in 2005. The Eritrean government explained the arrests of the journalists as occurring 'against a backdrop of war when the very existence of the nation was threatened' and, as a result, the government was 'duty bound to take necessary precautionary measures (and even suspend certain rights)'.[50] However, unlike certain other human rights instruments, the African Charter does not allow states to derogate from it in times of war or other emergencies. The precarious post-war situation in Eritrea at the time of the crackdown, the potential military threat posed by Ethiopia, and the possible political challenge posed by the reformist themselves, were thus not considered relevant by the Commis-

---

[47] Paragraph 28 in UN Working Group on Arbitrary Detention, *Opinion 23/2007 (Eritrea)*, adopted on 27 November 2007.
[48] African Commission on Human and Peoples' Rights, *Communication 275/2003 – Article 19 v The State of Eritrea*, (EX.CL/364 (XI)). Final ruling was made in 2007.
[49] The African Charter permits complaints by third parties on behalf of and not known to the individuals of concern (*actio popularis* approach). The journalists detained were: 1. **Zemenfes Haile**, founder and manager of the private weekly *Tsigenay*; 2. **Ghebrehiwet Keleta**, a news writer for *Tsigenay*; 3. **Selamyinghes Beyene**, reporter for the weekly *Meqaleh*; 4. **Binyam Haile** of *Haddas Eritrea*; 5. **Yosef Mohamed Ali**, chief editor of *Tsigenay*; 6. **Seyoum Tsehaye**, freelance editor and photographer and former Director of Eritrean State Television (EriTV); 7. **Temesgen Gebreyesus**, reporter for *Keste Debena*; 8. **Mattewos Habteab**, editor of *Meqaleh*; 9. **Dawit Habtemicheal**, assistant chief editor, *Maqaleh*; 10. **Medhanie Haile**, assistant chief editor, *Keste Debena*; 11. **Fessahye Yohannes** (or Joshua) Editor-in-Chief of *Setit*; 12. **Said Abdulkadir**, chief editor of *Admas*; 13. **Amanuel Asrat**, chief editor of *Zemen*; 14. **Dawit Isaac**, contributor to *Setit*; 15. **Hamid Mohammed Said**, EriTV; 16. **Saleh Aljezeeri**, Eritrean State Radio; and 17. **Simret Seyoum**, a writer and general manager for *Setit*. One of the 18 individuals originally listed by Article 19 had been covered by the ruling passed by the African Commission on the detention of the G-15 group (see above: *Communication 250/2002 – Liesbeth Zegveld and Mussie Ephrem v The Government of Eritrea*); thus, his name was excluded from the current case. Several of the journalists listed later died in prison.
[50] Paragraph 87 in African Commission on Human and Peoples' Rights, *Communication 275/2003 – Article 19 v The State of Eritrea*, (EX.CL/364 (XI)).

sion, which stated that 'Eritrea's actions must be judged according to the Charter norms, regardless of any turmoil within the State at the time'.[51]

Both the Eritrean government and Article 19 accepted the basic facts of the case (the actual arrest of the journalists and the closure of the press), but differed in regard to the motivations and justifications behind the action taken by the government. Article 19 argued in its complaint that the newspapers were closed and the journalists arrested since they had expressed their opinions and spoken out against the government. The Eritrean government, on the other hand, claimed that the arrests and the closure of the press were justified by Eritrean law since the measures occurred because 'the stated newspapers and the leading editors were recruited into the illegal network organised for the purpose of ousting the Government through illegal and unconstitutional means'.[52]

The African Commission rejected the Eritrean government's claim that its action was justifiable due to clauses in domestic legislation, which permit restrictions on basic human rights during times of political crisis.[53] The African Commission thus ruled that the arrests of the journalists were arbitrary (a violation of Article 6 of the Charter), and that their incommunicado detention for several years was a violation of the principles of due process of law (Art. 7(1)) and amounted also to a violation of Article 5, on the right to be free from torture and cruel, inhumane and degrading punishment and treatment. Furthermore, the Commission ruled that separating the detainees from their families over such a long period of time also constituted a breach of the right to family life (Art. 18). The government's banning of the press and targeting journalists was further deemed to be a violation of the right to freedom of expression and opinion (Art. 9), and an infringement of the public's right to information (Art. 9). The African Commission concluded its ruling by explaining:

> A free press is one of the tenets of a democratic society, and a valuable check on potential excesses by government. No political situation justifies the wholesale violation of human rights; indeed general restrictions on rights such as the right to free expression and to freedom from arbitrary arrest and detention serve only to undermine public confidence in the rule of law and will often increase, rather than prevent, agitation within a state.[54]

To support its conclusion, the African Commission made reference to a UN Human Rights Committee finding on the subject, which states that: 'The legitimate objective of safeguarding and indeed strengthening national unity under difficult political circumstances cannot be achieved

---

[51] Paragraph 87 in African Commission on Human and Peoples' Rights, *Communication 275/2003 – Article 19 v The State of Eritrea*, (EX.CL/364 (XI).
[52] Paragraph 89 in African Commission on Human and Peoples' Rights, *Communication 275/2003 – Article 19 v The State of Eritrea*, (EX.CL/364 (XI).
[53] As this constitutes a breach of Article 1 of the African Charter, which obliges states to recognize the rights, duties and freedoms enshrined in the Chapter and to undertake to adopt legislative or other measures to give effect to them
[54] Paragraphs 106 and 107 in African Commission on Human and Peoples' Rights, *Communication 275/2003 – Article 19 v The State of Eritrea*, (EX.CL/364 (XI).

by attempting to muzzle advocacy of multi-party democracy, democratic tenets and human rights.'[55]

The African Commission thus urged the Eritrean government to 're-lease or to bring to a speedy and fair trial the 18 journalists detained since September 2001, and to lift the ban on the press', and recommended that the 'detainees be granted immediate access to their families and legal representatives', as well as paying compensation to the detainees. Need-less to say, the Eritrean government ignored the ruling by the African Commission.

International actors and human rights organisations, like Amnesty International (AI 2002, 2004), government agencies, like the US State Department (USSD 2008a), and multilateral organs, like the EU[56] and the Inter-Parliamentary Union,[57] all consider the G-15 detainees and the journalists to be political prisoners.

FINAL REMARKS ON 'DEMOCRACY' AND PLURAL POLITICS

Since the 2001 crackdown, a large number of Eritreans voicing their dissent towards the authoritarian policies of the regime and advocating democratic rights have disappeared into incommunicado detention in Er-itrea's prison gulag. Little is known about the condition and whereabouts of thousands of ordinary Eritreans who are not sufficiently well-known internationally to attract support from international lawyers who can argue their case in front of the international system of justice. The rul-ings on the G-15 and journalists by the African Commission on Human and Peoples' Rights and the UN Working Group on Arbitrary Detention ought, in this regard, to be read as applicable to the vast number of anonymous Eritreans languishing in incommunicado detention due to their struggle for democracy.

It seems unlikely, considering the developments of the last decade, that President Isaias Afwerki and his regime will allow any true and realistic plural politics in the country, irrespective of what type of democratic model is suggested. Since the establishment of independent Eritrea, Isaias Afwerki has assumed the posts of party chairman (in a sin-gle-party state), head of state and government, chairman of the National Assembly, Commander in Chief of the armed forces, and in effect also the head of the judiciary (since he dismissed the Chief Justice at his own will in 2001). Eritrea today is the quintessence of a one-man dictatorship, as aptly described by a team of exiled Eritrean researchers who tried to

[55] Paragraph 107 in African Commission on Human and Peoples' Rights, *Communication 275/2003 – Article 19 v The State of Eritrea*, (EX.CL/364 (XI)).
[56] Council of the European Union: 'Declaration by the Presidency on behalf of the European Union on political prisoners in Eritrea', 20 September 2007, 12978/1/07 REV 1 (Press 201), P 074/07, Brussels.
[57] Inter-Parliamentary Union, Resolution on Eritrea adopted unanimously by the Governing Council at its 173rd session, Geneva, 3 October 2003.

create a directory of the power structure and organisational features of the Eritrean government:

> But to do so would imply that there is structure and organizational chart in the government. In reality, there is none: there is Isaias Afwerki, and then there is everybody else. He is indispensable, and everybody else is disposable. He is the snake, and the rest are its skin – that he sheds seasonally, and only he knows when the season begins and when it ends.[58]

Prior to the outbreak of the 1998-2000 Ethiopian border war, the Eritrean government functioned as a collective leadership where the top echelons of the EPLF/PFDJ were internally accountable to each other. There was periodic, although irregular, convening of party organisational congresses and deliberations in the National Assembly. Until the outbreak of war in 1998, this collective leadership was together responsible for laying the foundation of dictatorship in Eritrea. The G-15, eleven of whom are languishing in jail today, reluctantly admitted this in their open letter to EPLF/PFDJ members in April 2001: 'Just as we bear ultimate collective responsibility for our performance as leaders, we are obliged to bear equal responsibility for correcting our failures. Since our failure to lead properly has injured the people, we are prepared and determined to make amends ...'.

Today, President Isaias Afwerki reigns alone, with the help of a few loyal men at the top of the party, military and intelligence structures. By constantly reshuffling government and military officials, the president makes sure that no one can consolidate a power-base strong enough to threaten him.[59] How long he will last, however, is an open question.[60] On the other hand, as will be seen in Chapter 11, the attempted coup or the failed military mutiny of 21 January 2013 can also be seen as a signal of the potential challenge that may come from the rank and file of the army, as a result of a growing level of dissatisfaction.

---

[58] The Awate team: 'The Snake and Its Skin', 25 February 2009, at: http://www.awate.com/portal/content/view/5083/9/, accessed 3 March 2009.

[59] For example, President Isaias Afwerki made one of his latest re-shuffles of the government and military chiefs of staff in March 2009.

[60] Recently, for instance, scattered information about assassination attempts carried out on the president has been circulating.

6

The Eritrean Gulag Archipelago Prison Conditions, Torture and Extrajudicial Killings

INTRODUCTION

Eritrea is a country re-born out of suffering and human rights abuses. Its independence was hard won in 1993 after a 30-year-long war of liberation (Cliffe and Davidson 1988; Connell 1993; Iyob 1995). The massive and widespread human rights abuses experienced by the Eritrean people suffering under the yoke of the Derg military regime of Ethiopia, made them determined that they would 'never kneel down'[1] in their struggle against oppression (Firebrace and Holland 1987).

It is cause for despondency that the oppression and massive human rights abuses, now committed by their liberation hero-turned-dictator, President Isaias Afwerki, persist in Eritrea today. Promises of democracy and freedom offered by the liberation front (EPLF/PFDJ) during the war and at independence have all been broken.[2] Thousands of Eritreans are languishing in 'secret' detention camps throughout the country, government critics, veteran liberation fighters, civil servants, peasants, students, journalists, and religious believers alike.[3] No group or individual is unaffected – men and women, young and old, Christian and Muslim, rural and urban, educated and uneducated, all are liable to be regarded as a threat to the regime and thus susceptible to arrest, torture and disappearance (see Chapter 7). Eritrea, in the second decade of the twenty-first century, is a nation held hostage by its own government, with a population denied basic human rights and freedoms. Estimates of the number of political prisoners or victims of detention without trial and enforced disappearances, given by different sources, including Eritrean refugees and exiled civil society representatives, vary between 10,000 and 30,000. For

[1] 'Never kneel down' was a popular slogan of the EPLF. President Isaias Afwerki continues to use this metaphor, as during the recent war with Ethiopia he allegedly stated: 'Eritreans only kneel on two occasions; when they pray and when they take aim to shoot the enemy'.

[2] The *National Democratic Programme of the EPLF* of 31 January 1977 states that the aim of the struggle is to establish an independent democratic state, where 'freedom of speech, the press, assembly, worship and peaceful demonstrations' are protected (Article 1. D), and to ensure 'all Eritrean citizens' equality before the law' (Article 1. E). See also President Isaias Afwerki's first address to the UN General Assembly, Forty-eighth session, 10th Plenary Meeting, 30 September 1993.

[3] See, for instance, Amnesty International (AI 2002, 2004).

example, in a 2013 report Amnesty International notes that although it is impossible to know the exact number of political prisoners, the number is estimated as making at least ten thousand (UN Special Rapporteur on Eritrea 2013; Amnesty International 2013: 14).

The police are officially responsible for maintaining internal security and order in Eritrea; however, the army reserves and demobilised soldiers are also called upon to assist in operations targeting civilians, whom military personnel have the authority to arrest and detain.[4] Agents of the National Security Office (NSO), which reports directly to the president's office, are also responsible for detaining individuals who are considered to be a threat to the country's 'sovereignty' or security (USSD 2011: 6).

The Eritrean police corps, many of whose officers are conscripts, are riddled with corruption and they typically use their influence as government officials to assist friends and family. It is also reported that the police demand bribes to release detainees (USSD 2011: 21). The police, military and internal security forces continuously engage in arrests and detentions without due process. Despite a constitutional provision on administrative redress (Art. 24), there are no operative mechanisms to address accusations and cases of abuse by the police, internal security, or military forces (USSD 2011: 22).

The Eritrean Constitution prescribes that detainees must be brought before a judge within 48 hours of arrest, and may not be held for more than 28 days without being charged with a crime (Art. 17.4; also Art. 59 of the Criminal Procedure Code). This is an important safeguard against police abuse. The criminal procedure code requires that unless there is a 'crime-in-progress', police must conduct an investigation and obtain a warrant prior to an arrest (USSD 2011: 6). However, in cases involving national security, this process is often (mis)used or neglected by the authorities. In reality, most arrests are conducted without a warrant; the majority of the detainees are not presented before a court of law; and detainees are held for much longer periods than the law prescribes, often incommunicado (AI 2008b; USSD 2011: 7).

In practice, the accountability to the judicial system is non-existent. Former prison guard Mehari Yohannes, a veteran EPLF fighter who joined the front in the mid-1980s when he was 15 years old, managed to escape from Eritrea in 2002.[5] He describes a:

> 'sloppy' jail system with no accountability: one where orders are given orally (nothing in writing), people thrown in jail and forgotten, people asked to show up for 'five minutes' only to end up in jail for 4–5 years, a system without due process, a system that dumps prisoners in the cover of the dark every night, a system where family members are not notified of the arrest of their loved ones and if they inquire of the whereabouts of their children are given no information.[6]

[4] The legal foundation of this authority is unclear, however.
[5] Mehari Yohannes was responsible for guarding Semere Kestete, the imprisoned leader of the Eritrean Student Movement (see chapter 5), when he engineered the flight of both of them to Ethiopia in July 2002.
[6] Gedab News at Awate.com: '"The 'Executed": No smoking gun, but plenty of circumstantial evidence', Gedab Investigative Report on the alleged massacre of 150 people, 13 March 2003, at: http://awate.com/the-%E2%80%9Cexecuted%E2%80%9D-no-smoking-gun-but-plenty-of-circumstantial-evidence/, accessed 18 June 2012.

THE ERITREAN 'GULAG ARCHIPELAGO'

Like a chain of islands, the Eritrean political prisons, detention centres, and labour camps are scattered throughout the country. They are under the control of the military or the internal security service. Some are purpose-built as centres of incarceration; others may be converted store-houses or makeshift constructions (often metal shipping containers),[7] or may double up as military camps and detention centres. Many of the sites are underground, where detainees are kept hidden in specially dug cells and 'dungeon'-like structures. Reportedly, some political prisoners are held incommunicado in secret security sections of official police stations or of officially-designated prisons (such as in Sembel prison in Asmara). Members of the armed forces and national service conscripts are held in military prisons, including custodial 'rehabilitation centres' in army units (AI 2004). Some detention facilities in the army are known as 'rehabilitation centres' or 'tehadiso' to disguise the malpractice of arbitrary detention in the army.

The majority of the detention centres are secret, with access prohibited, and not officially designated as prisons. Several of the detention camps are located in some of the world's most inhospitable places, where soaring temperatures (above 50 degrees Celsius) and extremely rudimentary facilities make basic survival difficult. No outsiders are permitted access to these prisons/camps, and usually even close family members of detainees are denied visits.[8] The International Committee of the Red Cross – which has access to political prisoners in many dictatorial regimes throughout the world – is denied access to any Eritrean prisoners or prisons (AI 2004: 21).[9]

Of the numerous prisons and detention facilities throughout the country, the most frequently named are:

---

[7] The shipping containers are used both as an easy way to expand the capacity of the detention centres, and also as designated punishment since they work as 'ovens' and may reach extreme temperatures in the hot Eritrean climate. Amnesty International reports that metal shipping containers are used as prison facilities in Sawa military training centre, Adi Abeto prison, Dahlak Kebir prison, Mai Serwa, Alla near Decamare, Mai Edaga near Decamhare, Mai Temenei in Asmara, and Tehadasso army prison (in addition to other places) (AI 2004).

[8] Prisoners suspected of ordinary crimes and held in official civilian prisons and police stations are normally allowed three family visits per week and food, and their conditions broadly conform to international standards (AI 2004; USSD 2008a).

[9] The ICRC had permission to visit Ethiopian soldiers (who the Eritrean government claims are deserters from the Ethiopian army) and to visit and register Ethiopian civilian detainees in police stations and prisons (USSD 2008a). The Ethiopian inmates are usually held in separate prisons (AI 2004). On the ICRC's activities in Eritrea, see 'The ICRC in Eritrea - facts and figures 2007', at: http://www.icrc.org/Web/Eng/siteeng0.nsf/htmlall/eritrea-field-newsletter-310308/$File/facts-figures-eritrea-07-08.pdf, accessed 9 December 2008. As of 2009, the ICRC has been denied permission to visit Ethiopian prisoners. See the ICRC Eritrea Report 2011, available at http://www.icrc.org/eng/assets/files/annual-report/current/icrc-annual-report-eritrea.pdf, accessed 18 June 2013.

- **'Track B'** (or 'Tract B') is located near the airport in a western suburb of Asmara (a former US storage facility). It is a military-run prison reportedly containing about 2000 detainees,[10] mostly EPLF veterans, conscripts, alleged Islamists, and people accused of forging identity documents or smuggling army deserters out of the country (AI 2004: 21; AI 2013). Most of the prison camp's buildings are underground, in addition to extra 'storage' of detainees in metal containers. The camp is run by Col. Berhane, reportedly assisted by two notorious interrogators, Yosief Berhane and Fikre.[11]

- **Adi Abeto** army prison is just outside Asmara. A relatively large camp, it is reportedly used for conscripts, returned asylum seekers, and members of minority religions (AI 2004: 20).

- **Wia** military detention centre is located some 32 kilometres south of the Red Sea port of Massawa, at one of the hottest places on earth (it was used during the Italian colonial era as an incarceration site for extreme punishment). It is composed of several separate camps designated to hold two large groups of detainees: escaped military conscripts and draft evaders, and members of prohibited religious organisations.[12] The camp commanders are reportedly Lieutenant Colonel Jemal, Lieutenant Colonel Weddi Hale and Captain Ramadan. On 10 June 2005, reportedly, 161 detained youths were shot and killed trying to escape from Wia (USSD 2006).

- **Ira'iro** is a secret prison camp located near the village of Gahtelay (Northern Red Sea Province) in a mountainous desert region north of the Asmara-Massawa road.[13] It is composed of five main blocks, including two cell-blocks (of 62 cells each).[14] Allegedly, the camp was purpose-built in 2003 to receive the 'G-15' political prisoners (see Chapter 5). The camp is also used for other political prisoners, including many of the detained Eritrean journalists. The area is extremely inhospitable, making it difficult to escape, and the temperature can fluctuate from 40 Celsius by day to several degrees

[10] Reporters Without Borders, press release, 'Eritrea: Journalist employed by state-owned Radio Dimtsi Hafash held since 2006', 24 April 2008.

[11] Eritrean Center for Media Services (ECMS), 'Thirteen detainees escape Track B', 5 November 2007. It was not possible to ascertain the military ranks of Yosief Berhane and Fikre.

[12] Awate.com: 'Scores of Eritreans Die at Wi'a', 3 October 2007, at www.awate. com, accessed 14 March 2009. See also statements and information from the Open Doors International organisation (available at http://sb.od.org/).

[13] According to Reporters Without Borders, identified as 'hill 346' on the military high command's maps (RWB report 'New revelations about Eiraeiro prison camp - "The journalist Seyoum Tsehaye is in cell No. 10 of block A01"', 30 January 2008, available at: http://www.rsf.org/article.php3?id_article=25251 (accessed 18 April 2009.)

[14] According to Reporters Without Borders, the three sections holding the most politically sensitive detainees are A01, B01 and B03. (RWB report 'New revelations about Eiraeiro prison camp - "The journalist Seyoum Tsehaye is in cell No. 10 of block A01"', 30 January 2008, available at: http://www.rsf.org/ article.php3?id_article=25251 (accessed 18 April 2009).

below zero at night. The camp administrator is Lt Col. Isaac Araia, also known as 'Wedi Hakim'.[15]

- **Dahlak Kebir** detention centre is located on Dahlak Kebir Island, the main island of the Dahlak archipelago in the Red Sea, 7 kilometres from the main town of Nakua. It consists of eight large iron-sheet buildings, and holds about 800 inmates, mainly army deserters and draft evaders, and military and political prisoners (AI 2004: 20). The Dahlak islands are notorious for their extremely hot climate, and were used as detention centres during both the Italian and Ethiopian periods.

- **Me'eter** military detention camp is a quite new complex, located in Northeastern Eritrea. Reportedly, it is purpose-built to house religious prisoners and has received over 1500 adherents of 'banned' Christian churches. Some have reportedly died while in prison.[16]

- **Haddis Ma'askar** army prison is located close to the main Sawa military camp. It is also recently built, composed of underground structures. It holds about 1000 prisoners, mostly military personnel, but also returned asylum seekers (AI 2004: 20).

- **Ala Bazit** military prison camp is located in the middle of a desert behind the Ala Mountains, on the road between Dekemhare and Massawa.[17] It occupies the site of a former military training camp built by the US military in 1996, and consists of three groups of houses with corrugated sheet metal roofs that are surrounded by large brambles and overseen by three watchtowers.[18]

- **Mai Dima** military prison camp is located around Berakit Mountain (on the way to Obal), in Zone 3. It is run by the Intelligence Unit of the 25th Regiment. The camp is used to house Kunama detainees,

[15] A first-hand witness account of the Ira'iro camp has been obtained by Reporters Without Borders. The witness explains: 'About one kilometre after the barrier [check-point on the road to the camp] are the barracks of Eiraeiro's guards, then the outer perimeter of the camp itself, delineated by barbed wire on this side and by a minefield on the north side of the camp. After this second checkpoint, the prisoners are taken to the administrator's office in an L-shaped building on the edge of the complex. This building also houses a bakery, a medical post, a pharmacy and a bedroom for senior officials from Asmara such as President Isaias himself. In a flat area below the administration building, the prison camp is an E-shaped complex of three cement buildings, each containing a total of 64 separate cells separated by thick walls. Each cell is identified by a letter and a number. See Reporters Without Borders: 'New revelations about Eiraeiro prison camp - "The journalist Seyoum Tsehaye is in cell No. 10 of block A01"', 30 January 2008 (at: http://www.rsf.org/article.php3?id_article=25251, accessed December 2008).
[16] Information from the Christian-rights organisation Open Doors International (available at: http://www.opendoorsuk.org/resources/persecution.php?country=eritrea).
[17] It is one of five prison camps in the so-called 'Zone 3' of Eritrea, run by military Commando Unit No. 525.
[18] Reporters Without Borders, 'State TV journalist secretly sentenced in 2006 to five years of forced labour', 30 October 2008, at: http://www.rsf.org/article.php3?id_article=29140, accessed 8 December 2008.

and reportedly 26 Kunamas were killed in April 2007 by the authorities and buried in the camp (see Chapter 9).[19]

- There are several prisons in Asmara. **Sembel** prison is an officially-designated prison for political prisoners; **Tsetserat** prison holds mainly EPLF veterans in underground cells; **Wenjel Mermera** is a security section of the 2nd Police Station (known as *Karchele*), used as a special investigation centre; and likewise there is a special security section in the **6th Police Station** in Asmara holding political prisoners (AI 2004). Additionally, the national security service maintains many secret 'safe houses' in Asmara and other towns which are used for short-term detention and interrogation (AI 2004).

It is impossible to list all the political prisons and detention centres in Eritrea, not only due to difficulties in accessing information on this sensitive topic, but also due to the fact that a number of regular military camps and facilities double as centres of detention. Military units, from battalion up, have their own makeshift prisons. Often an outdoor space is marked off by large thorny branches from acacia trees where the detainees are kept in the open, day and night, sunshine or rain.

Some of the military camps have developed more specialised facilities to cater for political prisoners (like underground cells), others house detainees in ordinary military barracks. The most notorious military detention centre is at the main **Sawa** Military Training Camp in the western lowlands close to the Sudan border, where all new national service recruits are sent. Other military camps allegedly also functioning as detention centres are **Mai Temenai** (in Asmara), **Tessenei, Barentu**, **Mai Edaga** (near Dekhamare), **Galaalo** (at the Red Sea coast), **Alla** (near Dekhamare), **Gahtelay** and at **Assab**.

Military commanders are vested with the authority to try prisoners and pass sentences, including the death sentence. Reportedly, detainees have been executed in front of their unit members to intimidate others into accepting the discipline (see Chapter 7).[20]

CONDITIONS OF DETENTION

The conditions in the detention camps and prisons are harsh and life-threatening and the facilities are extremely primitive (USSD 2011: 4-5). Reportedly, scores of Eritreans die while in detention or under arrest.[21] It

---

[19] This event, according to the testimony of a former EPLF liberation fighter and later intelligence officer in the Eritrean army, Menghesteab Girmay Asres, given in October 2008, is discussed in detail in Chapter 9.

[20] Information given by Eritrean escapees. See also Amnesty International (AI 2004: 23; Amnesty International 2013).

[21] Reported by, *inter alia*, Amnesty International, Reporters Without Borders and US State Department. For instance, RWB reported that 'at least three of the journalists who were arrested in 2001, died in prison between 2005 and 2006. And on 11 January, Fessehaye Yohannes, known as 'Joshua', one of the most important figures in the country's intellectual life, died from the effects

is difficult to obtain official confirmation on deaths in prison, since there reportedly are no inquests into the deaths of prisoners and their families are generally not informed (AI 2004: 21).

In addition to ordinary prison blocks, many detention centres house prisoners in underground cells, in metal shipping containers, or in open-air facilities. Since several of the camps are located in areas where day-time temperatures rise to more than 40 degree Celsius, prisoners suffer an extra physical burden. For instance, in the Wia military detention centre, allegedly 16 prisoners died, while hundreds fell sick, by being exposed to extreme heat and subsequently suffering from dehydration, inadequate medical care and malnutrition, during the hot season of 2007.[22]

Prison guards who have fled Eritrea have recounted the horrible prison conditions. For instance, a former guard told Reporters Without Borders about the situation in Ira'iro:

> The cells are windowless rooms, 3 metres square, with ceilings high enough to be out of reach, and lit 24 hours a day by a bulb behind an opaque plastic globe. They have a numbered metal door with a 10-centimetre-square spy-hole through which the guards give the prisoner his food. Inside the cell, to the right of the door, a hole in the ground serves as a latrine. Above it is a pipe that delivers water but only the camp administrator can turn on the supply.

> A one-metre-high metal bar projecting from the floor at the far end of the cell, opposite the door, is used for punishments. If the guards think a prisoner has behaved badly (a look or comment to another prisoner or to a soldier, for example), the prisoner is bound to the bar by the feet and by the hands behind the back, in a squatting position. They are forced to remain like this 'for at least 40 hours' [...].

> The heads of the prisoners are shaved every two months by a barber, who is accompanied by a guard to prevent him talking to them. They are given food twice a day in a plastic bowl – a soup of lentils, vegetables or potatoes. They also have a glass of tea in the morning and six pieces of bread. They are only allowed one litre of water a day. Detainees in very poor health may be given an additional water ration, but only if prescribed by the camp physician, Dr Haile Mihtsun. If he issues a prescription, it is posted on the cell door. The administrator turns on the water in the pipe over the latrine for only 20 minutes a week. The prisoners have to wash themselves and their clothes in that short period of time.[23]

The testimony of a former Eritrean military intelligence officer corroborates the information given by the prison guard above, and describes the terrible conditions in Mai Dima military prison camp.

> The conditions for prisoners were awful. We didn't allow them to change their clothes, we didn't allow them to see their family, we always forced them to walk without shoes, and we always gave them small amounts of food and water – in

(contd) of appalling prison conditions in Eiraeiro' (see: *Eritrea – Annual Report 2008*, at http://www.rsf.org/article.php3?id_article=25386&Valider=OK). Furthermore, Open Doors International claims that eight Christians have died while in detention ('Christian deaths mount in Eritrean prisons', 21 January 2009, at: http://www. opendoorsusa.org/content/view/902/139/, accessed 23 January 2009).

[22] Awate.com: 'Scores of Eritreans die at Wi'a', 3 October 2007, available at www. awate.com.

[23] Reporters Without Borders: *Eritrea – Annual Report 2008*, at http://www.rsf. org/article.php3?id_article=25386&Valider=OK.

order to weaken them and to make them sick and die. When they got sick – we didn't give them medical treatment and because of this they were having mental and physical problems. We forced them to do hard work, and we were taking their private property like money, house, gold, and necessary documents, and other privately owned things. We would put 23–26 people in a small cell so that many would nearly die because of the shortage of fresh air. We scared and beat them continuously, and they couldn't escape. I have seen a lot of prisoners going crazy, and facing different kinds of diseases. I also saw some of the prisoners disabled because of the heavy beatings. I also saw prisoners die inside the prison.[24]

Food and water supplies to detainees vary from prison to prison and depending on the season. Generally, however, the amount and quality of the food is inadequate. Likewise, sanitation facilities vary, but are generally very poor. Testimony given to Amnesty International by a former detainee in Wenjel Mermera prison in Asmara, gives evidence of this:

The food was very poor and looked like washing-up water. It consisted of half-cooked bread, lentils, and half-cooked unsalted cabbage, in very small quantities. It was placed in a communal bowl in our cell where we had to eat by hand – about six spoonfuls' amount each for 26 prisoners. We were given half a cup of tea in the morning, and two meals a day at noon and 4pm. We had tap water to drink, but not enough. There was an open toilet in the cell. We could only wash once in two weeks. We slept on the floor, which was often damp, with two thin blankets. (AI 2004: 19-20)

The unhygienic conditions and absence of toilet facilities (only a bucket) and the prevalence of diarrhoea among prisoners help spread infectious diseases. It is also reported that detainees are forced to lie in diarrhoea as a punishment (AI 2004: 21). Reportedly, many detainees have died as a consequence of illness and unhygienic conditions (AI 2004; USSD 2008a).

The handling of detainees is part of an overall strategy, where inadequate facilities and mistreatment are part of an interrogation strategy to weaken the resistance among the detainees. 'Standard procedure' in this respect – beyond physical torture – is a six-point plan, as described by a defected Eritrean intelligence officer:

1. Confiscate personal assets like money, jewellery, necessary documents and gifts;
2. Forbid change of clothes and underwear;
3. Inflict pain and weaken them through meagre food, water, and medical supplies;
4. Harass them by applying strict, severe security and surveillance measures;
5. Deny family access;
6. Wear them out through rigorous labour.[25]

The severe physical and psychological stress in prisons has caused psychological problems for many detainees (USSD 2008a; 2011). Report-

---

[24] Recorded interview with Menghesteab Girmay Asres (conducted for this study on 25 October 2008 in Addis Ababa).
[25] Ibid.

edly, many have committed, or tried to commit, suicide to escape the gruesome prison conditions. A former detainee of the infamous Dahlak Kebir island prison off Massawa, who later managed to escape, recalls:

> Walta Haile, an ex-Malta deportee who had been tortured, tried to commit suicide at Massawa by tying his own hands and jumping into the sea [on 15 December 2003]. He got caught in the ship's propeller and his face was badly cut. He was taken out of the sea and we didn't hear of him again, maybe he died. (AI 2004: 22)

It seems clear that the Eritrean prison conditions, and the treatment the detainees receive, contravene the principles enshrined in the 'Basic Principles for the Treatment of Prisoners', adopted by the UN General Assembly Resolution 45/111 of 14 December 1990. Furthermore, conditions of detention in Eritrea are in clear violation of the standards as prescribed by the International Covenant on Civil and Political Rights (ICCPR), to which Eritrea is a party. Article 10 of ICCPR makes clear that detainees shall 'be treated with humanity and with respect', as well as in line with other standards which are routinely violated by Eritrean authorities. Further aggravating the harsh conditions of detention is the deliberate torture and cruel, inhumane and degrading treatment inflicted upon detainees.

TORTURE AND CRUEL, INHUMANE AND DEGRADING TREATMENT AND PUNISHMENT

During the liberation struggle against the Derg, Eritrean detainees were routinely tortured in Ethiopian prisons; a brutality which made the Eritrean people even more steadfast in their struggle for independence. Sadly, the torture, inhumane and degrading treatment and punishment sustained on a massive scale in Eritrea persist today; paradoxically by the very same liberation 'heroes' who were tortured by the Derg.[26]

During our work on this study, a number of Eritreans have retold their personal experiences of torture inflicted by EPLF officials, both rank-and-file soldiers, officers and professional 'torturers', as well as by high-level EPLF leaders themselves.[27] Reporters Without Borders interviewed escapees from the infamous Ira'iro prison, who told about their 'daily hell' and the involvement in torture by high-level government officials:

> The prisoners are kept day and night under the light of an electric bulb and in complete isolation. Some are manacled by the feet or hands. Others are not. When they are not shut up in their cells, the prisoners are taken to one of the three interrogation rooms. The interrogation sessions are often conducted by

[26] For instance, the vivid recollection of the EPLF fighter Girmai Haile of his torture experiences under the Derg as described in Bondestam (1989), could just as well be told by one of today's escapees from EPLF's detention centres.

[37] The Director of Suwera, Eritrean human rights NGO based in Khartoum, confirmed that the majority of the refugees interviewed who had been imprisoned told about experiences of torture. Interviewed 20 April 2008, Khartoum.

Abdulla Jaber, the security chief of the ruling People's Front for Democracy and Justice, or other senior officials such as Yemane 'Monkey' Gebreab, President Isaias' advisor [and political director of the government party]. The prisoners are tortured during these sessions. They are hit with plastic whips, for example. There are messages written over the doors of the interrogation rooms. One says: 'Did you see who died before you?' Another says: 'If you don't like the message, kill the messenger.'[28]

Former detainees tell about various types of torture and inhumane treatment inflicted upon them with or without a specific reason given. A 34-year-old who had been undertaking national service told what happened when he and his army friends did not manage to carry out a physical exercise as ordered:

They beat us and some were thrown in prison. They beat with a stick first. They beat as much as they could. Then when you are tired they tie you like a 'helicopter'. Afterwards, they throw you on the sand, in direct sunlight. You are left outside during night too, freezing.

Another national service soldier told about his friend: 'My friend Wedi Amir was tied by the hands and hung from a tree. His arms/tendons were 'broken'. He was sent to the hospital and [they] amputated both arms. I think he is a mental case now.' A young man in his mid-twenties explained his story:

I escaped the army in 2004, to Asmara. After a month I was working with house construction in Asmara. Then they [military] came and took me to Addi-Abeyto prison, in the vicinity of Asmara. They tied me in the 'no. 8' for two weeks. This is normal. [...] I was tortured continuously for several weeks. My own army friends had to torture me. The officers commanded them to do it. Now I have a nerve problem…[29]

The informants indicate that extreme methods of torture are frequently used by Eritrean interrogators. Based on numerous interviews with Eritrean torture victims, Amnesty International has listed the following standard torture methods used by the EPLF regime against their own people (AI 2004: 19).

- *'The helicopter':* the victim is tied with a rope by hands and feet behind the back, lying on the ground face down (sometimes even suspended in the air), outside in the hot sun, rain or freezing cold nights, stripped of upper garments. This is a punishment allocated for a particular number of days, the maximum reported being 55 days in the Dahlak Kebir island prison, but it is more often one or two weeks. The prisoner is tied in this position 24 hours a day, except for two or three short breaks for meals and toilet functions.

- *'Otto' (Italian for 'eight'):* the victim is tied with hands behind the back and left face down on the ground, but without the legs tied.

[28] Reporters Without Borders: 'New revelations about Eiraeiro prison camp - "The journalist Seyoum Tsehaye is in cell No. 10 of block A01"', 30 January 2008: http://www.rsf.org/article.php3?id_article=25251, accessed December 2008.
[29] All interviews conducted in Addis Ababa, 28 April 2008.

- *'Jesus Christ':* the victim is stripped to the waist, wrists tied, and standing on a block with hands tied to a tree branch; the block is removed, leaving the victim suspended with the feet just off the ground in a crucifix-like posture. Beatings are inflicted on the bare back. This is said to be an extremely severe torture, restricted to only 10–15 minutes to avoid serious lasting injury. This method was first reported from Adi Abeto prison in 2003.

- *'Ferro' (Italian for 'iron'):* the wrists are bound behind the back with metal handcuffs while the victim lies on the ground face down and is beaten with sticks or whipped with an electric wire on the back and buttocks.

- *'Torch' or 'Number eight':* inside a special torture room, the victim is tied up by wrists behind the back and with the feet bound; a stick is placed under the knees and supported on a framework on both sides horizontally, and the body is turned upside down with the feet exposed. The soles of the feet are beaten with sticks or whipped. (This was a common punishment in Ethiopia and pre-independence Eritrea under the Derg.)

- *'Almaz' (diamond):* the victim is tied and suspended from trees with arms tied behind his back (USSD 2007a).

Reportedly, detainees have also been exposed to torture by electric shocks and sexual violence (such as a soft-drink bottle filled with water and tied to the testicles) and rape of female detainees (USSD 2007a). A standard procedure, before and after active torture, is to tie the victim at the hands, elbows and feet for extended periods (up to several weeks), and leave them exposed to the sun (USSD 2007a). One former detainee recalled:

> I saw others tied too, some very tightly. I saw one whose veins in his arms burst and blood flowed out. They just left him there and forgot about him. When the veins burst they took him away and we didn't know what happened to him. Sometimes the veins swelled up because of the sun, and burst.(AI 2004: 22)

Another survivor gave the following witness account:

> They beat them in front of us until they were vomiting blood. They tied them in 'helicopter' method for 55 days outside in the heat. Ermias' skin colour changed, his body swelled and he couldn't walk. For the first two days he was refused food, but the prisoners fed him. I don't know if he is still alive. (AI 2004: 18)

For several years, Eritrea has been one of the top 'torture-victim' producing countries in the world, as documented by the annual review of the Freedom from Torture organisation (2006-2007). In the period under review the organisation received 150 referrals involving Eritrean victims of torture. Eritrea was preceded only by two other countries which have referrals of 193 and 235 each. These were DRC and Iran, respectively (Freedom from Torture 2006-2007). Furthermore, the UN Special Rapporteur on torture and other cruel, inhumane or degrading treatment or punishment has received considerable reports of torture in Eritrean detention camps and prisons, and also cases where detainees were tortured to death.[30]

Despite the widespread reports of systematic torture in Eritrea, committed by police, army, intelligence, party and government officials, no known action has been taken to punish the perpetrators of torture and abuse (USSD 2011: 3). This is in itself a clear violation of Articles 2 and 3 of the ICCPR (ratified by Eritrea), which require states to respect and ensure the civil and political rights of *all* individuals within its territory (for elaboration, see Novak 2005: 27-82).

The prohibition of torture has an extraordinary status in the protection of human rights under international law; it is nonderogable and ensured without any restrictions whatsoever (Novak 2005: 157). Furthermore, the Eritrean Constitution prohibits torture (Art. 16.2), and it is prohibited by Article 7 of the ICCPR and has now attained a status of customary international law and ranks as *jus cogens* (Novak 2005: 157-158). Clearly, the Eritrean government is in grave violation of both Eritrean and international law on this matter.

EXTRAJUDICIAL KILLINGS AND ENFORCED OR INVOLUNTARY DISAPPEARANCES

How many people have disappeared – or even been killed – in the Eritrean Gulag archipelago under the EPLF is impossible to estimate. There are numerous reports of summary executions or people being tortured to death, carried out by military personnel in the many military detention camps throughout the country (AI 2004; USSD 2011: 3). An eyewitness account given by an Eritrean refugee to Amnesty International, provides a glimpse into this brutal reality:

> One day while I was in the army, three soldiers were brought in front of us and shot. We were told they were traitors but we were not told what the charges were. They had no trial and we didn't know who they were or what they had done. (AI 2004: 23)

Enforced disappearances and extrajudicial killings have reportedly taken place in Eritrea on several occasions. In the immediate aftermath of military liberation of the country in May 1991, reportedly several hundred people were rounded up from the Dembelass and Qohain areas after being accused of serving the Ethiopian military junta and being members of the Ethiopian Workers Party.[31] To this day, there is no news of what happened to them or their whereabouts.[32]

---

[30] UN Human Rights Council, A/HRC/4/33/Add.1, 20 March 2007, Fourth Session, Agenda item 2; UN Human Rights Council, A7HRC/4/21/Add.1, 8 March 2007, Fourth session, Agenda item 2.
[31] Gedab News at Awate.com: 'The "Executed": No smoking gun, but plenty of circumstantial evidence', Gedab Investigative Report on the alleged massacre of 150 people, 13 March 2003. at: http://www.awate.com/cgi-bin/artman/exec/view.cgi/11/1090/printer, accessed 4 April 2009.
[32] Not all people 'disappearing' in detention die, however. Some of those who

In January 2003, TV-Zete, a television station founded by the Eritrean Action Group in Sweden, revealed that a massacre of Eritrean Muslims perpetrated by the Eritrean government had occurred on 18 June 1997. The group of 150 Eritrean civilians was rounded up on 23 January 1997 and accused of being collaborators of the Eritrean Islamic Jihad Movement. Allegedly all of them were executed without trial or formal sentencing. The killings were part of a retaliation offensive ordered by the chief of the National Security Office, Abraha Kassa, under the direction of President Isaias Afwerki, in response to the murder of five Belgian tourists, allegedly carried out by Eritrean Jihadists, in late December 1996. An investigation team by the Eritrean diaspora news site Awate. com has researched the alleged execution of the 150 civilian Eritrean Muslims. Although much circumstantial evidence exists, it is impossible to come to a definite conclusion on the massacre due to lack of concrete evidence and the fact that it is impossible to carry out investigation of this type in Eritrea.[33] However, immediately after the killings of the Belgian tourists, there were several reports about retaliation campaigns against villages in the area. Allegedly, villagers from Sheab, Gedged and Shebah were rounded up and disappeared – purportedly executed – in early 1997 by Colonel Osman Bekhit and his squad. Villagers from Seber also disappeared after a raid by General Wuchu and his men.[34] A more recent and equally brutal incident occurred in 2007 involving the persecution of the Kunama ethnic group. Owing to its peculiar characteristic features, this issue will be discussed as a separate case study in Chapter 10.

Extrajudicial killings take place not only in detention centres and prisons, but also in the context of everyday life in rural and urban areas. A number of people have been shot near the Sudanese and Ethiopian borders, allegedly for attempting to cross the border illegally (USSD 2008a). Apparently, military personnel on the border have standing orders to shoot on sight if people are attempting to flee the country. For instance, on 31 December 2008, six Eritrean teenage boys trying to cross the border to Ethiopia in the Mid-Mereb basin (Western lowlands)[35] ran into an Eritrean military border patrol. Five of them were rounded up and after identifying themselves, the soldiers reportedly shot and killed four of the boys at arm's length.[36] One of the five boys, Tekeste Woldu, who happened to stand behind the others, was shot lightly on his leg and fell to the ground first. The others fell on top of him, so the soldiers did not notice that he had survived. Later, Tekeste Woldu, despite his wound, managed to trek

---

(contd) were reported 'disappeared' have later been known to have received extrajudicial sentences to long prison terms (AI 2004).

[33] Gedab News at Awate.com: See Note 31.

[34] Ibid.

[35] In the forest area of Enda Azmatch Uqbit, in the environs of a place called DemBe Enda Seqal.

[36] The names of the victims are: Goitom Solomon (from Adi Quoray); Kiros Haile (from Adi Haber); Tesfai Debessai (from Adi Haber); and Mengistu Weldegergis (from Adi Yehdug); all from the district of Enda Azmatch Uqbit.

across the Eritrean border into Ethiopia, where he currently is a registered refugee.[37] Similar reports of abuse are also chronicled by the report of the UN Special Rapporteur on the Situation of Human Rights Eritrea. One particular example is that of a woman who 'was shot seven times, in the leg, foot, hand and breast, but still managed to escape,' and as a result 'had to be hospitalized for nine months' (Special Rapporteur 2013: 9).

The practice of extrajudicial killings by the Eritrean border patrols was confirmed by many of the Eritrean refugees interviewed in the Sudan and Ethiopia as part of the research undertaken for this study. This was also vividly described by Ethiopian soldiers in the trenches at Zalambessa frontline, as they explained how they were trying to give protective fire when Eritrean soldiers defecting were shot in the back by their own officers.[38] As a consequence of this brutal standing operational order, many innocent inhabitants in the border areas are killed too. Since many of the people living in the border areas are pastoral nomads, they are not accustomed to territorial borders as country demarcation lines and may thus be shot while tending to their daily activities, for instance, following their grazing animals.

Furthermore, the government has authorised the use of lethal force against anyone resisting or attempting to flee during military searches for deserters and draft evaders in the cities; a practice that reportedly has resulted in many deaths (USSD 2008a). Many individuals were beaten and killed during these forced recruitment roundups (USSD 2008a), possibly as a strategy to instil fear and compliance among the group of youth targeted. An Italian diplomat became an eyewitness to a forced conscription roundup in October 2005 in Asmara, where a young man was shot dead at point blank range. The diplomat recounts in his own words:[39]

> I was parking my car in the centre of the town when I saw a truck on the other side of the road. On the side of the truck, some soldiers were pushing twenty or so boys. I understood that it was a matter of a raid of young people to be sent to the infamous and hated military training army camp of Sawa. One of the boys managed to wrestle himself free from the group and tried to escape across the road. He did not reach the other side before he was hit by a burst of sub-machine gun fire. Subsequently a man in uniform approached the victim and ended his life with a grace shot. The body of the boy remained in the street for over an hour. To me it seemed like a warning to those who try to resist the orders of the regime.[40]

[37] Reported on the website of the organisation Connection e.V. (International Support of Conscientious Objectors and Deserters) by the Eritrean People's Party, 'Eritrea: The Shoot-to-Kill Heinous Policy Brings the Death of Four Innocent Teenager Boys', 11 February 2009, at: http://www.connection-ev.de/z.php?ID=582, accessed 4 April 2009.

[38] Tronvoll was visiting the frontlines and interviewing Ethiopian soldiers at Zalambessa in January 2013.

[39] *Corriere della Sera*: 'Speciale: in fuga dall'Eritrea: Massacri e repressioni', 25 October 2005, at www.corriere.it/Primo_Piano/Esteri/2005/09_Settembre/11/speciale_eritrea.shtml, accessed 16 January 2009.

[40] Italian diplomat, as cited in *Corriere della Sera* (Authors' translation).

FINAL REMARKS

There is no doubt that the Eritrean government's system of detention, the cruel and inhumane prison conditions, and the practice of torture and extrajudicial killings, are in clear breach of Eritrean national law and the international human rights obligations to which the government has subscribed. Witness statements (from individuals fleeing the country) and evidence of this brutal practice are found in abundance. The Eritrean population is no stranger to mass detention and torture, as the brutal Derg military regime of Ethiopia also used such a strategy to quell Eritrean resistance to their domination. The current human rights atrocities committed by the EPLF/PFDJ are probably on a larger scale than the Derg and this time it is their own liberation leaders and government – not an occupying regime like Ethiopia – who are committing the violations. The social and political impact is thus far more devastating on Eritrean society.

The totalitarian policies of the regime, their denial of any such practices, and their rejection of international calls for respect for human rights in Eritrea, make it impossible to undertake on-the-ground monitoring and investigation into the widespread and massive occurrences of grave human rights violations in the country. Thus, human rights violations on a massive scale are sustained and conducted with impunity. The international community has not taken upon itself the responsibility to intervene in Eritrea. Considering the scale of the atrocities committed, there may be a legal justification and foundation for an international humanitarian intervention (through the African Union or United Nations); however, to the authors' knowledge, this has not yet been either politically or juridically explored. The responsibility to investigate and press charges against today's perpetrators must therefore be followed up by the new regime replacing the EPLF/PFDJ sometime in the future.

7

Everyday Life of Detention and Disappearances: Vulnerable Groups in a Population Under Siege

INTRODUCTION

Memories of the detention and disappearances of loved ones by the brutal Ethiopian military dictatorship during the war of liberation still linger among the people of Eritrea. However, today those memories are overshadowed by the current brutal reality, that their own government is even more ruthlessly vicious than their former enemy.

Despite the fact that there is a fairly adequate formal legal framework for the protection of basic human rights in the country (see Chapter 2), widespread and systematic violations on a massive scale occur on a daily basis in Eritrea. Eritrean and international laws prohibit arbitrary arrest and detention, yet it remains a serious and pervasive problem in the country (USSD 2011: 5). No one knows how many individuals – men and women, old and young – are kept in detention or under arrest in Eritrea today, but estimates suggest 10,000 (UN Special Rapporteur on Eritrea, 2013). Today, *anyone* in Eritrea is liable to arrest and detention, irrespective of their age, gender, religion or ethnicity. *Any* reason – or *no* reason at all – may be given for their arrest or detention.

WHO IS DETAINED AND WHY?

Old age or youth is not an excuse for avoiding detention. Reportedly, detainees of over 80 years of age and in poor health are held under rudimentary conditions in prisons.[1] For instance, 82-year old Hassen Sheik Feres was arrested by the security forces in May 2007, without any charges. He is held in high esteem as a veteran liberation fighter for Eritrean independence in the 1960s.[2] Reportedly, just prior to his arrest,

[1] Amnesty International, for instance, reports the detention of Suleiman Musa Haji and Sunabera Mohamed Demenam, both over 80 years old and in poor health (AI 2004).
[2] Hassen Sheik Feres was a veteran seaman and captain plying the waters off the Eritrean coast. Under this natural cover, he was instrumental in smuggling food, medicines, arms and ammunitions from the countries of the region to the Eritrean coast during the period of the armed struggle.

he had met President Isaias and told him, 'Fear God and rule justly', a comment which apparently was not regarded favourably by the president.[3]

Children, too, are liable to arrest and detention in Eritrea. Reportedly, children as young as eight or nine years of age have been detained, with or without their parents. It has also been reported that child detainees have been sexually abused in prison (USSD 2008a). This is a clear violation of the UN Convention on the Rights of the Child (Art. 37), which Eritrea ratified in 1994. Although there is a juvenile detention centre in Asmara, usually children are imprisoned with adult prisoners (AI 2004: 21; USSD 2011: 5).

Having a trusted, high-profile position or a distinguished record as a veteran liberation war hero is no protection against the arbitrary punitive injustices committed by the government. Most famous and notable are the eleven top-level government ministers and party officials arrested in the September 2001 crack-down, all prominent EPLF leaders and veteran liberation war heroes. However, detentions of top-level EPLF members have occurred since 1991 when the party came to power. For instance, General Bitweded Abraha, a founding member of the EPLF, was arrested in 1992 and detained without charge for five years, apparently due to a falling-out with President Isaias Afwerki. He was re-arrested just weeks after his release and is reportedly still detained. Having served about two decades of imprisonment, often in solitary confinement in a dark cell, he is believed to have become mentally ill (AI 2004: 9). Furthermore, in the 1993 'fighter rebellion' – when some sections of the armed forces briefly took over key installations on the eve of independence as a protest against President Isaias Afwerki's tendencies to make his own decisions involving all fighters and Eritreans – several of the officers believed to be the 'ring leaders' of the protest were arrested and reportedly secretly detained without charge in Tsetsarat prison (AI 2002: 17).[4]

The arrest of further distinguished and prominent Eritreans continues. Taha Mohammed Nur was detained in November 2005. He was one of six founding members of the Eritrean Liberation Front (ELF) in Cairo in 1960, the first organised armed resistance to Ethiopian occupation of Eritrea. Taha was also an EPLF-appointed member of the Constitutional Commission of independent Eritrea, and served as a commissioner in the five-member Referendum Commission (as its secretary). Throughout his life, Taha Mohammed Nur fought for Eritrean independence and the well-being of its people – a personal history which was ignored by the regime. Taha was never released and died in prison in early 2008; his family was told to pick up his body from prison, without any explanation given for his death.[5]

[3] Awate.com: 'Hassen Feres, 82, Arrested in Massawa', 23 May 2007 (at www.awate.com).

[4] Including Tewelde Zemichael, Tesfaldet Tewelde and Hadera Kahsu, a medical doctor (AI 2002).

[5] Mr Taha Mohammed Nur was an early critic of the political developments in independent Eritrea. During an interview with Tronvoll in 1996, as a Constitutional Commission member he expressed a deep concern over the way the constitution-drafting process was handled (censoring and excluding views and opinions which differed from the EPLF view), and the monopolisation of power by the EPLF (see chapters 2 and 4).

Arrests and detentions can be ordered both with and without any specific reason given. Ordinary civic protest, not related to any specific 'sensitive' political or military matter, may unleash coercive reprisals from the authorities. For instance, 35 men (and two women who were later released) of high local standing were reportedly detained in the village of Halhal (close to Keren) on 27 November 2006.[6] They had alleg-edly been protesting against the distribution of land plots to individuals who were not residents of the area, a protest not accepted by the local authorities.[7] Furthermore, on 16-17 September 2006, in one coordinated operation, police reportedly arrested more than 2000 persons at several nightclubs in Asmara. The US State Department reports that in one of the nightclubs, police 'surrounded the club, entered, and began to check the identification cards of those inside. After initially arresting only specific individuals, police changed their approach and arrested without charge everyone inside the club – approximately 250 persons – using sticks and threats to control the crowd' (USSD 2007a). No trials were car-ried out in relation to the mass arrest, and most of those detained were subsequently released on bail.

In May 2006, 54 college students were reportedly imprisoned for refusing to participate in Independence Day celebrations.[8] The group, all evangelical and Pentecostal Christians, refused to participate in the state-organised activities marking Independence Day as they felt it was contradictory to their faith. Such an action challenges the extreme na-tionalistic ideology and praxis of the regime and is thus not taken lightly. For this 'disobedience', they were detained and allegedly suffered puni-tive measures for over ten days.[9]

Muslims are also arbitrarily targeted. For instance, on 13 and 14 August 2008, over 30 Muslim elders, community and religious leaders were reportedly arrested in Senafe town and surrounding villages.[10] No reason was given for their arrest, no formal charges have been made, and

---

[6] The following individuals have been identified; Mohammad Nur Hazut, Abubakar al-Haj, Sulaiman Ibrahim Humad, Mohammad Osman Mohammad Ali Ashkaray, Adam Farajalla Elos, Idris Mohammad Fikak, Jemae Karar Mohammad Nur Abilo (*Eritrean Center for Media Services, 'Eritrean authorities arrest 35 leading personalities in Halhal', 27 December 2006, http://www.adoulis.com/english/ details.php?rsnType=1&id=158, accessed 4 December 2008*.

[7] The Eritrean government seemingly intends a 'Tigrinisation' of lowland territories, where Tigrinya highlanders are given land rights in non-Tigrinya (lowland) areas. This, notably, has never been reported to happen the other way around, so that a Muslim lowlander has been given land rights in the Christian highlands.

[8] Cf. Release Eritrea, press release: 'Eritrean students imprisoned for refusing to participate in Independence Day celebrations', 23 May 2006, at: www.release-eritrea.org.uk/node/45, accessed 9 January 2009.

[9] This action is a clear violation of Article 18 of the International Covenant on Civil and Political Rights, ratified by Eritrea.

[10] They include the imam of the main mosque, Siraj Ona Ali; Awqaf leader and director of the Islamic Institute, Mohammed Saleh Abdella; a teacher and member of the Awqaf committee, Suleiman Ali; and a town dignitary, Pasha Mohammed Suleiman.

their whereabouts are still unknown.[11] Another example is the detention of 180 Muslims in 1993. After refusing to acknowledge the government-appointed Mufti, they were subsequently imprisoned and have yet to be released (USSD 2010). Generally speaking, Muslims residing in the lowlands (together with the Kunama minority group) are greatly at risk of abuses by the government. Historically these communities are regarded as sympathetic either to Ethiopia or to the ELF, the leaders of the latter being predominantly Muslim. As such, incidents of arbitrary arrest and detention are particularly felt by Muslims in the region (HRW 2009b: 24-25).

Mass arrest and collective punishment has become a common phenomenon in Eritrea. This is related in particular to preventing and punishing protests against the government's militarisation of society in general, and its much-hated national service programme.[12] After the 2000 peace agreement with Ethiopia, the Eritrean people looked forward to a general demobilisation of the army, and a return to 'normality' and civilian rule in the country. However, with the sustained full mobilisation and increasing militarisation of society,[13] people began to protest against and evade recruitment to the compulsory national service programme. As the protests spread, the government broadened its strategy and in 2005 started to detain and arrest relatives of draft evaders and escapees to prevent people fleeing. The authorities have no legal instrument that could justify such action (USSD 2007a). Furthermore, collective punishment is in itself a violation of Article 14 of the International Covenant on Civil and Political Rights, ratified by Eritrea. Since 2005, thousands of mothers and fathers, sisters and brothers, of draft evaders and escapees have been arrested throughout Eritrea. For instance, reportedly around 179 women and 26 men were detained on 24 October 2005 in the highland town of Dekemhare. The targets were parents whose children had fled the country over the last several years. If a parent was not found, the eldest available brother or the closest adult relative was detained. This wave of arrests followed earlier crack-downs in the region.[14] Furthermore, over 500 relatives, mostly parents, of young men and women who have avoided conscription or deserted the army,

[11] Information given to one of the authors by the Awate Team; personal communication, 2 April 2009.

[12] All Eritreans between the ages of 18 and 40 (both men and women) are required to undertake national service (6 months of military training and 12 months of 'construction work'). Since the Eritrean-Ethiopian war of 1998-2000, the national service has become neverending, as – due to the general full mobilisation of society – all recruits are kept under military command. Thus, individuals who enlisted for national service in 1998 are still serving in the army a decade later! The national service personnel are also used as forced labour for both public construction work and on the private enterprises of high-ranking military officers.

[13] For instance, the militarisation of the system of higher education in the country, and the abolition of Asmara University.

[14] Eritreans for Human Rights and Democracy, 'Hundreds more of Eritrean parents arrested in the Southern Region', 26 October 2005, at http//ehdr.org.uk/NE-26Oct05.htm.

were reportedly arrested and held under harsh conditions in Asmara in late 2006 (USSD 2007a). As the flight of Eritrea's young men and women today has reached about 3000-4000 per month, the regime has reportedly ceased the practice of arresting parents or relatives of the escapees, as this would have implicated an unmanageably large share of the population of the country.[15] According to Human Rights Watch, as of January 2010, the number of people who fled the country in recent years is estimated at about 200, 000 (HRW 2011: 8).

Residents of villages west of the town of Nakfa (Agaraa, Falket, Dejaya, and Gen) were prevented from farming and carrying out their jobs, reportedly due to local resistance towards the government military recruitment campaigns, in addition to refusal to celebrate Independence Day and commemorate Martyrs Day. According to the Eritrean Constitution (Art. 19.1), every person has the right to freedom of thought, conscience and belief, even in cases that contravene 'official policy'. This constitutional principle is ignored by the Eritrean government, which considers such actions as undue criticism and disobedience, warranting collective punishment in retaliation.[16]

PARTICULARLY VULNERABLE GROUPS AND INDIVIDUALS

Due to the enormity of human rights abuses in Eritrea, which affects the whole population, it may be difficult to single out certain individuals or groups that are more at risk of attack than the population at large. Nevertheless, certain groups or individuals are directly targeted by the government and exposed to grave human rights violations due to their particular status, profession or background. These prejudiced practices are partly a manifestation of the ideological underpinnings of the EPLF/ PFDJ (stressing a militant nationalistic ideology), but are also somewhat arbitrary, as all 'new' groups perceived as a threat to the regime's power will routinely be sanctioned. The groups are discussed below.

Individuals from the Kunama ethnic group are also in danger of being persecuted, apparently on ethno-political grounds. As noted before, due to its peculiar characteristic features, the persecution of Eritrean Kunamas will be discussed in Chapter 10 as a separate case study.

National service personnel and military conscripts
National service personnel and military conscripts, or youths liable to be called for national service, are in an extremely precarious situation. At independence, the leadership of the Eritrean defence forces was commended for its high morale and work ethic; high-ranking officers served without payment and special privileges, on the same footing as

[15] Information given to one of the authors by the Awate Team; personal communication, 2 April 2009.
[16] Eritrean Center for Media Services, 'Collective punishment against areas west Nakfa and arrest of a Liberation War wounded', 20 June 2006 (www.adoulis.com).

rank-and-file soldiers. Today, however, the Eritrean military leadership has reportedly become totally corrupted. Many of the army officers are extremely volatile and unaccountable in their execution of power. Since Eritrea is run as a military dictatorship, there are no checks and balances to the omnipresent power of the military leadership. In order to maintain its hegemonic position, the military leadership heavy-handedly cracks down upon all signs of dissent or questioning of its powers and no reasons whatsoever are tolerated to be excused from serving in the military. The military is strictly controlled from the top down without any democratic accountability. Sitting at the highest level of the structure is the state president, as the commander-in-chief of the armed forces.

National military service is compulsory in Eritrea, and there are no provisions for conscientious objectors.[17] According to law, Eritrean individuals between the age of 18 and 50, both men and women, must undertake national service for at least one and a half years (six months basic military training and one year of national service).[18] However, allegedly the upper age limit is frequently disregarded. In addition, numerous cases of under-age conscription are reported, making Eritrea a country with a pervasive practice of conscripting children into the army.[19]

Since the start of the Eritrean-Ethiopian war in 1998, national service recruits have been kept in the army for an indefinite period, as no demobilisation has taken place. The legal penalty for evading conscription or assisting in it is two years imprisonment (as per the National Service Proclamation of 1995). Amnesty International reports, however, that in practice offenders are being punished by their local commanding of-

---

[17] The right to conscientious objection to military service is not unequivocally supported by international law. Amnesty International argues that the right to conscientious objection is inherent in the rights to freedom of opinion and belief set out in Article 19 of the Universal Declaration of Human Rights and the International Covenant on Civil and Political Rights (AI 2004). Furthermore, paragraph 5 of resolution 1998/77 of the Commission on Human Rights emphasises that states should take the necessary measures to refrain from subjecting conscientious objectors to imprisonment. However, the International Covenant on Civil and Political Rights does not explicitly refer to a right to conscientious objection. Article 8.3.c.ii inserts a certain ambiguity into this matter, which the UN Human Rights Commission has also elaborated (see ICCPR General Comment No. 22 on Art. 18 para 11, at http://www.unhchr.ch/tbs/doc.nsf/(Symbol)/9a30112c27d1167cc12563ed004d8f15?Opendocument). In the case of Eritrea, however, according to the UN Special Rapporteur on freedom of religion or belief, 'Imprisoning conscientious objectors for more than 13 years is clearly a disproportionate measure which violates the individuals' right to freedom of thought, conscience and religion as laid down in A/HRC/7/10/Add.1 page 26 article 18 of the Universal Declaration of Human Rights as well as article 18 of the International Covenant on Civil and Political Rights (ICCPR)' (cf. Human Rights Council, A/HRC/7/10/Add.1, 28 February 2008, Seventh session, Agenda item 3).

[18] See the National Service Proclamation, Proclamation No. 82/1995 (23 October 1995).

[19] Information given to one of the authors by the Awate Team; personal communication, 2 April 2009.

ficers without any form of trial, legal recourse or opportunity to appeal, or redress. The forms of punishment may vary, but usually consist of torture and arbitrary detention for an indefinite period (AI 2004: 23). Such practices are unlawful and a clear violation of human rights (ICCPR Arts. 7, 8, and 9); however, it appears that no army officer has ever been investigated or punished for employing them.[20]

Reportedly, thousands of military service personnel are held in arbitrary detention without charge or trial (AI 2004: 23; AI 2013). Many of them are possible conscientious objectors; others are prisoners of conscience and individuals protesting against the brutality and destructiveness of the militarisation of society in Eritrea. Investigation carried out by Amnesty International reveals that there are a number of reasons for the arrest and detention of military conscripts (AI 2004).[21] Due to the brutality of the military service, many try to evade conscription by all possible means, including fleeing the country.[22] Thus, a number of individuals are detained while trying to evade conscription. Others have been arrested on opinion-based political grounds, such as criticising government policies or resisting military mobilisation and the conduct of war, and requesting demobilisation and a return to civilian life. Expressing support for democratic reforms has also led to arrests. Conscripts have also been detained for congregating in prayer meetings (AI 2004: 16). Some female conscripts have also reportedly been detained for rejecting sexual requests by officers (AI 2004: 26; ICG 2010: 30, Bailliett 2007).

In interviews carried out for this study in the Eritrean refugee camps in eastern Sudan and in the Shimelba camp of Tigray in Ethiopia, dozens of former military conscripts and national service personnel reported eyewitness accounts of human rights abuses, corroborating the findings of Amnesty International. For instance, a 28-year-old law graduate from Asmara University, who fled the country in 2007, explained how the system operates in the army:

> Whenever they conduct a meeting or a course of instruction, the commanding officers expect opinions and reactions from the soldiers. Whenever a person speaks out against the government leadership, or questions policy or strategy, no immediate action will necessarily be taken. But later at night they will come and pick them up and take them away for torture and detention. Many of my fellow soldiers disappeared in this way during night time.[23]

---

[20] Offences committed by conscripts and other members of the armed forces are in theory subject to military law, for which penalties are set out in the Transitional Penal Code which was adopted from Ethiopia in a modified version by Eritrea at independence (AI 2004).

[21] Some of these are arrested for 'regular' military offences punishable under military law, such as being absent without leave or disobeying an order. However, the punishments are imposed without due process of law.

[22] In 2008, about 700 and 400 Eritreans fled to the Sudan and Ethiopia respectively every month, the absolute majority of them national service personnel. In 2007, 14,100 new claims were registered in Sudan and 7800 in Ethiopia (UNHCR 2008). In 2009, however, the number of people fleeing the country reportedly increased to about 2000 per month. As of January 2010 the number of people who fled the country in recent years was estimated at about 200, 000 (HRW 2011: 8).

[23] Interviewed in Khartoum, 20 April 2008 (name withheld).

Adherents of prohibited religious groups

Adherents of prohibited churches and religious organisations or groups are constantly persecuted and restricted from practising their faith, which constitutes a clear violation of Article 18 of the International Covenant on Civil and Political Rights, ratified by Eritrea. Individuals belonging to churches and sects not officially approved and sanctioned by the government are likely to be arrested *en masse* if they congregate, and are likely to be exposed to torture and inhumane and degrading treatment.[24]

The EPLF, as a Marxist-Leninist-inspired liberation front, was a secular organisation and established independent Eritrea as a secular state. Today, only four main religions are officially recognised and allowed to organise and practise their beliefs (albeit controlled and under surveillance by the government): the Eritrean Orthodox Church (about 30 per cent of the population); the Eritrean Catholic Church (about 13 per cent of the population); the Evangelical Church of Eritrea (Mekane Yesus); and Islam of the Sunni rite (about 50 per cent of the population).[25] Although officially allowed to operate, their adherents may still risk government harassment and detention due to faith-based practices.

In addition to these four main religions, there are at least twelve smaller Christian denominations (totalling about 2 per cent of the population), mostly Pentecostal and evangelical in their orientation (generally known as pentes). These include the Jehovah's Witnesses (1600 members in the country), the Mullu Wongel Church, the Rhema Church, the Kale Hiwot Church of Eritrea, Meserete Christos Church and the Hallelujah Church. There are also small congregations of Buddhists, Hindus, and Baha'is, in addition to followers of traditional beliefs (USSD 2011). It is important to note that some of these religious groups have existed in the country for several decades, predating Eritrea's *de facto* independence in 1991.

There are various reasons to explain why Christians and members of other non-recognised religious communities are persecuted in Eritrea. For instance, Jehovah's Witnesses were victimised more or less immediately after the military liberation of Eritrea, since they do not engage in politics. As they refused to register to vote in the 1993 referendum on independence, they were targeted and harassed and sanctioned by the EPLF government from 1992 onwards. Their refusal, on the grounds of faith, to enrol in the national military service programme which was

[24] See UN Commission on Human Rights, E/CN.4/2006/6/Add.1, 21 March 2006, Sixty-second session, Agenda item 11(a); UN Commission on Human Rights, E/CN.4/2006/5/Add.1, 27 March 2006, Sixty-second session, Agenda item 11; UN Human Rights Council, A/HRC/4/21/Add.1, 8 March 2007, Fourth session, Agenda item 2; Amnesty International, 'Eritrea: Religious Persecution, (AFR 64/013/2005), 7 December 2005; Voice of the Martyrs, 'Eritrea: Police arrest 150 more Christians'. See also the comprehensive, compiled information reproduced by Howard Hughes in the unpublished report 'Power versus Prayer: Religious Persecution in Eritrea', May 2007. See also US State Department's annual country reports on international religious freedom.

[25] Number of adherents according to US State Department (USSD July - December 2010 Religious Freedom Report).

launched in 1994 further aggravated the situation, subsequently leading to stripping the Jehovah's Witnesses of their citizenship rights by
Presidential decree in October 1994 (AI 2004: 14).[26] Three Jehovah's Witnesses who refused the first call for military service have been held in
incommunicado detention in Sawa military training centre since 24 September 1994.[27] Although there are varying numbers on this, as is the case
in many other reports, the UN Special Rapporteur on freedom of religion
lists 25 Jehovah's Witnesses as having been detained 'solely on the basis
of their religious beliefs'.[28] Some have reportedly died in prison. The
particular history of the Jehovah's Witnesses in Eritrea has indicated
that the government singled them out 'for particularly harsh treatment'
(USSD 2007b; USSD 2009; USSD 2010; USSD 2011; AI 2012: 143).

The Eritrean government denies that there are any restrictions on
religion *per se*, and argues that the Jehovah's Witnesses are themselves to blame since they 'refuse to accept the Government of Eritrea
and the laws'.[29] Government spokesperson and senior cadre Yemane
Gebremeskel explained that since the Jehovah's Witnesses 'publicly said
they don't recognise the temporal government, the government's response was, okay, if they do not recognise the temporal government, the
government will also not recognise them'.[30] The statement exposes the
political immaturity of the EPLF/PFDJ in handling civilian governmental
affairs. In a formal response to an inquiry by the UN Special Rapporteur
on freedom of religion or belief, the Eritrean government claims that
the Jehovah's Witnesses are not being arrested due to their religious
beliefs, but because they refused to participate in the national service
programme, which is compulsory and universal in Eritrea.[31]

After the political crackdown in September 2001, the Eritrean government put further restrictions on the freedom of religion and belief. For
instance, it is now prohibited to hold a prayer meeting or to keep a Bible
or the Koran in military camps, denying hundreds of thousands of military service personnel their constitutional right to worship. In May 2002
the government ordered the closure of all religions and churches apart
from the four main faiths, and decreed that all religious groups needed to
register in order to operate in the country. According to the US State Department, however, the Eritrean government failed to register religious
groups who were willing to do so and infringes upon the independence
of groups who are registered (USSD 2008b; USSD 2010); this again is a
violation of Article 18 of the ICCPR.

---

[26] To withdraw citizenship rights from the Jehovah's Witnesses is a clear
violation of Article 16 of the ICCPR: 'The Recognition of Legal Personality'.
[27] They are Paulos Iyassu, Isaac Moges and Negede Teklemariam (AI 2012: 143)
[28] Human Rights Council, A/HRC/7/10/Add.1, 28 February 2008, Seventh
session, Agenda item 3.
[29] Statement issued by the Ministry of Internal Affairs in March 1995 (AI 2004).
[30] IRIN news: 'ERITREA: Interview with Yemane Gebremeskel, Director of the
President's Office', Asmara, 1 April 2004: http://www.irinnews.org/Report.
aspx?ReportId=49359, accessed 6 January 2009.
[31] Cf. UN Commission on Human Rights, E/CN.4/2005/61/Add.1, 15 March 2005,
Sixty-first session, Agenda item 11(e).

President Isaias Afwerki has rejected criticism of the policy to register religious groups. In one interview he explained his view on new religious groups in the following manner:

> There is no restriction on religion. What's new about the Bible that you want to teach me? What is new about the Koran? I say there is nothing new. Extremists who want to use Islam as a political end for their ambitions should be asked that simple question. What do you want to do with this ideology? I say it's a pretence of using religion for ulterior aims. Religion is by default restricted because you have nothing new to teach me. You do not have the right to impose your beliefs on another person. That creates discord and confusion in the society. Government is there to guarantee everyone is respected. I don't believe that's a restriction.[32]

Since early in 2003 there has been active persecution of members of Christian minority religions that continues to this day. For instance, on 28 May 2005, Eritrean security forces arrested a whole wedding party of over 200 people, including the bride and groom, in Asmara. All those arrested were members of the banned Meserete Christos Church. Several detainees were released the next day, but the majority remained in custody.[33] On 29 April 2007, the Mehrete Yesus Evangelical Presbyterian Church in Asmara was raided by the police during a service, and the pastor of the church (Zecharias Abraham) and 77 other persons attending the service were arrested.[34] More recently in 2012 two similar instances have been reported. In May 2012, sixty-four Christians were arrested in a village outside of Asmara. Fifty-eight of those arrested continue to be held arbitrarily. A month later, 26 college students believed to be practising a non-registered religion were arrested. Their whereabouts are unclear (AI 2012: 143). There are also reports of forced recantations of faith during torture (USSD 2011: 7; International Crisis Group 2010: 2).

The new government directive that requires all churches and religious communities to register in order to operate legally is used as a formal reason to crack-down upon 'non-registered' churches. The Eritrean government responded, following an inquiry by the UN Special Rapporteur on freedom of religion or belief, that members of the Rhema Church and other Christians were detained because they had 'deliberately, contemptuously and provocatively disobeyed the decision of the Government that no religious group could operate until after they had registered with, and acquired a permit from, the Government in accordance with the existing law'.[35] Like most authoritarian regimes, the Eritrean government at times uses a legalistic approach to 'justify' its own violations of human rights.

[32] Interview by Edmund Sanders: 'Q and A with President Isaias Afwerki', *Los Angeles Times*, 2 October 2007.
[33] Cf. UN Commission on Human Rights, E/CN.4/2006/5/Add.1, 27 March 2006, Sixty-second session, Agenda item 11.
[34] Amongst those arrested were two US citizens and a number of Indian teachers working in Eritrea. The US citizens were released on 3 May 2007 while the rest remained in detention at an undisclosed location, according to the UN (cf. Human Rights Council, A/HRC/7/10/Add.1, 28 February 2008).
[35] Cf. UN Commission on Human Rights, E/CN.4/2005/61/Add.1, 15 March 2005, Sixty-first session, Agenda item 11(e).

In 2008, reportedly more than 3225 Christians from unregistered groups were detained in prison; including 37 leaders and pastors of Pentecostal churches, some of whom have been under detention for more than three years without due process of law (USSD 2008b; USSD 2010).36 In December 2008 it was reported that the country's most senior paediatrician, Dr Michael Mehari, had been arrested among many other senior members of evangelical churches in Eritrea.[37]

Since 2006 the US State Department has designated Eritrea a 'Country of Particular Concern' for consecutive years under the International Religious Freedom Act for particularly severe violations of religious freedom (USSD 2008b). In 2008, the US State Department observed that the situation regarding freedom of religion and belief had further deteriorated, and listed Eritrea – together with North Korea and Iran – as 'among the world's leading violators of religious freedom'. The US ambassador responsible for overseeing religious freedom in the world stated: 'Eritrea has an abysmal record of abuses – arresting, detaining, torturing and even killing some of its citizens for attempting to worship outside the four officially-approved religious groups'.[38]

The UN Special Rapporteur on torture and other cruel, inhumane or degrading treatment or punishment has, for instance, reported that two detained members of the banned Christian Rhema Church, Immanuel Andegergesh and Kibrom Firemichael, were tortured to death in 2006 in order to make them abandon their faith.[39] Open Doors International reported in early 2009 that three Christians had died in prison due to torture during the previous four months, bringing to eight the total number of Christians known to have died up to that time while imprisoned due to their faith.[40]

---

[36] The exact number of people arrested due to their faith is impossible to calculate and estimates vary. Open Doors International (a Christian rights-based organisation), for instance, claims that in mid-December 2008, 2907 Christians were held in detention in Eritrea due to their faith (Open Doors International: 'Christian deaths mount in Eritrean prisons', 21 January 2009, at: http://www.opendoorsusa.org/content/view/902/139/, accessed 23 January 2009.

[37] Cf. Release Eritrea: 'Eritrean authorities arrest the country's most senior paediatrician on the count of his Christian faith', 19 December 2008, at: www.release-eritrea.org.uk/node/67, accessed 9 January 2009.

[38] US Ambassador-at-Large for International Religious Freedom, John Hanford. See also David Gollust: 'US Religious Freedom Report faults North Korea, Eritrea, Iran', 19 September 2008, Voice of America news website, Washington DC, at: http://www.voanews.com/english/archive/2008-09/, accessed 22 January 2009.

[39] UN Human Rights Council, A/HRC/4/33/Add.1, 20 March 2007, Fourth session, Agenda item 2. See also UN Human Rights Council, A/HRC/4/21/Add.1, 8 March 2007, Fourth session, Agenda item 2.

[40] On 16 January 2009, Mehari Gebreneguse Asgedom, a member of the Church of the Living God in Mendefera, died at the Me'eter military confinement centre from torture and complications from diabetes; Mogos Hagos Kiflom (aged 37), a member of Rhema Church, was also tortured to death in Me'eter military confinement centre (exact date unknown); and Teklesenbet Gebreab Kiflom (aged 36), died in October 2009 while imprisoned for his faith at the Wia military confinement centre (Cf. Open Doors International: 'Christian deaths mount in Eritrean prisons', 21 January 2009, at: www.opendoorsusa.org/content/view/902/139/, accessed 23 January 2009.

The UN Special Rapporteur on freedom of religion or belief[41] in 2007 sent a communication of concern to the Eritrean government stressing that: 'The right to freedom to worship is not limited to members of registered religious communities, since registration should not be a precondition for practising one's religion, but only for the acquisition of a legal personality and related benefits'.[42]

Persecution of Eritrean Muslims is also a widespread practice. In some cases, Eritrean Muslims are persecuted on the ground of perceived allegiance with armed opposition groups operating from neighbouring countries, and predominantly led by Muslim figures. In the 1990s, such groups included, among others, the Eritrean Islamic Jihad Movement (EIJM), which later changed its name to Eritrean Islamic Reform Movement (EIRM), and was fragmented into several other sub-groups, such as the Eritrean Islamic Salvation Movement (EISM) of the Eritrean Islamic Party for Justice and Development (EIPJD) (Mekonnen 2009: 110-113). In recent years, other groups include the two Ethiopia-based armed groups: Red Sea Afar Democratic Organisation (RSADO) and National Democratic Front for the Liberation of the Eritrean Saho (NDFLDS). One particular incident, among many others, involving religious persecution against Eritrean Muslims took place in September 2004. The incident involved the arrest of a dozen Muslim students belonging to the Wahhabi sect within Islam. Amnesty International recognises the believers as victims of incommunicado detention because their whereabouts have remained unknown (AI 2005: 15).

It is thus clear that the active religious persecution conducted by the Eritrean government is in violation of Article 19.4 of the Eritrean Constitution, which states: 'Every person shall have the freedom to practise any religion and to manifest such practice'. Furthermore, the Eritrean government contravenes a wide array of international human rights clauses. For instance, Article 18(2) of the ICCPR provides that '[n]o one shall be subject to coercion which would impair his freedom to have or to adopt a religion or belief of his choice'. Furthermore, Article 6 of the 1981 Declaration on the Elimination of All Forms of Intolerance and of Discrimination Based on Religion or Belief is also violated, as it provides that the right to freedom of thought, conscience, religion or belief includes the freedom: '(a) to worship or assemble in connection with a religion or belief'.[43] Finally, the basic freedom of religion or belief, as

---

[41] Jointly with the Chairperson-Rapporteur of the Working Group on Arbitrary Detention, the Special Rapporteur on freedom of religion or belief and the Special Rapporteur on the question of torture.

[42] The Eritrean government has not responded to any of the concerns expressed by the UN Special Rapporteur. Human Rights Council, A/HRC/7/10/Add.1, 28 February 2008, Seventh session, Agenda item 3.

[43] The UN Special Rapporteur on freedom of religion and belief, furthermore, made the following observation in relation to the Eritrean case in her 2005 report to the UN General Assembly (A/60/399, para. 50), with reference to international human rights norms and to the mandate practice concerning 'Freedom from Coercion' (para. 1, category I.2): 'The fact that the prohibition of coercion was made explicit shows that the drafters of the Covenant found the freedom provided by paragraph 1 to be so significant that any form of coercion

established in Article 18 of the Universal Declaration on Human Rights (UDHR), is regarded as customary international law and thus binding even upon states that have not ratified all relevant international human rights conventions. The Eritrean government has routinely rejected or ignored all criticism and calls from international agencies in relation to its violation of religious freedom in the country. This was the position of the government, for example, in its response given in the Universal Periodic Review in 2010.[44]

Returned refugees and asylum seekers

Returned refugees and asylum seekers are detained, usually incommunicado, and possibly tortured, immediately upon arrival in Asmara, . To have fled Eritrea and applied for asylum in another country is considered a form of treason by the Eritrean government and returnees are treated accordingly, even though detaining them violates both the Eritrean Constitution (Art. 19.9) and the ICCPR (Art. 12.2) which prescribes that everyone shall 'be free to leave any country, including his own'. The brutal handling of Eritrean returnees was brought to light in 2002 when Malta forcibly deported over 200 Eritrean refugees back to Eritrea. Upon arrival in Asmara, they were all immediately detained, as explained by one of the returnees who later managed to escape imprisonment and flee the country once again:

> When we landed at Asmara, the airport was quiet. The Maltese handed us over. There were no relatives meeting us. When the Maltese plane left, the soldiers took us in a military bus to Adi Abeto prison. The women, girls and children were separated. There were interrogation rooms and we were called one at a time, with two guards, one asking the questions, the other doing the beating. (AI 2004: 30)

(contd) by the State was impermissible, independently of whether the coercion was physical or in the form of State-sponsored incentives. According to the Human Rights Committee: "Article 18.2 bars coercion that would impair the right to have or adopt a religion or belief, including the use or threat of physical force or penal sanctions to compel believers or non-believers to adhere to their religious beliefs and congregations to recant their religion or belief or to convert. Policies or practices having the same intention or effect, such as, for example, those restricting access to education, medical care, employment or the rights guaranteed by article 25 and other provisions of the Covenant, are similarly inconsistent with article 18.2" (general comment No. 22, para. 5).' Furthermore, the Special Rapporteur would also: 'like to make reference to her framework for communications, more specifically to the international human rights norms and to the mandate practice concerning "Freedom to worship" (see above para. 1, category I. 3. a)'. As she noted in her 2005 report to the Commission on Human Rights, 'members of religious communities or communities of belief, whenever they find themselves in places of worship, are in a situation of special vulnerability given the nature of their activity. The Special Rapporteur is therefore of the opinion that States should pay increased attention to attacks on places of worship and ensure that all perpetrators of such attacks are properly prosecuted and tried.' (E/CN.4/2005/61, para. 49). Cf. UN Human Rights Council, A/HRC/4/21/Add.1, 8 March 2007, Fourth session, Agenda item 2.

[44] UN Human Rights Council, A/HRC/13/2/Add.1 para 32, 8 March 2010, para 32 (in response to recommendations 88-89).

The women, children and those over the age of military conscription (40 years) were reportedly released after some weeks of detention, while the rest were sent to different detention centres in Eritrea and kept incommunicado and 'subjected to forced labour, interrogated and tortured (e.g. by beating, tying up and exposing to sun...)' (UNHCR 2004: 6). Of the original 233 persons forcibly returned to Eritrea, 180 were imprisoned for a longer period, of whom 30 later managed to escape to Sudan. Reportedly, some Malta detainees were released from prison in 2006, while an unknown number have died in detention or have been killed while trying to escape since their incarceration in 2002 (USSD 2006).

The deteriorating human rights situation in Eritrea and the treatment of returnees or deportees led the UNHCR to issue a separate position paper on the 'Return of rejected asylum seekers to Eritrea' in January 2004, recommending that 'states refrain from all forced returns of rejected asylum seekers to Eritrea and grant them complementary forms of protection instead' (UNHCR 2004: 6). However, several countries have continued to deport rejected asylum seekers and refugees back to Eritrea. In October 2011, 300 Eritreans were deported from Sudan and 30 from Egypt. Some 118 returnees were 'asked' to sign forms indicating that they were voluntarily returning to Eritrea and were beaten if they refused (AI 2012). In June 2008 up to 1200 Eritrean asylum-seekers were forcibly returned to Eritrea from Egypt, despite an urgent appeal to cease deportations by the UN High Commissioner for Human Rights.[45] Apparently returned women with children and those who were pregnant were released after some weeks in detention.[46] However, as of December 2008, at least 740 of the returnees were still imprisoned under harsh conditions in military detention facilities throughout Eritrea.[47] European states also overlook the UNHCR recommendation not to return rejected asylum seekers to Eritrea, despite a recent landmark ruling by the European Court of Human Rights reaffirming the absolute prohibition on returning people to countries known to practise torture.[48] For instance, German immigration authorities forcibly returned Yonas Haile Mehari and Petros Aforki Mulugeta to Eritrea on 14 May 2008. Neither man has been seen since their arrival in Asmara.[49]

---

[45] UN News Centre: 'UN human rights chief urges Egypt to stop deporting Eritrean asylum-seekers', 19 June 2008; Reuters: 'Egypt deports 10 more Eritreans - airport sources', Cairo, 18 January 2009.

[46] Amnesty International, 'Egypt: Further information on forcible return/Fear of torture or other ill-treatment', MDE 12/018/2008, 7 August 2008. See also the comprehensive Amnesty International report on Egypt's treatment of African refugees (AI 2008a).

[47] Human Rights Watch: 'Egypt: Stop deporting Eritrean asylum seekers', 8 January 2009, at: www.hrw.org/en/news/2009/01/08/egypt-stop-deporting-eritrean-asylum-seekers, accessed 9 January 2009.

[48] European Court of Human Rights: Application no. 37201/06, *Saadi v. Italy*, 28 February 2008.

[49] Amnesty International, Urgent Action 145/08 (AI index: AFR 64/002/2008), 29 May 2008.

Journalists

Journalists, as defenders of human rights, are annihilated in Eritrea. The 'horrifying state of affairs' in relation to press freedom in the country led Reporters Without Borders, for the first time, to rank Eritrea last (as number 173) in its 2008 worldwide press freedom index, after North Korea.[50] In all subsequent yearly reports by Reporters Without Borders Eritrea has always been ranked the last in the world in media freedom (RWB 2012). In 2007, the International Press Institute characterised the developments in Eritrea as so dire that the nation was singled out as the year's 'most egregious suppressor of press freedom'.[51] The reality today is that the only news serving Eritrea beyond the state propaganda media is the diaspora media outlets, communicating news to Eritrea through radio and television broadcasting, and the internet.

All private and independent press in the country was shut down as part of the September 2001 crack-down (see Chapter 5), since it was accused by the government of contravening the 1996 Press Law (AI 2002: 10). Reportedly, thirteen leading editors and journalists were arrested in the operation,[52] but no formal charges have been made (RWB 2008). The harsh conditions in prison sites have supposedly led to the death of several journalists at different times. As a matter of routine

---

[50] On a score from 1 to 100 (where 1 is best), Eritrea received 97.5 points (on the other end of the scale Iceland, Luxembourg and Norway scored 1.5 points). Cf. Reporters Without Borders: *Press Freedom Index 2008,* at: www.rsf.org/article. php3?id_article=29031, accessed 9 January 2009.

[51] International Press Institute: 'World Press Freedom Review 2007: Eritrea', at: www.freemedia.at/cms/ipi/freedom_detail.html?country=/KW0001/KW0006/ KW0154/, accessed 9 January 2009.

[52] Amnesty International has published short biographies of ten of the arrested editors/journalists (AI 2002): **1. Said Abdulkadir**, Chief editor and founder of the newspaper, *Admas*; also employee of the Ministry of Information's Arabic-language newspaper, *Haddas Eritrea*; aged 34. **2. Yosuf Mohamed Ali**, Chief editor of the newspaper, *Tsigenay*; business studies graduate; aged 45. **3. Amanuel Asrat**, Chief editor of the newspaper, *Zemen* ('Time'); EPLF member since the 1980s. **4. Temesgen Gebreyesus**, Sports reporter on the newspaper, *Keste Debena* ('Rainbow'); amateur actor; aged 36. 5. **Mattewos Habteab**, Editor of the newspaper, *Meqaleh* ('Echo'); mathematics graduate, University of Asmara; aged 30. **6. Dawit Habtemichael**, Assistant chief editor and co-founder of the newspaper, *Meqaleh*; physics graduate, University of Asmara; full-time science teacher employed by the Ministry of Education; aged 30. **7. Medhanie Haile**, Assistant chief editor and co-founder of the newspaper, *Keste Debena*; law graduate, University of Asmara; full-time employee of the Ministry of Justice; aged 33. **8. Dawit Isaac**, Editor and co-owner of the newspaper, *Setit*; dual Eritrean and Swedish citizen as a result of being granted asylum in Sweden in the 1980s; education graduate; writer and theatre producer; aged 38. **9. Seyoum Tsehaye**, Freelance photographer; French language graduate and former French teacher; EPLF veteran since the 1970s; former director of Eritrean state television in the early 1990s; aged 49. **10. Fessehaye Yohannes** ('Joshua') Reporter and co-founder of the newspaper, *Setit*; EPLF veteran since 1977; poet and director of an amateur cultural dance group; studied in the UK in 2000; aged 46.

practice, the Eritrean government never confirms such reported deaths (AI 2012: 144).[53]

The last permanent foreign correspondent was expelled from Eritrea in 2004,[54] and journalists trying to enter the country are either denied a visa or are closely monitored by the Ministry of Information. Journalists working for the remaining government media are also being targeted. Government newspapers and broadcasting facilities in Eritrea have become 'Soviet-style instruments of propaganda', directly monitored, controlled and censored by the Minister of Information (RWB 2008: 12).[55] Government journalists are forced to publish whitewashing reports about developments in the country, and conceal all criticism of the prevailing extremely dire social, economic, and political conditions under which the population is suffering. This led the UN Special Rapporteur on freedom of expression and opinion, jointly with the Chairperson-Rapporteur of the Working Group on Arbitrary Detention, to send an urgent appeal in November 2006 to express 'grave concern' at the 'series of arrests which may be an attempt to intimidate their media related work. This concern is aggravated by the high number of currently detained journalists in Eritrea, which reportedly numbers at least 22'.[56] The Eritrean government habitually neglects to respond to the inquiries and criticisms raised by Special Rapporteurs. The government has also denied access to the Special Rapporteur on the Situation of Human Rights in Eritrea, who was appointed by the UN Human Rights Council in July 2012.

The dire situation has prompted many government journalists to flee Eritrea, as they can no longer tolerate the blanket censorship on the current state of affairs in the country. In November 2006, nine state media staff were arrested on suspicion that they planned to flee the country, after several other renowned government journalists had managed to escape.[57] All of them were reportedly beaten and tortured during

---

[53] Fessehaye Yohannes (known as 'Joshua') was the last reported to have died on 11 January 2008 (RWB 2008: 12). See also Committee to Protect Journalists: 'In Eritrea, a prominent journalist dies in a secret government prison', New York, 9 February 2007.

[54] Reporters Without Borders: 'Last permanent foreign correspondent expelled from Eritrea', 13 September 2004, Paris. In March 2008 a BBC journalist, who had worked in the country for a year, was expelled; see his valedictory article: 'Not so fond farewell to Eritrea', BBC, 10 March 2008.

[55] The only media outlets in Eritrea today are those controlled by the state or the ruling party: EriTV; *Dimtsi Hafash* (Voice of the Masses radio); a government newspaper printed in four languages: Tigrinya (*Hadas Eritrea*), Tigre (*Eritrea Haddas*), Arabic (*Eritrea al-Hadisa*), and English (*Eritrea Profile*); a government-run press service, the Eritrean News Service (EriNA); several small publications and radio programmes run by party-controlled social organisations (women, workers, youth); and a party-controlled website, Shaebia.org (Connell 2007).

[56] Cf. Report of the UN Special Rapporteur on freedom of opinion and expression, UN Human Rights Council, A/HRC/4/27/Add.1, 26 March 2007, Fourth session, Agenda item 2, p. 88.

[57] Cf. Report of the UN Special Rapporteur on freedom of opinion and expression, UN Human Rights Council, A/HRC/4/27/Add.1, 26 March 2007, Fourth session, Agenda item 2.

detention (RWB 2008: 13). Other government journalists have been arrested while trying to flee the country, such as Eyob Kessete (a journalist with the Amharic service of the state radio *Dimits Hafash*) and Johnny Hisabu (editor with *Eri-TV*), both caught trying to leave the country during 2008 (ibid.). In June 2008, Paulos Kidane, a journalist working for *Eri-TV*'s Amharic service, was captured trying to flee into Sudan and was later reported dead by the Eritrean authorities (ibid.).[58]

The harassment of government journalists continues unabated. Reporters Without Borders reported that on 22 February 2009 the authorities ordered a raid on the premises of Radio Bana, a small public station in the heart of the capital that broadcasts educational programmes under the sponsorship of the Education Ministry.[59] Without any formal charges pressed or reasons given, its entire staff of around 50 journalists were arrested and taken to the Dobozito detention centre on the edge of the city. Some of the staff were later released but several of them are still in custody as we go to press.[60]

The Eritrean Constitution guarantees the freedom of expression and the press and other media (Article 19.2) concomitantly as it ensures every citizen's right of access to information (Article 19.3). The Eritrean government blatantly ignores its own Constitution and international obligations in regard to these rights.

Furthermore, the violation resulting from the clamp-down and arrests of journalists in Eritrea was brought to the attention of the African Commission on Human and Peoples' Rights, to which Eritrea is a party. The complaint was filed by the human rights organisation, Article 19. The African Commission decided to take on the case and in a lengthy written deliberation the Eritrean government was found guilty of violating the African Charter (Articles 1, 5, 6, 7(1), 9 and 18), and the Commission urged the government to release, or bring to a speedy and fair trial, the detained journalists – and to lift the ban on the press (see Chapter 5).[61]

Human rights defenders

Any person perceived as a defender of human rights will immediately be arrested if voicing criticism of government violations. The Eritrean government does not recognise the legitimate role of human rights defenders, as set out in the UN Declaration on Human Rights Defenders of 1998 (AI

---

[58] See also commemorative article by Mohamed Hassim Keita, published in *Dangerous Assignments (Fall/Winter 2007 issue), a publication of the Committee to Protect Journalists.*

[59] Reporters Without Borders: 'Plea to EU to suspend development aid in light of fresh crackdown on journalists', 6 March 2009, at: http://www.rsf.org/article. php3?id_article=30491, accessed 10 March 2009.

[60] Among them, according to Reporters Without Borders, are Bereket Misghina, aka Wedi Misghina, a famous actor and playwright; journalist and essayist Yirgalem Asfha, former art critic for the newspaper *Zemen*; teacher Basilios Zemo, aka Wedi Zemo, and a young teacher Senait Habtu, working in the radio's production studio. Unconfirmed reports suggested they had been transferred to the military prison in Adi Abeito, north-west of Asmara on the road to Keren.

[61] African Commission on Human and Peoples' Rights, Communication 275 / 2003 – Article 19 v. The State of Eritrea, EX.CL/364 (XI), Annex II.

2004: 37), a situation also acknowledged by the UN Special Representative on human rights defenders.[62] No organisations monitoring or conducting advocacy for human rights are allowed to operate in the country, as the government perceives such activities to be subversive or treasonous.

The practical and political restrictions placed upon organising civil society activities in Eritrea contravene the Eritrean Constitution (Art. 19.6) and ICCPR (Art. 22). The EPLF's negative attitude towards human rights activism was visible immediately after liberation, when the Regional Centre for Human Rights and Development, an independent NGO established by a senior EPLF member and former head of the Eritrean Relief Association, Mr Paulos Tesfagiorgis, was closed down on government orders soon after its opening in 1993 (AI 2004: 37) (see Chapter 4).[63]

Since independence, no truly independent civil society organisations or activities have been allowed to operate independently of government control and monitoring.[64] The Marxist-Leninist-inspired 'mass movements' which were an integral part of the EPLF during the struggle – like the associations of women, youth, students and workers – continued to be controlled by the EPLF after they became so-called autonomous organisations after independence. They are not allowed to promote human rights work which criticises the government.[65] An example is the arrest of three trade union leaders who allegedly protested against workers' worsening standards of living in 2005.[66] According to the Observatory for the Protection of Human Rights Defenders, the arrest came about solely on account of their efforts to exercise their mandate as trade union leaders, a concern also shared by the UN Special Rapporteur on the rights

[62] See report by the UN Secretary General's Special Representative on human rights defenders, 'Promotion and protection of human rights: human rights defenders', Commission on Human Rights, E/CN.4/2006/95/Add.5, 6 March 2006.
[63] The NGO was never formally registered since at that time there was no NGO law implemented, but operated by permission given orally by President Isaias Afwerki.
[64] The organisation Citizens for Peace was established after the outbreak of war with Ethiopia in 1998, with the aim of reporting on human rights abuses inflicted by Ethiopian authorities on Eritrean deportees from Ethiopia, as part of the propaganda war. Although registered as an 'independent' NGO, the organisation was closely controlled by the Eritrean authorities. During its active years, it did not do anything to scrutinise human rights abuses by the Eritrean government.
[65] The Eritrean women's associations, for instance, have conducted gender awareness campaigns and anti-FGM (female genital mutilation) work, both of which fall within the EPLF's policies on these issues.
[66] The three leaders were: Tewelde Ghebremedhin (chairperson of the Food, Beverages, Hotels, Tourism, Agriculture, and Tobacco Workers Federation), Minase Andezion (secretary of the Textile and Leather Workers Federation), and Habtom Weldemichael (head of the Coca Cola Workers Union). See UN Commission on Human Rights, 'Civil and Political Rights, Including the Question of Freedom of Expression, Report of the Special Rapporteur' (E/CN.4/2006/55/Add.1), 26 March 2006, para. 334-339. See also The Observatory for the Protection of Human Rights Defenders (a joint programme of the International Federation for Human Rights and the World Organisation Against Torture), 'Eritrea: Arbitrary arrest and incommunicado detention of three trade union leaders', (ERI 001/0505/OBS 032), 13 May 2005.

to freedom of opinion and expression.[67] Hence, their arrest constituted a grave violation of international legal standards (Arts. 22 and 19 ICCPR), as well as explicit violations of Conventions 87 and 98 of the ILO (which Eritrea has ratified) regarding freedom of association which is legally binding on Eritrea as an ILO member state.[68] The three trade union leaders were later released in 2007 (USSD 2008a).

There is no Bar Association in Eritrea or any other independent forum for lawyers. The very few lawyers in private practice are unable to act as legal defence counsel for detainees, or to advise on other human rights grievances (AI 2004: 37). This reality undermines the emphasis put upon legal counsel and due process of law, as prescribed by ICCPR (Arts. 2.3 and 14). None of the international NGOs that operated in the country were allowed to undertake any human rights-related programmes or awareness building. Thus 'civil society' – as it is generally understood – is nonexistent in the totalitarian Eritrean state (see Chapter 5).

EPLF/PFDJ dissenters

High-ranking EPLF leaders and government officials, civil servants and military officers[69] are also under a constant threat of arrest or detention if they express dissent or criticise President Isaias Afwerki. Throughout the post-independence period, President Isaias was afraid of internal dissent and opposition to his increasingly omnipresent power ambitions. Thus, he regularly reshuffled his Cabinet without any warning or reason, to hinder ministers and top-level government officials from developing and cementing an 'autonomous' power-base which could challenge him later. If some top-level cadre fell into disfavour, he would be 'frozen' – stripped of all formal authority and generally placed under house-arrest awaiting the outcome of the process against him or her.

Nevertheless, in the aftermath of the Eritrean-Ethiopian war, government ministers and top-level EPLF leaders protested against the unaccountable and monopolistic power of President Isaias. The group of EPLF leaders commonly known as the G-15 (Group of 15) were all members of the Eritrean parliament (the National Assembly) and the party's Central Committee and several of them were also Cabinet ministers. At the end of March 2001 they sent a letter to the president (which

[67] Cf. Commission on Human Rights, E/CN.4/2006/55/Add.1, 27 March 2006, Sixty-second session, Agenda item 11(c). See also UN Commission on Human Rights, E/CN.4/2006/95/Add.1, 22 March 2006, Sixty-second session, Agenda item 17(b).

[68] The UN Special Rapporteur also notes in this regard that Resolution 2005/38 of the Commission on Human Rights calls upon states to refrain from imposing restrictions which are not consistent with Article 19.3 of the ICCPR, to which the Eritrean Government acceded in 2002, including restrictions on reporting on human rights, peaceful demonstrations or political activities. Cf. Commission on Human Rights, E/CN.4/2006/55/Add.1, 27 March 2006, Sixty-second session, Agenda item 11(c).

[69] Military officers are in danger of arrest mostly in relation to internal infighting between the army echelons, for instance, in relation to controlling the system of corruption/bribery within the army. *Awate.com: 'Secret Meetings, Defections, Refoulment and Expulsions', Gedeab News, 20 November 2007 (www.awate.com).*

later became public), which was described as a 'call for correction, a call for peaceful and democratic dialogue, a call for strengthening and consolidation, a call for unity, a call for the rule of law and for justice, through peaceful and legal ways and means'. The letter outlined several policy areas where the government had failed, most importantly in terms of establishing democracy, the rule of law and respect for human rights.[70] The president rejected the call for change, and in the September 2001 crackdown, 11 out of the 15 signatories to the letter were arrested, and have been held incommunicado ever since (their names are listed in Chapter 5).

The Eritrean government has labelled the G-15 as traitors who tried to 'sell-out' their country during the war with Ethiopia and oust the President, justifying the continued incommunicado detention of the former prominent EPLF leaders.[71] However, international human rights organisations such as Amnesty International (AI 2002; AI 2004), government agencies such as the US State Department (USSD 2008a), multilateral organs such as the EU[72] and the Inter-Parliamentary Union,[73] consider the G-15 detainees to be political prisoners.

Furthermore, the arrest of the G-15 was brought to the attention of the African Commission on Human and Peoples' Rights which ruled that the arrests were in violation of the African Charter on Human and Peoples' Rights, Articles 2, 6, 7(1) and 9(2), and urged the Eritrean government to release the prisoners immediately and offer them compensation (see Chapter 5).

FINAL REMARKS

In Eritrea today, all people – young and old, women and men, Christians and Muslims, civil servants and peasants, educated and illiterate – are susceptible to being detained and arrested. Generally, no reason is given nor formal charges presented.

Against the backdrop of a widespread and arbitrary detention policy, certain groups may be identified as particularly vulnerable to arrest and governmental harassment. This study has identified national service personnel, adherents of prohibited churches and religious organisations, individuals from the Kunama minority group, forcibly returned refugees, journalists and other human rights defenders, as well as government party dissenters, as being particularly prone to arrest.

The common denominator among these categories of people is the

[70] On the inception of the Eritrean dissent movement, see Plaut (2002).
[71] See, for instance, interview with Yemane Gebremeskel, Director at the President's Office, by IRIN 1 April 2004 (http://www.irinnews.org/Report.aspx?ReportId=49359, accessed 6 January 2009).
[72] Council of the European Union: 'Declaration by the Presidency on behalf of the European Union on political prisoners in Eritrea', 20 September 2007, 12978/1/07 REV 1 (Presse 201), P 074/07, Brussels.
[73] Inter-Parliamentary Union, Resolution on Eritrea adopted unanimously by the Governing Council at its 173rd session, Geneva, 3 October 2003.

reality that they are liable to pose a challenge to the regime's totalitarian control over Eritrean society. Any element, no matter how small, which is perceived to be 'independent' of the government, may be construed as a threat and must therefore be subdued or annihilated. Eritrea has now entered a vicious negative cycle; as the antipathy towards the regime grows, more and more people will be targeted, again fuelling aversion against the regime. So far, this has led to an ever-increasing stream of refugees fleeing the country. At the time of writing, however, this growing aversion has not been converted into active mobilisation and recruitment into the Eritrean politico-military resistance fronts. Comparative politics shows, however, that if such a brutal policy of human rights abuse is sustained over time, an armed resistance with the aim of toppling the regime will rise by any means possible.

8

Minority Marginalisation: EPLF's Policies of 'Cultural Superiority'

INTRODUCTION

In 1993[1] Eritrea became what was then Africa's newest state after a 30-year-long war of liberation against Ethiopia. The Eritrean People's Liberation Front (EPLF) organised its resistance around a stringent nationalist ideology, where identity markers of ethnicity, culture, religion or regionalism were banned. The particular colonial history of the country, EPLF's ideology and the brutal and protracted war itself – which impacted on all people in the region – were believed to help to foster and consolidate an all-embracing national Eritrean identity (Negash 1987; Iyob 1995; Pool 2001). Today, however, over two decades later, the Eritrean nationhood cherished and celebrated in 1993 seems hollow, as the sovereignty of the Eritrean citizen is usurped by a ruling party that pits the people against each other in order to perpetuate its position of power.

In independent Eritrea, the EPLF sustained and even reinforced its strict nationalist ideology, as *national unity* became the principal guideline to which all government policies and development plans were aligned (EPLF 1994: 3). Consequently, the cultural diversity of the country, inhabited by at least nine distinct ethnic groups (several of which are further divided into separate clans), appeared to suffer, as arguments and claims for the enhancement and protection of cultural or minority rights were interpreted as undermining and divisive in relation to the official nationalist policy (Tronvoll 1998b).

The main objective of this chapter is to go beyond an assessment of the situation of minorities in the country, in order to cast light on the historical and political contexts which influence the situation of minorities today. This will help to explain how and why the precarious minority situation in Eritrea has developed.

In order to understand the policy of EPLF/PFDJ on minority rights, a brief backdrop on the liberation war and the context of cultural diversity will be presented. Subsequently, the legal obligations of the Eritrean

[1] The EPLF overran the capital, Asmara, on 24 May 1991 and liberated the whole country from the Ethiopian army on 28 May 1991. After a UN-monitored referendum on independence in April 1993, Eritrea declared independence and gained formal international recognition as a new country on 24 May 1993.

state will be addressed, in relation to its own Constitution as well as binding international treaties. This will be followed by a brief outline of the ethnic diversity in the country. Finally, the government's policies on land rights/pastoral concerns and language rights will be discussed by way of illuminating how current government policies are apparently sustaining the superiority of the dominating Tigrinya culture.

BACKDROPS: WAR AND CULTURAL DIVERSITY

During the war of liberation from Ethiopia, the argument that the Eritrean people were historically and culturally distinct from Ethiopia gave legitimacy to the struggle of the Eritrean People's Liberation Front (EPLF). At that time, this was quite a controversial position, since the scholarly work on the region generally viewed 'Eritrean' history and culture as sub-categories of Ethiopian studies (Gebre-Medhin 1989). The 'Greater Ethiopia' thesis – which subsumed all cultures and ethnic groups of the region under an Abyssinian[2] tradition – was also instrumental in interpreting political developments in the region. From the point of view of Ethiopia and its successive regimes, Eritrea was an integral cultural-historical entity and local resistance developing in the area was framed in political – and not ethnic or ethno-nationalistic – terms. Hence, already at an early stage of the struggle in 1982, a group of fighters under the EPLF Department of Politicisation, Education and Culture launched a scheme to identify, gather, and document specific ethnic customs, cultural traditions and historical traits unique to the nine ethnic groups of the country, in order to prove their 'distinctness' from the Ethiopian cultural sphere. However, the EPLF presented the initiative as an effort to identify and understand the indigenous knowledge of the Eritrean peoples in a socio-economic context (World Bank 2001).

The project to gather and analyse indigenous knowledge from the many Eritrean ethnic groups continued after independence, although at a restricted pace due to the lack of formal scholarly training of the fighters responsible for the project. In 1995 the official Eritrean newspaper, *Eritrea Profile,* started to run the column 'Eritrean traditions and customs,' presenting bits and pieces of the many interesting and varied customs from the nine Eritrean groups. Likewise, at official occasions in Asmara, folklore and traditional dances of the Eritrean minority groups were displayed as exotic artefacts of the new nation. Beyond that, the interest and concern for the minority cultures of the country did not seem to penetrate deep into the policies of post-independence Eritrea, as the nationalist ideology of the EPLF – strongly influenced by highland Tigrinya cultural perceptions – defined the parameters of all development plans. That respect of ethnic minorities only extended to official government shows and the mere pretence of this was very clear. The late native

---

[2] The term Abyssinia is used to denote the historical polity that embraced both Eritrea and Ethiopia prior to the advent of the Italian colonial ambitions in the region.

Kunama anthropologist, Alexander Naty, noted that, 'We only have "dance-democracy" in Eritrea. The minority groups are allowed to make public appearances at government hosted cultural events. All other minority rights and political liberties are, however, brutally crushed.'[3]

The Eritrean government's strong emphasis on national unity – ideologically anchored in the liberation struggle, manifested through the Eritrean National Charter of 1994, and enshrined in the 1997 Constitution – apparently works as an impediment to protecting cultural and minority rights in the country. Minority rights, as defined by international instruments, are perceived as an antithesis to the strong nationalistic policies and practices of the Eritrean government.

THE EPLF/PFDJ'S POLICIES ON MINORITIES

The National Charter – the ruling party's vision of how to develop independent Eritrea – declares that *national unity* is the principal guideline to which all government policies and development plans will be aligned (EPLF 1994: 3). All 'divisive attitudes and activities' are condemned and rejected, and the Charter places 'national interests above everything else' (ibid.: 13). Within this ideological framework, diversity suffers and cultural and minority rights are portrayed as illegitimate claims threatening the coherence of the Eritrean nation. This may be illustrated by how President Isaias Afwerki himself described the emerging opposition towards the implementation of new regional divisions (*zoba*) in the country in 1995, which deliberately broke down old administrative borders partly aligned along ethnic lines:

> The history of regional boundaries in Eritrea does not go back more than 100 years. All Eritreans are born equal. No ethnic group is superior or inferior to any other group. Eritrea belongs equally to every Eritrean. No social group is more closely related to land than the rest. There was a time when people thought in terms of 'we' and 'they' using religion and regional [ethnic] boundaries as bases. However, such notions have been put aside during the 30-year-long struggle, and it is because the fighters struggled as one person by uniting their hearts that we were able to achieve our goal of liberation. A person should be judged not by his place of origin but by his mental capacity, good manners and sense of altruism. Those who think otherwise are mentally sick and we should not allow them to impose their will on us. The government will not restrain itself from taking appropriate measures regarding those who misinterpret and misconstrue any administrative or developmental policies in order to create religious and regional conflicts. (Quoted in *Eritrea Profile*, 27 September 1995)

The Eritrean government's position on minority rights reflects the ideological origin of the liberation struggle. The Eritrean People's Liberation Front (EPLF) defined its war against Ethiopia on a nationalistic basis, struggling to liberate the territory of Eritrea and all its culturally diverse inhabitants. The EPLF in principle rejected all notions of ethnicity in the struggle (as was the predominant organisational platform of resistance

[3] Extracted from an interview conducted by Tronvoll with Dr Naty in Asmara, in September 1996.

in Ethiopia), and fought as *Eritreans*, not as Tigrinya, Afar, Tigre or some other ethnic group. Ethnicity, and in particular minority concerns, was in this regard perceived as irrelevant and as a possible obstacle to the formation of a coherent national front. Thus, 'minorities' is not even a term recognised or used by the government: in the official language of the state, ethno-linguistic communities are identified as 'nationalities'(Pool 1997: 5).

The EPLF liberation strategy was clearly successful, both militarily and ideologically. Through the struggle for independence, it managed to forge an Eritrean consciousness and identity among the many ethnic groups in the country (Iyob 1995; Pool 2001). However, this does not mean that other sub-national identities, based on ethnicity, clan, descent or locality, were 'replaced' or 'forgotten'. A national identity was created on top of, or parallel to, other culturally-defined identities which still are perceived as residual categories of identity in the country today (Tronvoll 1998a; Naty 2002b).

MINORITY RIGHTS/OBLIGATIONS OF THE STATE OF ERITREA

The legal protection of cultural and minority rights in Eritrea is inadequate. No specific act or proclamation is drafted with the aim to protect minorities or their cultural traditions. Hence, as a starting point, we need to turn to the Eritrean Constitution in order to acquire an understanding of the Government's legislative position on this issue.

The Eritrean Constitution on minority and cultural rights
The Eritrean Constitution makes limited references to cultural and minority rights. The first and most important one is Article 4(3), which states that 'the equality of all Eritrean languages is guaranteed'. Furthermore, Article 6(1) points out that 'as the people and government struggle to establish a united and developed Eritrea, within the context of the diversity of Eritrea, they shall be guided by the basic principle 'unity in diversity''. In Article 6(2), however, the Constitution downplays the 'diversity' of the people, and stresses that: 'The State shall strengthen the stability and development of the country by encouraging democratic dialogue and national consensus through participation of all citizens; by building strong political, cultural and moral foundations; and by promoting national unity and social harmony.' This principle is followed by Article 9 of the Constitution, covering 'national culture'; no mention whatsoever is made of the many minority cultures of Eritrea, as all attention is focused on developing unity and a *national* culture of identity.

The principle of non-discrimination and equality under the law is enshrined in Article 14(2), where it is explicitly stated that: 'No person may be discriminated against on account of *race, ethnic origin, language, colour*, gender, religion, disability, age, political view, or social or economic status or any other improper factors' (emphasis added).

The principle of non-discrimination and equality is also emphasised under Article 21 of the Constitution, covering 'economic, social and cultural rights and responsibilities'. Under Article 21(4), it is prescribed that: 'The State and society shall have the responsibility of identifying, preserving, developing, as need be, and bequeathing to succeeding generations, historical and cultural heritage; and shall lay the necessary groundwork for the development of the arts, science, technology and sports, thus encouraging citizens to participate in such endeavours.' The Constitution does not, however, specify if this 'historical and cultural heritage' relates to minority cultures *per se*, or if it should be interpreted as Eritrean national cultural heritage.

Eritrea's international obligations to protect minority and cultural rights

The protection of cultural diversity may be approached from two different angles: from a universalistic or a particularistic viewpoint. Based on the fundamental principles in human rights of equality and non-discrimination, all peoples, irrespective of their cultural or ethnic background, may freely maintain and develop their culture, language and ways of life while participating on an equal footing in societal activities, economic progress and development. As such, the other ethnic minority groups in the country should be put on an equal footing with the majority Tigrinya group in all spheres and activities of society. Seen from a particularistic perspective, furthermore, it may be argued that certain particularly vulnerable groups may need special attention and measures and positive action in order to protect, maintain and develop their culture. Inspiration for positive action and special measures can be found in the two UN Declarations; the Declaration on the Rights of Persons Belonging to National or Ethnic, Religious and Linguistic Minorities[4] and the Declaration on the Rights of Indigenous Peoples.[5] In the former declaration, emphasis is placed on the obligations of the state to 'protect the existence and the national or ethnic, cultural, religious and linguistic identity of minorities within their respective territories and ... encourage conditions for the promotion of that identity' (Article 1); whereas the latter, for instance, also emphasise the important principle of indigenous peoples to 'consider themselves different' from the majority, and 'to be respected as such' (preamble).

The principle of equal value and dignity of all cultures has been reaffirmed by the UN General Assembly resolution on 'Human Rights and Cultural Diversity'.[6] This holds true for prevention and mitigation of cultural homogenisation, as well as tolerance towards cultural diversity as a means for the advancement of peace (Iovane 2007: 249). The former UN Commission on Human Rights stressed this too, in its resolution,

---

[4] UN General Assembly Resolution 47/135, 1992.
[5] UN General Assembly Resolution 61/295, 2007.
[6] A/RES/58/167 'Human Rights and Cultural Diversity', 4 March 2004. Moreover, UN General Assembly Resolution 60/1 (of 24 October 2005) endorsing the 2005 World Summit Outcome, also underpins the rights aspect of cultural diversity, confirming it as 'one of the key values of contemporary international relations' (Iovane 2007).

'Promotion of the Enjoyment of the Cultural Rights of Everyone and Respect for Different Cultural Identities'.[7]

The United Nations Educational, Scientific and Cultural Organization (UNESCO) is particularly dedicated to promoting respect for cultural diversity. In the Universal Declaration on Cultural Diversity (unanimously adopted in November 2001), UNESCO aims, *inter alia*, to preserve cultural diversity, since the 'defence of cultural diversity is an ethical imperative, inseparable from respect for human dignity' (UNESCO 2001: Article 4).[8]

The above declarations and resolutions are not legally binding on states, but should be seen as general aspirations to be followed by UN member states. Eritrea is bound, however, by the three international conventions relating to cultural and minority rights[9] that it has ratified. They are the International Covenant on Civil and Political Rights (ICCPR),[10] the International Covenant on Economic, Social and Cultural Rights (ICESCR),[11] and the International Convention on the Elimination of All Forms of Racial Discrimination (ICERD).[12]

ICERD is the most important international legal instrument aimed at the prevention of discrimination and inequality along ethnic and racial lines. In Article 1, racial discrimination is defined as:

> [...] any distinction, exclusion, restriction or preference based on race, colour, descent, or national or ethnic origin which has the purpose or effect of nullifying or impairing the recognition, enjoyment or exercise, on an equal footing, of human rights and fundamental freedoms in the political, economic, social, cultural or any other field of public life.

State parties to the Convention are thus obliged to follow up and work actively to protect and enhance racial/ethnic equality in all sectors of society and fields of policy and governmental activity (Article 2). State parties must also guarantee fundamental human rights to everyone, without distinction of ethnicity or origin (Article 5). As shown in this study, some of these rights are violated systematically in relation to the

---

[7] UNHRC Resolution 2005/20, 14 April 2005.

[8] These intentions are further enshrined and elaborated on in the Convention on the Protection and Promotion of the Diversity of Cultural Expressions (adopted 2005, entry into force March 2007) (UNESCO 2005). The Convention states that 'cultural diversity can be protected and promoted only if human rights and fundamental freedoms, such as freedom of expression, information and communication, as well as the ability of individuals to choose cultural expressions, are guaranteed' (Article 2.1); and the fact that 'the protection and promotion of the diversity of cultural expressions presuppose the recognition of equal dignity of and respect for all cultures, including the cultures of persons belonging to minorities and indigenous peoples' (Article 2.3). Eritrea has not ratified the UNESCO Convention on cultural diversity, and is thus not obliged to comply with its rules.

[9] Some of the legal instruments geared to granting special prerogatives to minorities and indigenous peoples – like ILO Convention no. 169 – are not ratified by Eritrea, however, and are thus not relevant for discussion in this chapter.

[10] Ratified by Eritrea in 2002.

[11] Ratified by Eritrea in 2001.

[12] UNGA Res. 2106 (xx). Ratified by Eritrea in 2001.

Kunama minority group in Eritrea, such as the right to equal treatment before the law, the right to security of persons against violence, the right to freedom of movement and residence, and the right to nationality (see Chapter 9).

Article 27 of the ICCPR provides that persons belonging to minorities 'shall not be denied the rights, in community with the other members of their group, to enjoy their own culture, to profess and practise their own religion, or to use their own language'.[13] Importantly, though, these are rights granted to individuals in a group and not to the group collectively as such. The individual rights depend on the ability of the whole minority group to maintain its culture, language and religion (Novak 2005: 655).[14] The substance of the rights guaranteed by Article 27 focuses on 'ensuring the survival and continued development of the cultural, religious and social identity of the minorities concerned, thus enriching the fabric of society as a whole'.[15]

The right of minorities to the common enjoyment of their specific culture creates directly applicable duties on State parties to refrain from actions which might limit and destroy the exhibition of 'cultural life' of the group, for instance, in practising their customs, traditions and rituals, as well as traditional economic activities such as pastoralism and hunting (Novak 2005: 658-659). Of direct relevance to the Kunama case discussed in Chapter 9 is the interpretation that Article 27 of the ICCPR prohibits State parties from denying minorities access to and residence in their traditional home areas; and 'all measures which threaten the way of life and culture of a minority, such as large-scale expropriations of minority lands for commercial purposes' constitute a violation (Novak 2005: 659).

ETHNIC DIVERSITY IN ERITREA

Eritrea is officially described as being inhabited by nine ethnic groups, all diverse in culture, religion, and activities of production. Dividing ethnicity into fixed categories of population groups is, however, difficult from a scholarly viewpoint. For instance, the classic study on ethnic groups and clans in Eritrea, conducted by the anthropologist S.F. Nadel while he served as a military administrative officer in the country during the Second World War, illustrates this point well, as he lists a number of groups and clans not officially recognised as distinct groups today (Nadel 1944).

Tigrinya is the language of the highland (*kebessa*) population, which is the largest population group in the country, possibly constituting around 50 per cent of the total population. They usually refer to themselves

[13] The right of persons belonging to majority groups, such as the Tigrinya speakers of Eritrea, to protect and advance their culture is to be found in Article 15 of CESCR. For elaboration, see Eide 2001.
[14] See UN Human Rights Committee, General Comment No. 23 (1994), paragraph 6.2.
[15] UN Human Rights Committee, General Comment No. 23 (1994), paragraph 9.

as 'highlanders' (*deki kebessa*), but the term describing their language (Tigrinya) is generally used to denote the ethnic group also. The Tigrinya speakers are also to be found in the urban centres of the lowlands and the ports of Massawa and Assab, and in neighbouring Tigray regional state of Ethiopia. They are mostly sedentary agriculturalists, and share a common tradition of Orthodox Christianity, but also include groups of Roman Catholics and a small minority of *Jeberti*, Tigrinya-speaking Muslims. Muslims have traditionally been denied access to land in the Christian Orthodox highlands, thus today the Jeberti are mostly merchants and urban dwellers. The Jeberti are not, however, recognised by the government as a distinct ethnic group.

The *Tigre* group consists of diverse peoples inhabiting parts of the western lowlands, the northern highlands, the northern coastal plains, and parts of the Dahlak islands. The ten or so different clans speaking the Tigre language, of which the largest is the Beni Amer, do not form a distinct ethnic entity, although they share a common adherence to Islam (cf. Fegley 1995).

The *Rashaida* speak Arabic and form the smallest ethnic group, population-wise, in Eritrea. They are a nomadic people who migrated from the Arabian Peninsula in relatively recent times. They are found in small shifting concentrations in north-eastern Eritrea and the Sudan.

The *Afar* is the largest of the Cushitic-speaking groups in Eritrea, inhabiting the lowland coastal strip of Dankalia and they are also to be found in Ethiopia and Djibouti. The Afar are agro-pastoralists and are organised on a clan basis.

The *Saho* is another ethnic group based on a shared East Cushitic language. The Saho inhabit the escarpment region between the eastern lowlands and the *kebessa*. They are clustered in small pastoral nomadic and semi-nomadic groups. It is believed that the origins of the diverse groups speaking Saho are mixed, including elements from the Afar, Tigrinya, Tigre, and others. The *Bilen* ethnic group also speak a Central Cushitic language. They live in and around the town of Keren. The Bilen are sedentary agriculturalists, though some who live in Keren are traders.

Two languages spoken in Eritrea belong to the Nilo-Saharan language group. One is *Nara*, previously also known as Baria, a language spoken by people living in the eastern Gash region in the western lowlands.[16] They are sedentary agriculturalists, and live in small villages, divided in a clan structure. *Kunama* is the other Nilo-Saharan group in Eritrea. They too inhabit the western lowlands between the rivers Gash and Setit, living today predominantly as sedentary agriculturalists, although traditionally they were hunters and gathers. The social structure of the Kunama is based on a division into six clans. The clans are strictly exogamous, and they are the only group in Eritrea where descent is recognised through the maternal line. The *Beja*, in newer literature called the *Hedareb*, is a

---

[16] *Baria* is an Amharic/Tigrinya term for 'slave', thus seen from the dominant population group this is a derogatory term. However, many informants from the lowlands state that the people themselves use Baria as a self-descriptive term, not implying any servile connotations at all.

nomadic group living in the north-east and north-west border region (and is also to be found in Sudan).

In terms of religion, the Tigrinya ethnic group is entirely Christian, except the minority Muslim community of Jeberti, which is officially regarded as a sub-group of Tigrinya. The Afar, Saho, Hedareb and Rashaida are entirely Muslim communities. The Tigre is a predominantly Muslim community with a small Christian minority group, known as Mensa'e. The Bilen are Christians and Muslims. The Kunama include Muslims, Christians and adherents of indigenous belief. The Nara is a predominantly Muslim community with some adherents of indigenous belief.

There is no reliable data on the precise nature of ethnic configuration in Eritrea. However, based on 2010 estimates, *The World Fact Book* (2013) offers the following figures in percentages: Tigrinya 55%, Tigre 30%, Saho 4%, Kunama 2%, Rashaida 2%, Bilen 2%, other (Afar, Beni Amer, Nera) 5%. Apparently, Hedareb is referred to as Beni Amer in *The World Fact Book* (2013).

SUSTAINING CULTURAL SUPERIORITY: PERPETUATING MINORITY DISCRIMINATION

Within certain areas, the Eritrean government's development policies reflect a socio-historical and cultural bias. The reality is that the highlanders have throughout history maintained hegemony over what the state is supposed to be, whom it should embrace, and how its policies (whether military or domestic) ought to be designed. The sedentary Christian Orthodox highlanders of Eritrea and Ethiopia (*habesha*) have always dominated the Abyssinian realm (Eritrea and Ethiopia) and thus been instrumental in designing the political attributes of the state and the dominant culture of the nation (cf. Tronvoll 2009b).

In the Eritrean case, this hegemony was even exacerbated after independence, as the demographic weight of the Tigrinya population increased considerably in relation to the population of the state. As part of Ethiopia, the Tigrinya-speaking population constituted about 8 per cent of the population, in independent Eritrea about 50 per cent. The tradition of rule by the highlanders – in combination with what they perceive as their more advanced mode of production (sedentary agriculture), more developed culture, and being morally enlightened through Christianity – has had a negative impact on the accommodation of true cultural diversity in the independent state of Eritrea. Cases in point may be the lack of protection of pastoral rights under the new land tenure regime and the implementation of mother tongue as the medium of instruction in public primary schools in a way which is perceived by some ethnic groups as oppressive (see below).

The neglect of pastoral rights: eradicating 'backwardness'
The Eritrean land reform law (Proclamation No. 58/1994) adopts a sedentary agriculturalist's view of landed property, disregarding pastoral

and nomadic rights. During the liberation war, the EPLF encouraged the nomads to settle, and provided for education, health services and vaccination of cattle in the liberated areas.[17] The rival Eritrean Liberation Front (ELF), on the other hand, supported the nomads' traditional way of life and defended their rights of livelihood, a stance which was, to a certain degree, reciprocated by segments of the lowland agro-pastoralist groups with political support and backing.

After independence, the government of Eritrea designed a macro development policy which favoured agricultural rights over pastoral ones, and pastoralism was never mentioned as a potential area of growth and sustainable development.[18] The land reform proclamation furthermore included no special provisions protecting the grazing rights or rights of movement of herds of the lowland groups who traditionally practise pastoral nomadism and mixed agro-pastoralism. This may be seen as a violation of the cultural rights of these groups.

The diverging interests between agriculturalists and agro-pastoralists ('pure' pastoral nomads account only for about 5 per cent of the total population) might be read as a political discourse, displaying the contrasting political priorities of the EPLF/PFDJ vis-à-vis the political opposition, historically represented by the ELF. New settlement schemes are being planned and implemented in the western lowlands, directly infringing on traditional pastoral areas. The settlers include returning refugees from the Sudan and Tigrinya highlanders. Therefore, giving legislative protection to agriculturalists and not to agro-pastoralists sustains and broadens the cultural influence of the Tigrinya mode of production, at the expense of the economic activities pursued by minority groups.[19] It is thus plausible to argue that the regime aims to transform the pastoral nomadic

---

[17] Cf. *National Democratic Programme of the EPLF* (1977), Article 2.A.5: 'Provide the nomads with veterinary services, livestock breeding experts, agricultural advisors and financial assistance in order to enable them to *lead settled lives*, adopt modern techniques of agriculture and animal husbandry and improve their livelihood' (my italics). The same article is repeated in the *National Democratic Programme* of 1987 (Art. 2.A.5), adopted at the second congress of the EPLF.

[18] See, for instance, the state of Eritrea's *Development Letter*, prepared for the World Bank's Consultative Group Meeting for Eritrea, in Paris, 10-20 December 1994, and the government's *Macro Policy* document, November 1994, which lists the main objectives of the new land policy as: 'encourages long-term investments in agriculture and prudent environmental management; assures women's right to land on equal basis with men; promotes commercial agriculture' (p. 34).

[19] One informed observer of Eritrean politics told one of the current authors that one of the main reasons behind this narrow-minded development strategy is that there are more or less no policy-makers or decision-makers in the regime with a nomadic-pastoralist background. The regime's bureaucracy is predominantly drawn from the highland sedentary population, and is ignorant of pastoralist values and mode of life. Therefore, 'the EPLF/PFDJ believes that what is good for the sedentary agriculturalist must be good for the pastoralist', according to the informant (personal communication, 28 February 2009). On a different note, not giving pastoral rights proper legislative protection is also questionable in terms of sustainable development (Joireman 1996) and the possible negative environmental impact, a point stressed by Alexander Naty in his research on environmental degradation in Eritrea's western lowlands (1998, 2002a).

groups into sedentary agriculturalists, and mould them into replicas of the traditional Tigrinya production system.

The contradictions of language rights

Language rights are a vital medium for enjoying, preserving and developing minority cultures. International treaties binding on Eritrea grant minorities the right to use and develop their languages.[20] Similar to the land policy discussed above, the main 'official' objective and motivation for the new language policy in Eritrea is to foster national unity and identity in developing the country, while respecting cultural diversity (Woldemikael 2003). Or, as phrased by the head of Organisational Affairs of the EPLF/PFDJ: 'The EPLF's policy in the past and the government's policy at present has been and is [...] based on objective realities. This policy has served and serves national identity, unity and interest, and puts into consideration and safeguards the rights of the individual.'[21]

At an early stage, the Provisional Government of Eritrea (PGE)[22] emphasised the 'diversity in unity' argument and declared that: 'Every nationality has the right to its own language or any other language of its choice at the primary school'.[23] The Eritrean government justified its policy by referring to UNESCO's argument explaining that the use of the mother tongue in primary schools enhances the learning capacities of children. Furthermore, it was also emphasised that the use of mother languages in schools has the 'advantage of preserving minority languages and folk traditions that would be threatened if the government were to pursue policies and practices emphasizing the principle of "one state, one nation, one language"'(Woldemikael 2003: 122). This argument has, however, been questioned by Eritreans belonging to the minority groups, claiming that the 'so-called mother-tongue policy was adopted in order to sustain the marginalisation of the minority groups since they would not be fluent in the dominant language of the state, Tigrinya'.[24] This will sustain discrimination against the minority students in admission to institutions of higher education, as well as possible employment careers in the civil service, where a fluent command of Tigrinya is compulsory.

In all sectors of governance, the EPLF has attempted to modify 'traditional' society by developing the educational system as a tool of centrally planned processes of social and cultural change (see also Tronvoll 1998b; Woldemikael 2003: 120). It is thus important to contrast the formal policies ('law in books') with the implemented practice ('law

[20] Article 27 of the ICCPR.
[21] Abdulla Jaber, quoted in 'Unity in linguistic diversity', *Eritrea Profile*, 27 July 1996, p. 2.
[22] The PGE acted during the interim period running from the military liberation of the country on 24 May 1991 until the declaration of formal independence on 24 May 1993.
[23] Provisional Government of Eritrea, 'Declaration on Education in Eritrea', Legal Notice, No. 2/1991, 2 October 1991, Department of Education, Asmara (cited from Woldemikael 2003).
[24] One noted observer illustrated the devious use of the policy by the government with the Arabic proverb, 'A word of truth intended to serve falsity' (*Kilmet haq yuradu biha batil*). Personal communication, 2 April 2009.

in action'), in order to assess the use and development of minority languages in a human rights perspective.

The education policy encourages using the mother tongue as the language of instruction in elementary school (up to grade 7). Practice shows that not all languages are adequately taught in schools. In addition, all elementary school children are required to learn Tigrinya and/or Arabic (the two languages which are considered to be the working languages of the Eritrean government),[25] and English, which is the medium of instruction in all schools beyond primary school level (Woldemikael 2003: 122). This implies that Tigrinya children must learn Arabic and English in addition to Tigrinya, while Rashaida children (the only group speaking Arabic as their mother language) will learn Tigrinya and English in addition to Arabic; and the rest, that is children from the seven remaining minority groups, must learn Tigrinya, Arabic and English, in addition to their mother tongue.

The designation of Tigrinya and Arabic as the official working languages of the state (it is questionable, though, whether one can call Arabic a working language in practice in Eritrea), and English as the medium of instruction beyond grade 7, grants these languages a special status above minority languages in the country. In effect, this implies that the government is contradicting its own stated commitment to the equality of all Eritrean languages (Woldemikael 2003: 123). Woldemikael notes further that the application of the education policy has been fraught with difficulties, as the principle of the right to use one's 'own language or any other language of ... choice at the primary school' has been subject to local interpretation and negotiation (Gottesman 1998: 225-229; Woldemikael 2003: 124).

Apparently, the implementation of the language policy in Eritrea creates a threefold pattern, aligned more along religious lines than ethnicity (Woldemikael 2003: 124-128). The Christian population groups accept fully the aim of instruction in the mother tongue. To the dominant ethnic group, the Tigrinya speakers, this comes as no surprise, since their mother tongue is also the main language of the state. However, the Kunama, who are predominantly Christian (Lutheran Protestants), have also adopted the Kunama language as the medium of instruction in the schools.[26] The minority Christian Tigre speakers also prefer to use Tigre as their language of instruction. Most Muslim communities, on the other hand, including Tigre, Nara, Afar, Saho, Bilen, Hedareb and Jeberti, have chosen Arabic

[25] Arabic was justified by its historical position in the region, as well as the fact that it is used as a language of commerce and trade in the western lowlands and as the language of their religion among the Muslims.

[26] The Swedish evangelical mission started its work among the Kunama in the mid-1860s. Also the Roman Catholic Church conducted missionary activities among the Kunama during the Italian colonial period. One of the main tasks of the missionary work was focusing on establishing schools among the Kunama, and to develop their language into a written script (Normark 1972; Woldemikael 2003). It should be noted, however, that it is extremely difficult to divide and classify the Kunama, like other groups in the region, into categories of specific religious denominations, since religious syncretism and ambivalence are inherent in these communities.

instead of their ethnic languages. A cause, or an effect, of this is that there are no schools in Eritrea offering instruction in the minority languages of Nara, Bilen, Afar, and Hedareb. Consequently, the use and sustainability of these minority languages has reportedly been neglected.[27]

Reactions to the new Eritrean language policy can be explained from both historical and contemporary viewpoints. First, the structural discrimination against the lowland Muslim minority groups has been sustained for centuries, as they have been perceived as 'alien' to positions of power and authority in relation to the Abyssinian feudal system.[28] Furthermore, most of the urban centres are located in the highlands; hence public institutions and the infrastructure of the state tend to be overrepresented among Tigrinya highlanders. For instance, as late as 1958, there was not a single school in the Muslim areas of Eritrea (Pool 1997: 9).

The overrepresentation of Tigrinya continues. It was estimated in 1996-7 that the Tigrinya constitute about half of the Eritrean population; but 82 per cent of school pupils are taught in Tigrinya and 68 per cent (370 out of 549) of the total number of schools teach in Tigrinya (in 1996-7) (Woldemikael 2003). Hence, the absolute dominance of Tigrinya as a medium of instruction in Eritrean schools does not reflect the demographic composition of the population. Furthermore, Tigrinya is the sole language of instruction during military training and the language of command of the Eritrean army,[29] which bestows on it unprecedented importance in the highly militarised Eritrean society. In reality, Tigrinya is the dominant working language of the state, as it operates as the working language of the bureaucracy, the courts, the arts, and among the literati.

Possibly as a reaction to the dominant Tigrinya culture, the Muslim lowland groups have turned to Arabic as a medium of instruction rather than their minority languages. This is most noteworthy among the Tigre group, which is the second largest group in Eritrea, constituting about 30 per cent of the total population of the country. Despite this, just 5 per cent of schools (29 out of 549) used Tigre as a medium of instruction in 1995-6. Furthermore, only 3 per cent of the pupils in elementary schools were learning in Tigre, while 12 per cent chose Arabic as the language of instruction[30] (Woldemikael 2003: 127). The Saho and Jeberti as Muslim highland groups have shifted from mother-tongue to Tigrinya schools in the absence of schools which provide Arabic as a medium of instruction.

[27] *Landinfo* note, Norwegian Immigration Authorities, Oslo, August 2007: at http://www.landinfo.no/index.gan?id=834&subid=0, accessed October 2008.
[28] Non-Christian lowlanders (non-*Habesha*) could obtain high office under the feudal Abyssinian state by converting to the Orthodox faith, learning Amharic/Tigrinya and assimilating into the Christian Amhara/Tigrinya culture.
[29] After grade 12, all educational institutions in Eritrea are administered by the military. All Eritreans of 18 to 45 years of age have to undergo 18 months of national service, including 6 months of rigorous military training. In effect, though, the national service programme has been never-ending since 1998 and the general mobilisation of Eritrean society as a consequence of the Eritrean-Ethiopian war.
[30] Only the Rashida, constituting about 2.4 per cent of the population, have Arabic as their mother tongue.

Arabic is increasingly regarded as a lingua franca among Eritrean Muslims, however. They pray in Arabic; it is used by religious leaders in mosques as well as by teachers in Koran schools; and traditional judges use it in administering *Shari'a* law. Arabic is also the language of trade and business among Muslim communities. Thus, the demand for Arabic is driven by both local and public needs, as is reflected in the growth of the language as a medium of instruction. From 1993/4 to 1996/7, 32 new schools started to use Arabic as a medium of instruction, surpassing the growth rate of all other languages, including Tigrinya (which had a 22 per cent net increase) (Woldemikael 2003: 127).

The government seems to interpret the increased interest in Arabic as a medium of instruction as an expression of opposition to its language policy and ultimately its nationalistic ideology, as it is interpreted against the historical discourse on Eritrea after the collapse of Italian colonialism in 1941. At that time certain national and international actors argued that the country should be divided into an Arabic-speaking Muslim low-land sector (which could be united with Sudan) and a Tigrinya-speaking Christian highland sector (which could be united with Ethiopia).[31]

In spite of the growing popular demand for Arabic as a medium of in-struction, the government is accused of denying certain groups its use as a medium of communication. Mohammed Salih Ibrahim, a representative of the Eritrean Islamic Party for Justice and Development, explained that Muslims living in the highlands (the Jeberti) were particularly discrimi-nated against in this regard:

> The government tells people to use Tigrinya not Arabic. I speak and understand Tigrinya as well as Arabic. We, the Muslims in the highlands, were not oppressed by the dominant people of the Tigrinya; we like and are used to speak Tigrinya. But what is important here is that the government stopped our language and is forcing us to speak Tigrinya. The government is using this tactic to make trouble between us and the Eritrean people.[32]

As a major regional and international language, Arabic may appear more attractive to learn than ethnic minority languages. Hence, resist-ance to the policy of using the mother tongue in Eritrean schools by Muslims is probably related to a conscious decision to pursue broader strategies of social and economic upward mobility, since economic and political rewards and benefits are more likely to accrue to those who are fluent in Arabic rather than an Eritrean minority language. Additionally, Eritrean Muslims may turn to Arabic and their common faith as a strat-egy to resist the political domination of the Tigrinya culture projected by the EPLF/PFDJ government. As this brief discussion of the implementa-tion of government language policy illustrates, the divide between highlands and lowlands, Christians and Muslims, Tigrinya and minority groups, still largely prevails in Eritrea (cf. also Pool 1997: 9). Lately, the old Hamasien-Akele Guzay dichotomy seems to be resurfacing with a re-newed vigour, particularly in Eritrean diaspora communities. Hamasien

---

[31] 'Unity in linguistic diversity', *Eritrea Profile*, 27 July 1996, p. 2.
[32] Quoted from an interview with Tronvoll, on 19 April 2008 at Khartoum (Sudan).

and Akele Guzay are two of the three (traditional) highland provinces in Eritrea, the third being Seraye. In the 1970s, atrocious violations are believed to have been committed within the EPLF emanating from an alleged skirmish between individuals or groups originating from Hamasien and Akele Guzay. A full-scale analysis on this particular topic will, however, make material for future academic inquiry.

The government's contradictions on ethno-linguistic and religious equality have now become a cause for concern among Eritrean Muslims and non-Tigrinya segments, who accuse the government of a flawed policy that promotes the Tigrinisation (and by implication Christianisation) of the Eritrean society at the expense of Eritrean Muslims in general. This issue is best articulated in no other document than *The Eritrean Covenant* (2010), a document authored by an anonymous group of Eritrean Muslims who identify themselves as Mejlis Ibrahim Mukhtar, borrowing the name of a prominent Eritrean religious leader from the 1940s. *The Eritrean Covenant* debunks the rhetoric of the Eritrean government on ethno-linguistic and religious equality by citing credible statistical data on the ethnic and religious make-up of high-ranking government officials. At least two glaring examples analysed by *The Eritrean Covenant* can be briefly discussed here.

The first example is related to the composition of the government's Steering Committee on Cultural Heritage, which designated the Debre-Bizen Monastery (built in 1361) as national heritage, while excluding from such designation Missjid Abu Hanafi (built in 1203) and other historical mosques. The only logical explanation *The Eritrean Covenant* could imagine is that the Steering Committee on Cultural Heritage is made up of eleven members who are all Tigrinya highlanders, as if the issue is of exclusive concern to them.[33] On the thorny issue of Tigrinisation, similar observations were also made by the late Kunama anthropologist, Alexander Naty, who laments that 'reference to places by non-indigenous names is an indication of the dispossession of indigenous people's culture and identity'. In support of this argument, Naty mentions the following glaring examples:

> The names Gash and Setit for the two rivers in the region are misnomers. The Kunama (who are indigenous to the region) refer to the rivers Gash and Setit by the names Sona and Tika respectively. Many localities in Kunamaland have been given alien or misspelt names. Dokimbia has been renamed Tokumbia. The village of Delle in Aymasa has been called Addi K'eshi. Likewise, the original Kunama name of Badumma (one of the contested places in the current Ethio-Eritrean conflict) has been given the distorted name of Badme. (Naty 2002: 569)

The second example discussed by *The Eritrean Covenant* is about the staffing of the Ministry of Defence, which is one of the most important

[33] According to email correspondence with the authors of The Eritrean Covenant, members of the Cultural Heritage Commission are: Naigzy Gebremehdin (Chairman), Eritros Abraham, Yohannes Tecle Haimanot, Alemseged Tesfai, Zemhret Yohannes, Azeib Tewelde, Solomon Tsehaye, Yosef Libsikel, Kidane Solomon, Daniel Tesfalidet, Kesete Abraha.

state institutions in Eritrea. The Ministry has a total of 247 military officers above the rank of lieutenant-colonel, whose names and ranks are properly detailed in *The Eritrean Covenant*. Out of the total figure, only 22 are Muslims, making a mere 8.9% of the total number. In a society which prides itself as 'evenly divided between Christianity and Islam,' such figures are disproportionately unrepresentative. This imbalance should be one of the priority concerns to be addressed in any transitional political plan that could be envisaged for Eritrea.

FINAL REMARKS

The Eritrean government's strongly nationalistic ideology and policies, in combination with the ruling party's highland Tigrinya cultural inclination and dominance, make minority rights and protection a marginalised field in Eritrea today. Although certain policies on paper appear to follow the state's motto of 'Diversity in Unity', in reality they apparently sustain the Tigrinya cultural and political domination of Eritrean society.

Furthermore, as certain groups defined along ethnic (e.g. Kunama), cultural (e.g. pastoralist), or religious (e.g. Muslim) lines are construed as a threat to government policies and societal order, special protection or incentives to cater for the rights of these groups and their demands are negated.

In spite of the government's rhetoric on ethno-religious and linguistic equality, the reality on the ground shows an imbalance between the dominant ethnic group of Tigrinya and the rest of the eight officially recognised ethnic groups. The divide also has religious connotations, as the dominant group (Tigrinya) is an entirely Christian community, with the exception of the Jeberti who claim recognition as a distinct ethnic group. As shown by the examples discussed in *The Eritrean Covenant*, the prevailing imbalance is so skewed that it requires urgent remedy and rectification before it develops into the irreversible cause of a conflict. The challenge is also underscored by Ahmed Raji's *Lost Rainbow* (2010), where he notes that the fundamental question in Eritrea today is not simply one of removing a dictatorship, but also that of dealing with structural societal problems. A core element of the democratic agenda should be ensuring changes that involve healthy and sustainable relationships among the cultural components of Eritrean society (Raji 2010).

9

Diversity Diminished:
Targeting the Kunama Minority Group

INTRODUCTION

The consolidation of nationalist sentiments in Eritrea and the construction of a centralist, unitary state after independence in 1991 have led to a growing tension between the dominant nationalist ideology – which partly reflects the cultural sentiments of the Tigrinya majority group – and minority groups. This is aggravated by the fact that the EPLF/PFDJ government is perceived by many minority representatives to be a predominantly 'Tigrinya' government as the language and political culture of the government stems from the Tigrinya group inhabiting the Eritrean highlands and urban centres throughout the country.

Of the many minority groups in Eritrea, the government has seemingly singled out the Kunama group as of special concern to the state. The history of the Kunama population can be read as a narrative of sustained violations of minority rights, in addition to a general contravention of basic human rights, such as the right to life and the prohibition of torture and collective punishment. In order to highlight concerns about Eritrea's minority populations, this chapter will analyse the situation of cultural and minority rights in Eritrea exemplified by the case of the Kunama group and based on the framework for the general protection of minority rights as developed by the UN Independent Expert on Minority Issues (McDougall 2007: 334). A human-rights-based approach to the protection of minority rights should include the following four aspects:

1. protecting a minority's existence, including the physical integrity of persons belonging to minorities;
2. protecting and promoting cultural and social identity;
3. ensuring non-discrimination and equality, including ending structural or systemic discrimination; and
4. ensuring effective participation of minorities in public life, especially in decisions that affect them.

First, the historical marginalisation and suppression of the Kunama will be highlighted, followed by an in-depth analysis of the stigmatisation of the Kunama in independent Eritrea. Emphasis will be put on the

government campaign against the Kunama in the wake of the 1998-2000

Eritrean-Ethiopian war, the erosion of Kunama land rights, and the attack on their cultural sites and symbols which has led to an increasing stream of Kunamas as 'cultural' refugees to neighbouring Ethiopia.

THE KUNAMA

The Kunama is one of the smallest ethnic groups in Eritrea, and is estimated to number between 50,000 and 140,000 people.[1] They live in small scattered communities in the areas around the Setit and Gash river basin (western lowlands), which extends up to and along the Eritrean and Sudanese border in Eritrea and the adjacent districts of Humera and Adi Abo in the Tigray regional state in north-western Ethiopia.[2] The town of Barentu in the Gash-Setit area has traditionally been viewed as the Kunama 'capital'.

The frontier location of the Kunama group has positioned them in a precarious political situation. The anthropologist Dominique Lussier describes the consequences of their location: 'The advent of Eritrea as a newly created state has put the Kunama in the position of a double periphery now that the national borders have divided them on the ground' (Lussier 1997: 441). Although Lussier seems to be indicating that the Kunama people are divided by the borders of Eritrea and Ethiopia, as is the case in many cross-border African communities, Weldehaimanot and Mekonnen have a different view on this. Citing unequivocal findings of the Eritrea-Ethiopia Boundary Commission, they assert that the traditional territory of the Kunama does not cross the international boundary; hence, they reside wholly within Eritrea (Weldehaimanot and Mekonnen 2013).

The Kunama people are today nominally divided into four main groups: Kunama Aimasa, living in the western part of the provincial capital town of Barentu; Kunama Barka, living along the river Gash in the south-eastern part of Barentu; Kunama Marda, residing in the north-eastern part of Barentu; and Kunama Tika, living along the river Gash in the southern part of Barentu (USCIS 2003: 2). The traditional political structure was territorially defined, dividing the Kunama into six political

---

[1] No national census with categories for ethnicity is available. Estimates of the size of the Kunama population thus vary accordingly. The authoritative language database, Ethnologue, reports that 142,000 people speak the Kunama language, of which 140,000 reside in Eritrea (*Ethnologue.com*: 'Kunama: a Language of Eritrea'). The UN information agency (IRIN) estimates that there are around 100,000 Kunama people in Ethiopia and Eritrea, of which 70,000 reside in Eritrea (http://www.irinnews.org/PrintReport.aspx?ReportId=38494). The Catholic Near East Welfare Association (CNEWA) is much more conservative in estimating the Kunama population of Eritrea and Ethiopia to be between 50,000 and 60,000 (Molidor 2001). It is claimed that the Kunama population has been decimated by the recent Eritrean-Ethiopian war.

[2] The most comprehensive anthropological study of the Kunama was conducted by Dominique Lussier in 1994 (Lussier 1997). The Italian ethnographer Gianni Dore has also recently done research on the Kunama.

divisions, which are divided in turn into three to four sections corresponding to well-defined localities.

A history of oppression

Throughout history the Kunama have been exposed to conflict and subjugation from neighbouring groups (Longrigg 1945; Naty 2004). A native Kunama anthropologist, the late Alexander Naty, stressed in particular the hostile historical relationship between the Kunama and the 'Abyssinians', i.e. the ruling highlanders in current day Eritrea and Ethiopia. The highlanders viewed the Kunama as secondary people, since they were originally non-Christians and their livelihood differed from the sedentary agriculturalist practice dominant in the highlands. Repeated raids against Kunama villages where people were enslaved, cattle stolen and villages torched, have left an imprint in Kunama collective memory of the highlanders as enemies (ibid.: 2).

Historians have documented repeated massacres on the Kunama throughout history, and in successive raids by Abyssinian forces towards the end of the nineteenth century (and in particular the 1886 campaign by Ras Alula, the governor of Tigray). During the latter conflict, it is estimated that the Kunama was decimated from about 200,000 to only 10,000–15,000 people (Longrigg 1945: 68-72; Erlich 1996: 101; Kibreab 2008: 80-82). With the advent of Italian colonialism, the raiding of the Kunama ceased. Italian colonial rule brought relative peace and stability for the Kunama people, a memory which is still cherished by Kunama elders. Despite the Italian presence, however, irregular Abyssinian raids into Kunama territory continued (Naty 2001). Moreover, with the collapse of the Italian colonial empire in 1941, the Kunama were once again exposed to the whims of their neighbours.

The 'continuity in the Kunama experience of brutal domination' (Lussier 1997: 441) has thus been experienced up to recent times. For instance, it is reported that during the British Military Administration (BMA) of Eritrea (1941–52), the Kunama were exposed to conflict and subjugation from many neighbouring groups with the apparent consent of the BMA (ibid.: 444). In particular, during 1949 and 1950, organised warfare was conducted against the Kunama by neighbouring groups, ironically driven by Idris Awate, the person who later became famous as the rebel who commenced the armed struggle against Ethiopian domination of Eritrea in 1961.[3] An Italian journalist working in Eritrea at

---

[3] Like all interpretations of historical events in the region, the role of Idris Awate is also severely contested. Thus, his possible role in Kunama raids could be exaggerated as part of a conscious defamation campaign against Idris Awate and his role as the 'first Eritrean resistance fighter', first by Haile Selassie and later by the Derg, all of whom referred to him as a *shifta* (bandit) in order to undermine his political legitimacy and discard his representativeness as a Muslim 'lowlander'. The controversy about Idris Awate's involvement in the Kunama genocide still haunts the Eritrean political discourse, as the Kunama front was recently expelled from the opposition umbrella organisation Eritrean Democratic Alliance when the Kunama leader criticised and rejected the symbol of Awate as an Eritrean hero.

the time, Lussier reported that: 'I am positive that there is an on-going process of genocide directed against the Kunama, whether or not the parties or neighbouring groups are conscious of this, but there is no doubt that this is being done with the assistance of the British Administration responsible for the territory' (ibid.: 445). These historic events feed into current sentiments of fear, scepticism and enmity towards neighbouring groups and central authorities among many Kunama.

During the Eritrean liberation war, the Kunama were accused of being the only group that largely and consistently supported the Ethiopian government (see also Gilkes 1983: 203; Bondestam 1989: 183-4; Markakis 1990: 116), even though there were Kunama recruits to the EPLF in the last phase of the war (Pateman 1990: 20-21). The Derg military junta armed the Kunama and used them to help defend towns like Barentu and Tessenei from attacks from the EPLF. It is claimed that the Kunama military support for the Derg army was instrumental during the EPLF siege of Barentu in 1976/77, when hundreds of Kunama fought alongside the garrison and were recruited into the Derg army (Gilkes 2005: 235).[4] When the EPLF finally captured Barentu from the Ethiopian army in mid-1984, the Kunama as a whole suffered. It is reported that as 'Kunama women and children fled the town they were shot down by advancing EPLF fighters' (Gilkes 2005).

Although many Kunama found the Derg's policy of ethnic equality appealing – considering the unequal power relations that existed between them and other groups, in particular the Tigrinya highlanders (Naty 2001: 587) – this was probably not the main motivating factor for supporting the Derg. More than being ideologically anchored, the support for the Derg was probably pragmatic, as a Kunama elder explained: 'We had no choice, we joined whoever came: when these came we said 'father', when those came we said 'father' and we just stayed alive' (Lussier 1997: 443). The seeking of Ethiopian patronage by the Kunama may thus be interpreted as a survival strategy, as the Eritrean liberation fronts also joined in the raids on the Kunama by neighbouring groups, forcing the Kunama to seek protection from Ethiopian forces stationed in Barentu (Markakis 1990: 116; Gilkes 2005: 235).

A similar interpretation of the Kunama political allegiances is also supported by the British government fact-finding mission to Eritrea in 2003, which found that:

> The Kunama has traditionally relied on the Ethiopian Army when larger and more powerful ethnic neighbours attacked them. For historic reasons, although the majority of the Eritrean population strongly supported Eritrean independence, the Kunama still maintained their support for the Ethiopian army. (BIA 2008: 42)[5]

[4] It is estimated that some 6000 Kunama in total served in the Ethiopian army during the 1970s and 1980s (Gilkes 2005), a relatively large number considering the small size of the group.
[5] In interpreting these allegiances and sentiments, it is important to distinguish between the perceptions of the Tigrinya highland population and Eritrean nationalism. In certain contexts and discourses these two categories fuse and overlap, in others they are separate and conflicting.

THE STIGMATISATION OF THE KUNAMA IN INDEPENDENT ERITREA

After independence in 1991, the Eritrean government included the Kunama in the compulsory national service programme, and by that means is trying to enforce and consolidate a Kunama loyalty to the Eritrean state. However, the tense relations between the Kunama and the EPLF government have been sustained in the post-independence period (USCIS 2003). The Kunama's history of supporting the Derg during the liberation war was a stigma which immediately put them in jeopardy of government sanctions after independence. According to Kunama representatives, the discrimination against the group was felt immediately after the EPLF takeover in May 1991. Endrias Sisto Nada, a Kunama spokesperson, explained that, when coming to power, the EPLF accused them of working for Ethiopia and being Ethiopians.[6]

The decisive and brutal arrest immediately after the EPLF takeover of Eritrea in 1991 of at least 55 Kunama serving as administrators and civil servants under the Ethiopian government signalled the continuation of hostile relations between the EPLF and the Kunama. Allegedly, these people had been involved in human rights abuses under the Derg. None of the 55 persons have been released or been seen since then, and it is unclear if any formal charges have been pressed, or any trials held (BIA 2008: 44). Hundreds, and possibly thousands, of Kunama ex-soldiers were also detained for at least two years after independence; some were kept for longer and it is even claimed that some may still be in detention (Gilkes 2005: 236).

The immediate clampdown on Kunama representatives after the EPLF takeover in Eritrea in 1991 was soon followed by other apparently discriminatory actions directed against the Kunama. On 11 March 1995 in the town of Shambuko (also written Shambakko), two Kunama brothers were shot and killed by police officers (who were ex-EPLF fighters of Tigrinya origin). The anthropologist Dominique Lussier was doing fieldwork in the area at that time and interviewed a number of eye-witnesses to record the event (Lussier 1997). The Kunama brothers were in town to market their harvest. A Tigrinya woman complained to the police about the price they demanded, and the police officer ordered the brothers to sell at a lower price. One of the brothers refused, saying he was not forcing anybody to buy his harvest, and instead started packing it on his camel. The police officer prevented him from leaving, and a fight broke out between them. A second police officer (also Tigrinya) then reportedly shot the Kunama man dead on the spot. His brother, shocked by the incident, grabbed the gun and while running away emptied it in the air. According to Kunama witnesses, the surrounding Tigrinya people all pulled arms and chased after the brother and shot him dead too. In the aftermath of the event, several Kunama were arrested (accounts vary between nine and twenty) and put in jail for months, while none of the Tigrinya involved in the incident were questioned. It is not reported whether the police officer who shot the first brother faced any consequences for his action.

[6] Interviewed on 29 April 2008, in Shimelba refugee camp, Tigray, Ethiopia.

This incident was deeply felt in Kunama society, and Lussier reports that 'it reached momentous proportions as a source of concern' (Lussier 1997: 444). The incident is also corroborated by the Eritrean anthropologist Alexander Naty as a source of increased tension between the Kunama and Eritrean authorities in the post-independence period and a symbolic reminder of the historical animosity between the Kunama and the Tigrinya highlanders (Naty 2002b: 3).

The outbreak of the new war between Eritrea and Ethiopia in May 1998 further worsened the already tense relations between the Kunama and central Eritrean authorities, as it revived the image of the Kunama as Ethiopian collaborators and spies. Unlike people of other ethnic groups, the Kunama did not flee their home villages when the Ethiopian forces occupied Eritrean territory during the war. They remained in their villages and the majority ignored the Ethiopian presence. Eritrean authorities thus accused the Kunama first of failing to resist the Ethiopian military offensive, later of allegedly assisting the Ethiopians and showing them secret unguarded border-crossing points on the Mereb river (Naty 2001: 588; Gilkes 2005: 237).

The existence of the Kunama resistance movements – the Democratic Movement for the Liberation of the Eritrean Kunama (DMLEK) and the Eritrean Democratic Resistance Movement-Gash Setit (EDRM)[7] – and Ethiopia's support for their politico-military operations, have furthermore reinforced such a view among highlanders and the Eritrean government. Endrias Sisto Nada, a Kunama spokesperson, claims: 'Today the Government has one aim: they say that we are siding with the opposition and they kill us and imprison us.'[8]

This view is corroborated by a recently defected Eritrean intelligence officer, Mr Menghesteab Girmay Asres.[9] His security unit (the Third Operational Unit) was responsible for following and targeting the Kunama community around Mendefera. Menghesteab Girmay Asres offered two reasons for the government's campaign against the Kunama:

> The first reason is that the government has for a long time quarrelled with the Kunama; and the second reason is that the Kunama have strong opposition groups who struggle for the rights of Kunama people. These opposition groups are strong enough to attack military camps and they are destroying government properties. The government is really concerned about this group. The problem is that the government can't destroy the opposition group as they can't find them. The government knows that the Kunama people as a whole are the base and the supporters of this opposition group and that is why the government attempts to eliminate the Kunama.[10]

[7] British government fact-finding mission to Eritrea, 4-18 November 2002 (BIA 2008).
[8] Interviewed 29 April 2008, in Shimelba refugee camp, Tigray, Ethiopia.
[9] Mengesteab Girmay Asres joined the EPLF in 1990 and served with the Front until 1993. He was re-enlisted in the Eritrean army in 1998, first with the 16th Military Intelligence Unit of Regiment 161, subsequently serving as an expert of information and cartography with various military sections until 2004. He was then transferred to the Intelligence Unit of the Third Operational Zone, working as an investigator in the internal security/counter-intelligence section until he defected in September 2007.
[10] From a recorded interview conducted for this study on 25 October 2008.

During the Ethiopian military offensive, Operation Sunset, in February/March 1999, Kunama resistance forces allegedly joined behind the Ethiopian troops. As large parts of the Eritrean western lowlands fell into the control of Ethiopian military, including the regional capital Barentu, the Kunama front was given delegated administrative authority by the Ethiopian Army in their home areas. When Ethiopia withdrew from uncontested Eritrean territories in 2000 after signing the cease-fire agreement, this created anxiety and fear among the many Kunama who had assisted or accepted the Ethiopian military presence in the Eritrean western lowlands. Immediately after the Ethiopian pull-out, it was reported that Kunama who had helped in administering Barentu under Ethiopian control were arrested and killed (AI 2001). Further, in its comprehensive country study of Eritrea of 2004, Amnesty International reports that:

> An unknown number of Eritrean civilians were detained in fighting zones during the war on suspicion of collaborating with the Ethiopian army, especially when the Eritrean army regained areas captured by the Ethiopian army in southern Eritrea. This was particularly the case with members of the Kunama ethnic group (or 'nationality') in south-western Eritrea. The Kunama have historical connections with Ethiopia and were as a result suspected of Ethiopian sympathies during the war. Scores of Kunamas are allegedly still secretly detained on suspicion of welcoming the Ethiopian army when it captured parts of south-western Eritrea. (AI 2004: 11)

In a letter sent to Amnesty International in November 2000, Kunama representatives claimed that immediately after the war ended, some 600 Kunama men, women and children were forcefully taken and transferred to Sahel (the mountainous and barren region of north-eastern Eritrea), after which their whereabouts was unknown (Gilkes 2005: 237). The US State Department corroborates these reports, and writes in its country study on Eritrea for the year 2002 that: 'There was no information available, nor is any likely to become available, on the several members of the Kunama ethnic group who were detained without charges on suspicion of collaborating with Ethiopian forces in 2000' (USSD 2003).

It thus seems plausible to argue that the Eritrean government's retaliation against the Kunama after the Ethiopian pull-back in 2000 was not only directed against the Kunama resistance movement *per se*, but was intended as a collective punishment. It appears that a considerable proportion of the Kunama community was perceived as Ethiopian collaborators and spies. This perception is further strengthened by the fact that, unlike people of other ethnic groups, the Kunama did not flee their home villages when the Ethiopian forces occupied Eritrean territory during the war. They remained in their villages and the majority ignored the Ethiopian presence (Naty 2001: 588; Gilkes 2005). What is important to note is that a similar pattern of persecution was also noted within certain segments of the Saho ethnic group, who did not evacuate their villages in the areas of Senafe, Soira, and Hazemo during the Eritrean-Ethiopian border conflict. The same is true about returnees from Sudan who had been settled in Gash Barka. All of these groups were categorically labelled as traitors because they were not harmed by Ethiopian troops during the limited period that their respective localities fell under Ethiopian control (Hirt 2010; Mohammad 2013: 329). For whatever reason, violence towards the Kunama people appears to be disproportionate to that of any others.

A Kunama woman explained that: 'When the Ethiopians left, we were suspicious about revenge the Eritrean [authorities] might take on us saying we helped the Ethiopians'.[11] Hence, more than 4000 civilian Kunama fled Eritrea alongside the Ethiopian army when it pulled back under the cease-fire agreement.[12] These Kunama were mostly from the villages of Fode and Anugulu, whose districts fell under the control of the Ethiopian army during the war. From the point of view of the Eritrean authorities, this action confirmed the accusations that the Kunama had sided with Ethiopia during the war. In this context, it must be remembered that tens of thousands of Kunama remained in Eritrea, and did not flee alongside the Ethiopian army. Furthermore, thousands of Kunama youth fought in the Eritrean army against Ethiopia during the war. The native Kunama anthropologist Alexander Naty questioned why, on these grounds, only the Kunama are stigmatised as 'not true Eritreans' by the Eritrean government, since other segments of the Eritrean population have also collaborated with different Ethiopian regimes.

REGIME REVENGE: THE 2007 KUNAMA CRACKDOWN AND MASSACRE

The Kunama's fear of revenge after the 1998-2000 war was well founded. A former EPLF liberation fighter and later intelligence officer in the Eritrean army, Mr Menghesteab Girmay Asres, has described in detail how the military intelligence and interrogation system operates in general, and how the Kunama were targeted in particular. The following account is based on Mr Menghesteab's testimony given in October 2008.[13] At the beginning of 2007, a special intelligence operation was ordered against the Kunama, while army security units in Shambuko, Bushuka, Maidima and Mendefera started 'collecting Kunama and abusing them horribly'.

At the beginning of 2007, seventy Kunama were imprisoned under harsh conditions in Barentu. The Eritrean army continued its persecution

[11] UN Integrated Regional Information Network for Central and Eastern Africa (UN IRIN-CEA), 'Plight of the Kunama Refugees', 2 December 2002, at http://www.irinnews.org/PrintReport.aspx?ReportId=38494.
[12] On the grounds of their particular collective motivation for fleeing and the risk of returning to their country of origin, all of the more than 4000 Eritrean Kunama in the Shimelba refugee camp were granted the right of resettlement in the United States as a group (CORC 2007).
[13] Menghesteab Girmay Asres gave his testimony, in a broadcast on the exiled Eritrean television channel, 'Eritrean Voice TV', on 18 October 2008. He repeated his testimony in a recorded interview conducted in Addis Ababa on 25 October 2008, by Anna Little, on behalf of Tronvoll and for the Eritrea Human Rights Study, organised by the Oslo Centre for Peace and Human Rights.

of the Kunama in areas such as Faulina, Boshoka, Shambuko, Bimbina, Tolegamuja, Aymaba and Koyta Biya, as they were accused of being sympathisers of the Kunama resistance front (DMLEK). Allegedly, children as young as nine were taken into custody in these operations, where a total of 300 Kunama were detained. Menghesteab asserts:

> The prisoners were bloodily harassed, molested and tortured in order to say yes to the accusations which were alien to them and they knew nothing about. [...] If you are going to arrest someone you should have some evidence against them, but for those people there was no evidence or a reason for us to interrogate them. They were innocent and there was no reason to interrogate them – we just brought them to beat and to kill them and we were treating them very badly – beating them till they died. In general, the aim of the government is to kill and beat the Kunama, not to interrogate.

Prison conditions worsened the plight of the Kunama, as explained by Menghesteab:

> The conditions for [the Kunama] prisoners were awful. We didn't allow them to change their clothes, we didn't allow them to see their family, we always forced them to walk without shoes, and we always gave them small amounts of food and water – in order to weaken them and to make them sick and die. When they got sick we didn't give them medical treatment and because of this they were having mental and physical problems. We forced them to do hard work, and we took their private property like money, house, gold, and necessary documents, and other privately owned things. We would put 23 to 26 people in a small cell so that many would nearly die because of the shortage of fresh air. We scared and beat them continuously, and they couldn't escape. I have seen a lot of prisoners going crazy, and facing different kinds of diseases. I also saw some of the prisoners disabled because of the heavy beatings. I also saw prisoners die inside the prison.

Menghesteab reports that the fate of the nearly 300 Kunama detained during the period of January to May 2007 differed:

- Ten children aged 9–13 years were sentenced to 6 months custody at Halhale rehabilitation centre in the Third Operational Zone;

- Thirteen individuals aged 13–18 were sentenced to between one and four years incarceration in Adi Quala;

- Around 250 Kunama of all ages, including mothers with infants, were sentenced to between one and 20 years incarceration in Adi Quala;

- Two individuals died during interrogation (names withheld by the author); and

- 26 individuals were poisoned and killed (the names of 18 of them are withheld by the authors).

The most shocking incident reported by Menghesteab Girmay Asres was the brutal killing by poison of some of the detained individuals. All of them were Kunama men and many were known to have close relatives in the Kunama resistance front (DMLEK). The alleged killings of these individuals were not only committed to intimidate the Kunama collectively, but also to cover up a propaganda initiative by the Eritrean government. In order to justify and divert attention from the Kunama crackdown, twelve Kunama prisoners (detained in Mendefera) who spoke Tigrinya well were forced to confess and testify on camera that they were part of the Kunama front (DMLEK) and were responsible for planting anti-vehicle mines in Shambuko, Geze, Erab, Bimbina, Sinshale and Adi Tekleheimanot at the beginning of 2001. The Eritrean government wanted material evidence to expose Ethiopia's proxy war by using the Kunama front to undermine its legitimacy in the eyes of the Eritrean people. Allegedly, the Minister of Information Mr Ali Abdu personally escorted both a journalist and a cameraman to the operational command run at the time by Major-General Omar Tewil who was commander of the Third Operational Zone.[14] The Kunama prisoners did as they were instructed and 'confessed' their misdeeds and praised the EPLF/PFDJ for the adequate, and even good, treatment they received while in custody.

Afterwards, the prisoners were taken to the prison camp at Mai Dima, run by the Intelligence Unit of the 25th Regiment. In the camp, they were told to dig a hole in the ground 5 metres deep and 4 metres square. In order to assist in this work, an additional 14 Kunama prisoners were brought from Adi Quala. After the hole was complete, the officer in charge of the case, Major Tekleberhan Hagos (Wedi Aynei), brought two containers of 20 litres of a certain poisonous chemical from Meandefera to the Mai Dima camp. He then dismissed the regular camp security, and brought in a special team of six intelligence officers from Mendefera to carry out the massacre. All the 26 prisoners were then allegedly poisoned on one day in April 2007, and dumped in the hole they had dug.[15] After the operation, the officers of the intelligence unit were ordered by the commander of the Third Operational Zone to send all personal documents and belongings of the victims to his headquarters. Reports about the massacre were later filed with the Third Operational Zone and the Ministry of Defence. The Minister of Information was also later informed about the incident, as he wanted to use the prisoners for another propaganda mission. The minister is reported to have expressed dissatisfaction and regret about the measures taken.

Considering the extremely abhorrent and grave accusations reported above, one should be very cautious about stating them as facts. Although Menghesteab Girmay Asres appears to be a credible eye-witness of the events, the only other concrete information we have on the Spring 2007 crackdown on the Kunama is provided by the Kunama resistance front (DMLEK). This may, however, also serve as an illustration of how totalitarian and authoritarian Eritrean society has become, as possible information about such a grave incidence of human rights abuse did not filter through to the international community until one year after it allegedly took place.

---

[14] Ali Abdu defected from the regime in the fall of 2012.
[15] Menghesteab recollects the names of 18 of the 26 persons killed. The names are not published here, but may be provided upon request. The location of their grave is inside the prison premises of the 25th Regiment Intelligence Unit in Mai Dima. The camp is located around Berakit Mountain, on the way to Obal.

ENCROACHMENT ON KUNAMA LAND RIGHTS

The tense relations between the Kunama and the EPLF are not only grounded in perceived opposing political allegiances, but also stem from the new development policies drafted after independence. Within a matter of months after liberation, the new government sought land on which it could resettle both demobilised fighters and returning refugees from the Sudan. The lack of fertile agricultural land in the overpopulated highlands was also a concern, and settlement areas for Tigrinya-speaking highlanders were needed. In the eyes of the government, the agro-pastoral lands of the Kunama in the fertile region of Gash-Setit were significantly under-utilised, and thus were an appropriate area to exploit development-wise (Gilkes 2005: 236).

The Gash-Setit area has not until recently experienced any considerable settlement flows. The area was perceived to be on the periphery by political decision-makers and remained under-developed and marginalised; the local inhabitants were basically left in control of their own land. Only some of the urban centres (Barentu, Shambuko, Dokimbia, Tessenei and Omhajer) experienced some new settlers from other ethnic groups, mainly highland Tigrinya speakers and people from the Tigre group (Naty 2002b). These individuals were either posted to the western lowlands as government administrators or attracted to these areas for small-scale business purposes (as shop and bar owners).

After independence, the Eritrean government abolished, in principle and by law, all traditional land tenure forms, and made all land the property of the state.[16] The rationale behind the reform as stated in the preamble of the new land proclamation was that the old land tenure systems were not compatible with the modern needs for development of the new state. In the government's development outlook, landed resources are viewed as a commercial factor – as a means to increase production output – so as to enhance Eritrea's food security. Within the government's nation-building strategies, moreover, land is viewed as an impediment to creating a mobile and homogenous population, as traditional land tenure arrangements tie people to a certain locality through descent rights in land (Tronvoll 2000).

One of the key changes introduced by the new proclamation is that, although priority to usufruct of land will be given to local villagers, any person may ask for land in any place where he or she wants to live (Tronvoll 1998b). Traditionally, land rights in Eritrea are traced through descent and habitation rights. By severing people's connection to land through descent, the government wanted to make them more geographically mobile, which again would encourage commercial farming and a better exploitation of the land resources. The government-appointed land commissioner assumed that 'the whole concept of

---

[16] Land Proclamation (Proclamation No. 58/1994).

attachment to land will change resulting from this', and viewed this as an important intended effect of the reform (ibid.: 472).[17]

The new legislation requires that the land administration take local conditions into consideration, including available areas of agricultural land and the number of inhabitants in the area, in order to distribute the usufruct rights equally. From the capital, the vast Kunama plains of Gash-Setit were perceived as semi-vacant, and large areas of land were put aside for resettlement and agricultural plantation schemes.[18] The only snag was that the land was not vacant; the Kunama perceived this to be their ancestral land (USCIS 2003). The Kunama thus claim that the new land policy of the government undermines their clan-based traditional ownership rights (Naty 2002b). The government-sanctioned encroachment on Kunama land is thus a violation of Article 27 of the ICCPR on the protection of minorities (ratified by Eritrea). The interpretation of the article is clear on the matter that when minorities reside primarily in a certain bounded geographical area – like the Kunama – their members may not be denied access to and residence in this area (Novak 2005: 659). Furthermore, 'All measures which threaten the way of life and culture of a minority, such as large-scale expropriations of minority lands for commercial purposes' constitute a violation of Article 27 of the ICCPR (ibid.: 659).[19]

Most of the ethnically-mixed groups of returnees from Sudan (refugees from the war of liberation) have settled in the Gash-Setit region.[20] Moreover, the Ali Gidir area in western Gash became the centre of large-scale agricultural development projects, and Gilkes reports that 'thousands of highlanders moved into Barentu and other Kunama towns and villages, over 30,000 into the area of Barentu alone' (Gilkes 2005: 236; see also Naty 2002b).[21] The new settlers compete with the local population over the utilisation of resources, leading to increased tension in the area. As the big mechanised farms are mostly owned and operated by Tigrinya highlanders, the conflicts between the Kunama and the new development initiatives of the state inevitably embody an ethnic component.

The rapid change of local control of land – perceived as land

[17] Whether it was intended or not, the land policy has opened up the western lowlands in general for migration by Tigrinya highlanders, as on the one hand pastoral lands are perceived as un-exploited by the authorities and thus suitable for sedentary cultivation; and to urban centres where Tigrinya speakers fill the roles of administrators and civil servants. It is, however, more or less impossible for outsiders to settle in the highland Tigrinya area, since all the land is cultivated by sedentary agriculturalists.

[18] See, for instance, Government of Eritrea, Department of Agriculture (December 1992): 'A Proposal of Rehabilitation and Settlement Scheme for Returning Refugees in Eritrea (Agricultural Component)', Asmara, Eritrea.

[19] ILO Convention 169 furthermore substantiates minorities' claims to land.

[20] According to Alexander Naty, they have been settled in the villages of Alabu, Fanko, Garsat, Gergef, Tabalida, Dokimbia, Omhajer and Samunait.

[21] Tronvoll first visited this area and Barentu town in September 1991, just months after the military liberation of Eritrea. At that time, Barentu was predominantly a Kunama settlement. Today, the Kunama do not constitute a strong visible presence in Barentu.

encroachment by the Kunama – was conducted in such a manner that even the EPLF-appointed Kunama governor of Gash-Setit region, Germano Nati, protested. His objections were all in vain, and he was immediately 'frozen'[22] and in 1996 replaced by a loyal appointee described by the Kunama as 'our main enemy' (Gilkes 2005: 236-7). Germano Nati was later arrested as a member of the G-15 group and part of the 2001 dissent process and is still languishing in incommunicado detention (see Chapter 5).

The anthropologist Lussier claims that the 'forced removal of local communities partly because of refugee resettlement, is an on-going process *specific to Kunama land*' (Lussier 1997: 443, our emphasis). If so, it is an even worse case of minority rights violation, according to Article 27 of the ICCPR. However, other areas of the Eritrean western lowlands are also used for re-settlement programmes (affecting the Beni Amer/Tigre and other groups), which dilutes Lussier's claim. On the other hand, in addition to the 'villagisation' programme, there are also other state interventions on Kunama land, like industrial plantation schemes, 'wiping out the existence of time-honoured strategies of coping with hunger' (ibid.). Other observers of Eritrea note that the seizure of Kunama land continues (Gilkes 2005), and Kunama representatives interviewed as part of the research for this study stress this point.[23]

In the wake of the new Eritrean-Ethiopian war (1998-2000), encroachment on Kunama land was sustained. Internally displaced Tigrinya from the highlands were settled in the Kunama villages of Delle, Tolegamaja and Karkon (Naty 2002b: 3). Furthermore, the Kunama villages of Fode and Anugulu and the surrounding fertile agricultural lands – whose population had fled alongside the retreating Ethiopian army – were allegedly given to around 500 displaced Tigrinya speakers from Adi-Bare (near Badme village).[24] The US State Department corroborates in general this information in its 2002 human rights *Country Report* on Eritrea:

> In 2001 there were unconfirmed reports that the Government took land from Kunamas without compensation and gave it to other ethnic groups on the grounds that the land had not been efficiently exploited. There also was an unconfirmed report that Eritrean refugees returning from Sudan were resettled on Kunama fields after evicting the native Kunama (USSD 2003).

Furthermore, a British fact-finding mission to Eritrea also took note of a number of land disputes between the government and the Kunama, 'whereby the Kunama are pushed into ever-diminishing tribal lands, as the non-Kunama population expands to relieve pressure in the more densely populated parts of Eritrea' (BIA 2008: 42).

---

[22] 'Freezing' means that the person is deprived of all politico-administrative powers, and sometimes even put under house-arrest, until President Isaias Afwerki is once again comfortable with the individual's loyalty. It is a strategy frequently used by the president towards people who question or protest against his decisions.
[23] Endrias Sisto Nada, a Kunama spokesperson, interviewed on 29 April 2008, in Shimelba refugee camp, Tigray, Ethiopia.
[24] Interview by Tronvoll with Kunama representatives in Shimelba refugee camp, Tigray, Ethiopia, on 28 April 2008.

Denied the possibility to do on-the-ground research and surveying of the Eritrean government's encroachment of Kunama land, it is difficult to give estimates of the impact (area- or population-wise) on the Kunama of the Eritrean government's development and resettlement schemes in Gash-Setit. It appears, however, these plans are in breach of Article 27 of the ICCPR. Furthermore, it seems relevant to argue that any government, which claims to act in the interests of its people, ought to consult with relevant groups about their interests and viewpoints on specific development policies affecting them directly or indirectly. The Kunama objections have apparently, in this regard, been overlooked or ignored.

NEW WAR: KUNAMA CULTURE BELEAGUERED

Kunama land is not only encroached upon by new civilian settlers, but also by military intervention. The Kunama claim that the Eritrean army is deliberately and consciously establishing bases in Kunama villages and on Kunama holy sites, in order to violate their cultural heritage.[25] The unsettled border dispute and the failed peace process with Ethiopia requires Eritrea to maintain full mobilisation along the Ethiopian-Eritrean border. Since the Kunama home areas lie close to or straddle the border, many Kunama villages and towns have been converted to military bases. Reportedly, the following Kunama villages in the vicinity of Barentu are or have been used as base areas for various military divisions; Prima-Kanteri, Maʻra-rarata, Laˇwsiʻ, Duta, Gulul, Balak, Shilibo.[26] Confiscation of land for military purposes is allegedly not limited to the Barentu area alone, but is taking place throughout the Gash-Setit region, thus impacting on many Kunama communities. The Kunama argue that it is a deliberate strategy by the Eritrean government to confiscate land for military purposes and locate military facilities in civilian Kunama villages, in order to dilute Kunama cohesion and cultural distinctness. As part of the strategy to break down Kunama culture – and political resistance – Kunama refugees claimed that Kunama girls are either raped or lured into sexual relations with military personnel from the Tigrinya group so that their children will be considered Tigrinya offspring and not Kunama.[27]

The perception that Kunama culture is deliberately beleaguered is corroborated by reports that Kunama holy sites are being occupied for military purposes by the Eritrean government. Kunama culture venerates specific locations for specific ritual purposes during certain

---

[25] The religious rights and protection of holy sites of minorities are integral to Article 27 of the ICCPR, in addition to being protected as a separate right under Article 18.

[26] Communicated to Tronvoll via e-mail from Kunama refugees in Shimelba refugee camp in Tigray, Ethiopia, August 2008.

[27] Interviews by Tronvoll in Shimelba refugee camp, Tigray, Ethiopia, 28-29 April 2008.

time-periods.[28] These locations are considered holy by the Kunama, and are not supposed to be used for purposes other than the specific cultural rituals. For instance, in Koˇna, close to Shambuko, the *kuˇnduˇra* ritual is celebrated annually. During this event, traditional leaders of the Kunama will pass on cultural knowledge to new generations. In Koyta (in Soˇsoˇna'district), the *indodagalba* ritual is performed. On this occasion, Kunama ritual leaders accept sacrifices offered by the community and pray for rain and protection of the forthcoming harvest. Furthermore, twice every decade (in the ninth and tenth years) the *tu'ka* ritual is celebrated at Soˇsoˇna'. On this occasion the Kunama make sacrifices for the communal well-being and increase of the group. Finally, the *ana-ila* ritual is celebrated in Agisha and Alay-Saglia (close to Shambuko) and in Odase (in Fode district). This is a rite of passage where young Kunama boys are initiated into adulthood. A group of boys (from 10 to 100) are collectively accompanied by elders to the sites of worship, where they are instructed about cultural ethics, moral stature, traditions and discipline. Passing this ritual is crucial for Kunama boys, as it prepares them for adult responsibilities (i.e. marriage) and grants them access to further cultural rites and events.

On all these holy ritual sites, the Eritrean government has allegedly established some type of military presence. This prevents the Kunama from performing their cultural rituals at the traditionally designated holy areas; or if they try to do so, it is claimed that Kunama boys when they attend at the place of veneration have been forcefully conscripted into the army.[29] This is a particularly severe breach of the protection of minority rights enshrined under Article 27 of the ICCPR.

One other concern raised in relation to the performance of Kunama cultural traditions is the government's treatment of the *Sanga-Na'ne*. The *Sanga-Na'ne* are honoured individuals (descendants of the Nataka clans) who function as mediators and peace-makers in Kunama society. When conflict occurs among the Kunama, over land or individual grievances (even in cases of fatal wounds), the *Sanga-Na'ne* intervene in order to stop a cycle of revenge and to reconcile the conflicting parties. The Kunama accuse the central authorities of undermining the position of the *Sanga-Na'ne* in Kunama society, having prohibited their role as 'peace-makers'.[30] The targeting of traditional authority among the Kunama has forced

[28] Generally, military use of land (including minority groups' homelands) may be acceptable under human rights law, as there is a wide margin of appreciation in relation to the needs of the state (in times of emergency and war and state security). However, if there is abuse in a specific situation in order to violate minority rights (or people belonging to a minority), the 'necessity argument' will no longer be valid.

[29] Based on information gathered through interviews with Kunama in Shimelba refugee camp, Tigray, Ethiopia, and subsequent written statements from refugees through e-mail to Tronvoll .

[30] From a human rights non-discriminatory perspective, the Eritrean government may want to prevent 'multi-jurisdication', but only if they do so with a similar policy towards all groups in the country. Since the government encourages traditional community courts among the dominant Tigrinya highlander group, this seems to be a case of discriminatory practice against the Kunama, which thus constitutes a breach of the government's human rights obligations under ICCPR.

many *Sanga-Na'ne* to flee to Ethiopia, or to renounce their ritual practices. Consequently, it is argued that intra-Kunama conflicts have been on the increase, since their traditional mechanism of conflict resolution is banned and, due to lack of trust, few Kunama view government-sanctioned conflict resolution mechanisms as an alternative.

EXIT KUNAMA: POLITICAL REPRISAL
AND CULTURAL CONSEQUENCES

There is a steady, and increasing, flow of refugees fleeing Eritrea every month. The figure changes constantly. As of June 2013, it was indicated that more than 4000 Eritreans, including unaccompanied minors, are fleeing the country every month (UN Special Rapporteur on Eritrea, 2013). As a result, Eritrea has been consistently ranked one of the top refugee-producing countries in the world (such as Iraq and Somalia) (UNHCR 2008: 15).[31] Considering the small population size, a total of about 4.5 million of whom about 2.5 to 3 million are left inside Eritrea, the number of people fleeing the country is worrisome.

In order to curtail the increasing flow of refugees, the Eritrean government has declared draconian measures on border control (where border patrols can open fire on sight on people believed to be fleeing the country), in addition to severe penalties imposed on family members left behind in Eritrea. For every person fleeing the country, the remaining family must pay a fee of 50,000 Nakfa (approximately US$3500), serve three months hard labour in detention camps, or alternatively languish in one-year's imprisonment. If two or more family members are caught fleeing, the punishment increases correspondingly. It has been reported that mothers and fathers over 70 years of age, without the capacity to pay the fee, have been thrown into jail as retaliation for escaping sons or daughters.[32]

The collective pressure and reprisal campaign against the Kunama is reportedly being intensified, as the Eritrean government, according to the Kunama opposition (DMLEK), allegedly ordered the Kunama farmers to give half of the produce they harvested during the 2008 season to the government.[33] This will further undermine the collective sustainability of the group.

The majority of the current refugees are national service personnel (UNHCR 2008), mostly men, who flee the country based on personal

[31] An unknown number of Eritreans flee the country (across the Red Sea, through Somalia or over the deserts of Sudan) without registering with any refugee authority.

[32] Since these sanctions are imposed on all Eritreans no matter their ethnic origin, it is not a violation of minority rights, but it is in contravention of civil rights principles in general (collective punishment, the right to leave the country, rule of law, etc.).

[33] Waltainfo: 'Eritrea orders Kunama farmers to hand over half produce', 4 November 2008, at: http://www.waltainfo.com/walnew/index.php?option =com_content&task=view&id=4249&Itemid=45. Walta Information Center (WIC/Waltainfo) is run by the the Ethiopian –government. As such, the report may not be taken as entirely reliable.

motivations (for a better future with hope for continued education or employment) or grievances (fear of arrest and torture). Since the majority of the national service personnel are drawn from the largest ethnic group, the Tigrinya highlanders, they also constitute the bulk of the refugees. With the exception of the Kunama, there is seemingly no other ethnic group whose members cross the border *en masse* with their entire families and possessions.

Considering the brutal and unfair reprisal strategy employed by the Eritrean government against the family members of refugees who were left behind, the Kunama as a group is particularly affected. With the exodus of thousands of Kunama, this places a potentially heavy financial burden on the remaining families, both for payment of 'fees' and the costs of incarceration. The policy of collective retaliation towards families of Eritrean refugees has reportedly engendered great consternation among the Kunama. This has prompted even more Kunama families to flee the country, despite the inherent dangers of crossing the borders.[34]

In the eyes of many Kunama, the combined impact of the Eritrean government's discriminatory policies and actions threatens to make the Kunama cultural heritage extinct in Eritrea. This notion is further fuelled by a statement allegedly offered by President Isaias Afwerki in response to the massive flight of Kunamas in 2000 alongside the Ethiopian army: 'Eritrea is now home to nine ethnic groups, minus one'. Kunama refugees in the Shimelba camp had gathered the same impression, as they claimed: 'We are no longer considered to be Eritreans'.[35] This information corroborates the orders to 'eliminate the Kunama' allegedly given to the Eritrean internal security forces, as referred to above.

UNHCR began discussions with Eritrean and Ethiopian authorities in 2004 on the possible voluntary return of the Kunama to Eritrea. The Eritrean government was allegedly prepared to welcome the Kunama back to their homeland; however, the refugees were sceptical and reluctant to take up the offer (BIA 2008: 80). Considering the particular collective motivation for fleeing and the risk of returning to their country of origin, the more than 4000 Eritrean Kunama in the Shimelba refugee camp were granted collective resettlement rights in the United States as a group (CORC 2007). To the bewilderment of many, the majority of the Kunama in Shimelba refugee camp – about 2800 individuals – chose not to be included in the UNCHR referral (ibid.). Of the 1200 Kunama who accepted the offer, over 700 were scheduled to be resettled in the US by the end of 2008.[36]

The reluctance shown by many Kunama to go to the US may be influenced by the position of the Kunama resistance front, the Democratic Movement for the Liberation of the Eritrean Kunama (DMLEK), who fear

---

[34] Interviews by Tronvoll with Kunama refugees in Shimelba refugee camp, Tigray, Ethiopia, 28-29 April 2008.

[35] Interviewed by Tronvoll, 29 April 2008.

[36] US Department of State/US Department of Homeland Security/US Department of Health and Human Services: 'Proposed Refugee Admissions for Fiscal Year 2008: Report to the Congress', submitted to Committees on the Judiciary, US Senate and US House of Representatives, p. 23.

that their people may become culturally extinct if a mass exodus to the US occurs. Thus, they try to persuade the Kunama refugees to stay in the camp in order to be ready to return to Eritrea after the fall of Isaias Afwerki. Different means are used to communicate this position by the DMLEK, including a 'fear campaign'.[37] Allegedly, the Kunama front is using the Shimelba refugee camp as a recruiting pool for their resistance against the Eritrean government. They have allegedly told the refugees that if they go to the US, they will be sold as slaves and treated badly. In order to illustrate their possible fate in the US, the television drama series *Roots* (1977), about African slavery in America and featuring the historical individual, Kunta Kinte, and his descendants, has been screened in the camp.[38]

The majority of the Eritrean refugees in Shimelba are fed up with war and terror, and there is the same feeling among the Kunama. A group of young Kunama men interviewed in the camp gave a response in unison on the issue of resistance to the Eritrean regime:

> We hate to fight; so the Kunama Front is not that attractive to us. But we are still blamed and punished for their activities by the Eritrean government. We are even insecure here in the camp, since the Front [DMLEK] has good contacts with Ethiopian authorities. So we feel insecure here. We see that people are being kidnapped from the camp. Maybe they are taken by the Front to become soldiers.[39]

Stories about abductions, forcible recruitment and threats to the Kunama in the camp are rejected by the DMLEK. They claim that all recruitment is voluntary, based on the wish to remove President Isaias Afwerki from power: 'We want a change in Eritrea by all means. We want democracy and development for our people.'[40] The DMLEK claims, as also stated by the defected security officer Menghesteab Girmay Asres, that the Eritrean government has recently intensified its operations against the Kunama with the aim of eliminating the group, as a response to the resistance exhibited by the movement.[41]

It appears that the Kunama refugees in the Shimelba camp are caught between a rock and a hard place: forced to flee their country in fear of persecution and possibly death at the hands of the Eritrean government; concerned that their cultural heritage may become extinct due to government campaigns and land encroachment; anxious about being resettled to an unknown life in the US; and, while remaining in the camp, constantly insecure about possible coercive recruitment into the Kunama resistance front.

[37] These abuses are of course not attributable to the Eritrean government. However, they may constitute abuses or violations by non-state actors.
[38] Paul Salopek, 'Refugees fear sharing same fate as Kunta Kinte', *Chicago Tribune*, 17 July 2007.
[39] Interviewed by Tronvoll in Shimelba refugee camp, Tigray, Ethiopia, 29 April 2008.
[40] Interview with the DMLEK leader Kornelious Adolay Osman by Tronvoll in Addis Ababa on 26 April 2008.
[41] Walta Information Center: 'DMLEK condemns growing barbarity of Eritrean government', 5 August 2008, at: www.waltainfo.com, accessed 23 September 2008.

Although the history of atrocities against the Kunama and their current disadvantaged position in relation to the Eritrean authorities are
quite unique in an Eritrean context, other minority group grievances are
also expressed against the EPLF government. The limits of this study
prevent an in-depth coverage of all ethnic groups in Eritrea, but for the
sake of illustration the situation of the Jeberti is worth mentioning (Bariagaber 2006: 18).[42]

BEYOND THE KUNAMA: THE DERECOGNITION OF THE JEBERTI

The history and plight of the Jeberti people is somewhat parallel to the
situation of the Kunama.[43] The Jeberti are Tigrinya-speaking Muslims
living in urban centres in the highlands of Eritrea and Tigray. Since their
conversion to Islam centuries ago, they have been marginalised and persecuted by the majority Christian Orthodox highlanders. For instance, being
Muslims in the Christian highlands, the Jeberti were barred from tenure
of agricultural land, forcing them to settle in small towns and concentrate
on crafts and trade. In the deeply sedentary agriculturalist culture of the
highlands, lacking access to land perpetuated the marginalisation of the
Jeberti. Over time, the group has thus developed a distinct culture separating them from the other Tigrinya-speaking Christian highlanders.

Due to their marginalised position in society, the Jeberti sought to be
recognised as a distinct ethnic group (nationality) under the 1987 constitutional reform in Ethiopia, which in principle emphasised their rights
to cultural autonomy. On the recommendation of a special task group,
President Mengistu Hailemariam granted the Jeberti status as a distinct
ethnic group, entailing *inter alia* separate representation in the Ethiopian
parliament (*shengo*).[44]

---

[42] Another group worth mentioning is the Afar. Since Afar territory straddles
the borders between Eritrea, Ethiopia and Djibouti, added to which there are
various political movements among them advocating a special Afar homeland,
they appear to be a potential threat to the nationalistic policies of the Eritrean
government and are thus susceptible to government sanctions. This issue
deserves treatment in a separate academic exercise.

[43] There are other small unrecognised minorities in Eritrea. Forgotten in most
academic discourse is the minority community of Tekurir, who live in the
Anseba and Gash-Barka regions. Perhaps the first serious academic treatment
of the plight of the Tekurir is that of Weldehaimanot (2009). He describes the
Tekurir as recently-settled descendants of the Hausa tribe in Nigeria, who speak
Arabic with an accent, and whose date of arrival in Eritrea is presumed to be
between 100 and 150 years ago. Compared even to the smallest ethnic groups
in Eritrea, the Tekurir is very small in size. However, socially and politically, it
is marginalised (ibid.: 3-4). As noted above, the Jeberti are officially regarded as
part of the Tigrinya ethnic group. In contrast, 'the position of the Tekurir is not
altogether clear' (ibid.: 6). In popular perception and semi-official narratives,
they are regarded as part of the Nara and/or the Kunama ethnic groups.

[44] Information given to Tronvoll by the late Dr Assefa Medhane, Professor at
the Department of Political Science and International Relations, Addis Ababa
University. Dr Assefa headed the Derg task force to assess the request by the
Jeberti for recognition as a nationality.

The Jeberti case apparently goaded the EPLF on several aspects. First of all, both during the struggle and in particular after independence, the EPLF's ideological and policy emphasis has been on creating national congruence, opposing all ethnic, sectarian, religious, or parochial claims and sentiments. Thus, an argument for recognition from a sub-group which the EPLF perceived to be part and parcel of the Tigrinya highlanders appeared nonsensical. In the eyes of the EPLF, ethno-nationalities are mainly defined by linguistic criteria; hence the Jeberti should be classified as belonging to the Tigrinya group. The Jeberti argument of distinctiveness was thus interpreted as subversive of their national liberation struggle. This view was underpinned by the fact that the Jeberti turned to the Ethiopian government for acceptance as a culturally distinct group, and was subsequently granted such status. The 'cooperation' with the Ethiopian government by representatives of the Jeberti collectively stigmatised the group in the eyes of the EPLF. Consequently, towards the end of the liberation war, the EPLF deliberately targeted the Jeberti community. Their leader, Dr Yassin Aberra, was allegedly assassinated by the EPLF outside his own house in Asmara in January 1991, just four months prior to liberation.[45]

The killing of the Jeberti leader made it clear that their claim for ethnic minority status would not be tolerated by the EPLF in independent Eritrea. After independence, many Jeberti fled the country and their struggle to be recognised as a distinct cultural minority is carried on by Jebertis in exile. The exiled Eritrean al-Nahda Party is predominantly composed of Jeberti, and is part of the broader coalition of Eritrean opposition movements supported by the Ethiopian government.[46]

FINAL REMARKS

The Eritrean Constitution states that 'all persons are equal under the law' (Art. 14.1) and that no person may be discriminated against on account of race, ethnic origin, or language (Art. 14.2). A similar prescription is found in both the ICERD and ICCPR, which Eritrea has ratified. It seems clear that the Eritrean government is violating its own Constitution and international law with its apparent discriminatory practice against the Kunama minority group, and possibly other minority groups too.

The apparent governmental targeting of Kunama cultural sites and traditions, in addition to harassment, intimidation and detention of Kunama representatives which has driven several thousands of families into refuge in Ethiopia, is raising concern among the Kunama that their unique culture is under threat and dying off in Eritrea today. The suppression of minority rights is one of the core violations discussed in the

---

[45] Information given to Tronvoll by Dr Yassin's family.
[46] See press release, 'Constituent Congress of a new Eritrean mass party opens sessions (media team at site of Congress)', 25 July 2008, at: http://www.nharnet.com/July_2008/RC_Party_Congress_E_1_July2708.pdf, accessed 26 September 2008.

report of the UN Special Rapporteur on the Situation of Human Rights in Eritrea (2013: 15).

It seems apparent that the Kunama case, in addition to the general human rights abusing context in the country, amounts to crimes against humanity. Whether or not one may invoke a genocide clause based on the persecution of the Kunama, needs further investigation. However, based on the information available today, without conducting investigations inside Eritrea, the scale of atrocities perpetrated against the Kunama does not seem to meet the requirements to allow the matter to be legally pursued as a case of genocide.

10

The Militarisation of Eritrean Society: Omnipresent and Never-Ending Military Service

INTRODUCTION

In our introductory chapter, we outlined how the concept of the garrison state could be used as an explanatory framework to understand Eritrea's post-independence development. In this chapter, we will further explore this assertion in terms of its relation to the high levels of militarisation in the country, both past and present. The country has been further militarised, particularly since the 1998-2000 border conflict with Ethiopia. The latest move by the president pushes the militarisation of society to the extreme, by ordering the establishment of a 'peoples' army', supplying arms directly to households throughout the country. This involves the arming of civilians and ordering them to military training and to carry guns wherever they go. Senior citizens, up to the age of beyond 80 years, are reportedly forced to carry Kalashnikovs, without any adequate explanation given for this draconian and dangerous policy. In order to fully understand the challenge of the militarisation of Eritrean society, we will start our discussion by exploring the root cause of the current pervasive level of militarisation. This analysis will confirm Eritrea as a sustained African garrison state.

PROLONGED HISTORY OF MILITARISATION

Eritrea is one of the most militarised countries in the world. As a country with a long history of political violence, this may not come as a surprise. In fact, referring to a claim made by Richard Reid, Tricia Hepner argues that militarisation is not a recent phenomenon in Eritrea (Hepner 2013: 158). In this sense, militarisation is characterised as a fundamental facet of the process of identity creation that has been taking place in the region for over two centuries (Reid 2011: 4; Tronvoll 2009b). As noted earlier, in the late 1930s, during the Italian occupation of Ethiopia, Eritrea was probably one of the world's most militarised societies with a large share of the adult male population under arms in the colonial army. In a region which has been influenced by long-term instability and violence, militarised cultures and identities have been continuously nurtured and have manifested themselves firmly in organised structures (Reid 2011: 201; Hirt and Mohammad 2013: 145; Tronvoll ibid.: 36-60). There are also others, such as Shinn (2010), who describe the Horn of Africa as the most conflicted corner of the world since the end of the Second World War.

An extreme level of mobilisation

On the other hand, Hepner notes that 'the shape of states and the dynamics of militarization in the Horn have also changed over time, sometimes producing dramatic changes in relatively short periods' (Hepner 2013: 158). The level of militarisation currently experienced in Eritrea is remarkably intense, and cannot be simply overlooked as a part of the long-term pattern in the region. Beyond its short-term ramifications on fundamental rights and freedoms, the phenomenon is eroding societal fabrics of the Eritrean society, as noted by Hirt and Mohammad (2013), at a pace experienced by only a few comparable instances.

On the particular issue of militarism, one of the most authoritative sources is UNHCR's yearly *Eligibility Guidelines for Assessing the International Protection Needs of Asylum-Seekers from Eritrea*. In its 2011 publication, UNHCR notes that 'with an estimated strength of between 200,000 and 320,000 men and women, Eritrea has the largest army in sub-Saharan Africa' (UNHCR 2011: 6). As will be seen later, this number appears somewhat conservative given that the Eritrean government has been conscripting virtually every adult inhabitant of the country continuously since 1994. Connell, a long-time scholar in Eritrea studies cites 500,000 as the total number of people enlisted in the national service programme (Connell 2011; 7), while the Bertelsmann Foundation reports 600,000 conscripts. On the other hand, citing the Immigration and Refugee Board of Canada, UNHCR also indicates that an estimated 35 per cent of Eritrea's population is reported to be in military service. It is not clear, however, how the figure constitutes 35 per cent of the population, since UNHCR did not give an indication of the estimated population numbers in Eritrea.

Knowing the exact number of the total population of Eritrea is problematic, since the government has never released an official census or other statistical data. As a result, most reports and analyses are based on estimates. In most cases, the total population number fluctuates between 3 and 5 million, although in some cases it also inflated up to and above 6 million. In a recent work on this particular topic, Hepner cites 4.5 million as being the population of the Eritrean society (2013: 153). *CIA Factbook*, on the other hand, offers the number of 6,233,682 Eritreans. These numbers most probably derive from various population projections based on the last population survey Ethiopia carried out in the province of Eritrea in the 1980s. Hence they are totally unreliable in accounting for the Eritrean population of today, particularly the population remaining within Eritrea.

A better starting point is the comprehensive census the EPLF conducted in 1992 in order to develop the referendum electoral roll. In it about 1,173,000 people were registered, of whom 800,000 were resident inside Eritrea and the rest mainly in Sudan and Ethiopia (but also Eritreans in the global diaspora registered to vote).[1] With an estimated 60 per cent of the population below the age of 18 (registration age for the referendum), it indicates that about 2 million Eritreans were within the country's borders in 1993.

Thenceforth we have had both a high population growth in the 1990s, followed by lower fertility rates since 1998 due to full military mobilisation, and a high level of flight since the 2001 crackdown. Eritreans have in recent years been fleeing the country in unprecedented numbers, making Eritrea one of the leading refugee-producing countries in the world. This has been widely reported, in the periodic reports of UNHCR among others. Eritrea's rank in this regard fluctuates every year. In 2008 in particular Eritrea was ranked the second-highest refugee-producing country in the world in absolute numbers. To be exact, by the end of 2008, Eritrea produced 62,700 new asylum-seekers around the world (UNHCR 2009). The simplest arithmetical model translates this into 5225 refugees per month. In this regard, Eritrea was preceded only by Zimbabwe which had 118,500 new claims in 2008. Even failed or conflict states, such as Somalia and Iraq, which have a much bigger population than Eritrea, were preceded by Eritrea in relation to new refugee outflow. While there are fluctuations in the monthly or yearly refugee outflow, the trend has not changed in significant proportions. In the last ten years, Eritrea has always remained among the top refugee-producing countries in the world. For example, in 2013 it was reported that around 4000 people were fleeing the country every month (Special Rapporteur 2013: 16). Seen against the country's small population, the amount of refugee outflow is alarming. The following analysis by Hepner, which builds on a diverse pool of statistics, is insightful for the issue at hand.

> The United States, for example, experienced a 166% increase in asylum applications filed by Eritreans between 2005 and 2010, and more Eritreans applied for asylum in 2009 than Iraqis or Somalis (UNHCR Statistical Database). Many European countries also witnessed dramatic upturns in first-time applications between 2005 and 2010: Sweden's rate of increase was 276%, Switzerland's was a whopping 974% and Norway's was more than 1000% (ibid.). Unknown numbers of Eritreans have disappeared while trying to cross the Sahara or Sinai deserts, perished at sea en route to Europe or the Middle East, or been captured by traffickers to feed the underground trade in organs and slaves thriving in Egypt and the Gulf States (HRW 2010). (Hepner 2013: 153)

Attention needs to be focused here on one crucial point. The increasing level of forced migration has a direct relationship with the alarming level of militarisation in the country. According to the UN refugee agency, most of the refugees who fled the country recently are very young and 'virtually all have claimed to be fleeing because of military service' (UNHCR 2009: 9). The same sentiments are confirmed through our work in the Eritrean refugee camps in Ethiopia and the Sudan for this study.

Demographers who have worked in Eritrea in recent years suggest

[1] See Norwegian Institutte of Human Rights (1993): *The Referendum on Independence for Eritrea. Report of the Norwegian Observer Group in UNOVER*, December 1993, Oslo, p. 12.

that, when balancing population growth with the exodus of refugees, a relatively similar number of inhabitants resides in the country today as was recorded in 1992 based on the referendum registration.[2] Hence, based on available knowledge from both internal as well as external sources, the best estimates of the Eritrean population remaining in Eritrea today is somewhere between 2 and 2.5 million people. Consequently, Eritrea has one of largest diaspora communities in the world owing to its long history of forced migration, and possibly more Eritreans are residing in the diaspora than are left within the country's borders. This distinctive history has made Eritrea one of the best examples of transnational nation-states (O'Kane and Hepner 2009; Bernal 2013)

With about 500,000 men and women in the armed forces, this suggests that about 25 per cent of the Eritrean population in total are directly under the control of the military machinery, and more than 50 per cent of the population above the age of 18 years. According to the International Crisis Group (ICG), the maximum limit of military mobilisation is normally believed to be 10 per cent of the total population of a given country. If the figure goes beyond this limit, as is the case in Eritrea, a society ceases to function normally (ICG 2010: 13). This is precisely what is happening in Eritrea, resulting in the structural failure of societal fabrics, described by Hirt and Mohammad (2013) as an instance of 'anomie'.

In theory, the Eritrean army is made up of two major segments, known as the regular army and the reserve army. In practice, there is no meaningful difference between the two categories, which include senior EPLF ex-freedom fighters and national service conscripts who are regularly enlisted in the army as part of the 18-month requirement of national service. The national service requirement includes a six-month military training and a twelve-month unpaid service, which can be done either in a military or a non-military establishment. During this 18-month period of time, regardless of the place where a person is stationed, they are accountable to the Ministry of Defence and formally they are considered members of the national defence forces. In practice, however, there is also no meaningful distinction between the military and non-military component of the 'national service', as was intended originally. This is clear from the following official government position on the issue:

> As a national service participant as well as a member of the reserve and regular army, almost every able-bodied person in Eritrea is armed. As a result who is going to fight whom? And who is going to mobilize whom? Therefore, unless somebody is stupid or crazy he/she will not attempt a military coup that is destined to fail from its inception. (Asmerom 2013)

The above statement was given by the Eritrean Ambassador to the African Union in an effort to discredit 'the incident' of 21 January 2013, the so-called Forto Operation 'attempted coup'. Regardless of the motive for the comment, it admits the factual situation on the ground as regards the excessive level of militarisation in the country, by explicitly stating

[2] Interviewed by Tronvoll. Due to project work inside Eritrea, they prefer to remain anonymous.

that the entire able-bodied section of the Eritrean society is indeed militarised, as has been claimed by many other sources for quite a long time. In order to get a clear picture, it is important now to take a look at the genesis of the problem since its early inception in the post-independence era.

THE GENESIS AND SUSTAINED CAUSE OF THE CRISIS: THE NATIONAL SERVICE PROGRAMME

Without forgetting the contribution of the long history of political violence in the region, the prevailing high level of militarisation in Eritrea is linked with the official commencement of a national service programme in the early 1990s. In principle, the policy of national service was officially proclaimed in 1991.[3] However, it was fully implemented only in 1994, when the military training of the first batch of national service conscripts (popularly known as *kedamay zuriya* or first-round conscripts) began in Sawa Military Training Centre, amidst a great deal of anxiety among conscripts and their family members. Because of the belated implementation date of the policy, often times the initial law that introduced the national service programme is cited as Proclamation No. 82/1995. However, this is only one of four different laws on national service that were promulgated between 1991 and 1996.[4]

Although the first law which introduced the national service programme is Proclamation No. 11/1991, the purpose of the programme was defined only in Proclamation No. 82/1995. The Preamble and Article 2 of the latter are the most important parts of the law as regards the motivations of the policy. The Preamble opens the proclamation by reiterating the difficult time the Eritrean people had to undergo under occupation forces, including the 30-year-long struggle to achieve national independence and sovereignty. It also underscores the heavy sacrifice that was

[3] One of the current authors (Mekonnen) belongs to the first conscripts of national service, who were enlisted as adult education teachers in 1991. This batch was enlisted before the official promulgation of the first National Service Proclamation (Proclamation No. 11/1991). The law became effective on 6 November 1991. The author was deployed in Assab in October 1991.
[4] The law, which introduced the policy of national service for the first time, is Proclamation No. 11/1991, which was promulgated on 6 November 1991. It can be designated as the 'First National Service Proclamation.' The 'Second National Service Proclamation' is Proclamation No. 71/1995, which was promulgated on 20 March 1995. The main objective of this law was amending some aspects of Proclamation No. 11/1991 or the 'First National Service Proclamation.' The 'Third National Service Proclamation,' Proclamation No. 82/1995, was promulgated on 23 October 1995. This law repealed and replaced all previous laws on national service. The 'Fourth National Service Proclamation' is Proclamation No. 89/1996, which was promulgated on 6 May 1996. This proclamation aims at regulating the possible demobilisation process of national service conscripts who have accomplished the 18-month requirement set by law. This was followed by Legal Notice No. 27/1996, which was promulgated on 28 October 1996. This is a subsidiary legislation (regulation) meant to supplement the demobilisation process envisaged by Proclamation No. 89/1996.

made to achieve the Eritrean people's aspirations. The Preamble then enjoins current and future generations of Eritreans to honour the pledge of their fallen heroes by ensuring the sustainability of Eritrea as an independent and sovereign state. This resonates with the preoccupation of the new government, noted by Kibreab as that of 'creating a cohesive national identity, as well as moulding a political community,' based on the EPLF's liberation-struggle legacy, characterised by 'a highly organised, disciplined, committed and cohesive army with an impressive organisational and fighting capability' (Kibreab 2009b: 41-42).

The main objectives of the national service programme are further explained in Article 5 of Proclamation No. 82/1995 as follows:

- To establish a strong defence force with a solid popular base that can guarantee the maintenance of a sovereign and independent Eritrea;

- To preserve and bequeath to the next generations the legacy of courage, perseverance and bravery the Eritrean people have shown in the 30-year struggle;

- To cultivate a new generation characterised by hard work, discipline, and active participation and readiness to build the nation;

- To strengthen and develop the national economy by utilising the reservoir of national wealth and our human resources in an organised and civilised manner;

- To provide participants of training centres with regular military training in order to acquire and advance professional skills and physical fitness;

- To fight sub-national sentiments and enhance coherence among our people by nurturing unity in nationalism.

In spite of its declared noble intentions, the national service programme would soon become one of the most draconian government policies in Eritrea, causing immense suffering and vulnerability to a large number of Eritreans. In the initial years, the programme was implemented with little objection from the general public, except in some instances which involved the conscription of females, particularly from communities which are predominantly Muslim. Afar elders protested intensely against the conscription of Afar girls and the fact that they had to live together with male conscripts, and Afar girls were excused from recruitment for a while in order to pacify the Afar protesters . It is important to remember that, like all other laws, the national service legislation was not adopted in a democratic decision-making process (Weldehaimanot and Mekonnen 2009). The far-reaching ramifications of the national service programme were felt widely in the aftermath of the 1998-2000 border conflict with Ethiopia. The crisis that ensued has now become a subject of abundant academic and non-academic literature (Weldehaimanot 2007; Kibreab 2009; O'Kane and Hepner 2009; HRW 2010; Hirt and Mohammad 2013; AI 2013; Mehreteab 2001).

A major problem with the national service programme is that with the commencement of the Eritrean-Ethiopian war the government refused to respect the limitations stipulated by legislation. Two important limitations envisaged by the national service law are on age and the duration of service. The maximum age limit of recruitment to national service stipulated by the initial law, Proclamation No 11/1991, was 40 years of age. This was extended to 50 years of age by Article 6 of Proclamation No. 82/1995, a law which repealed and replaced Proclamation No. 11/1991. According to Article 31 of Proclamation No. 82/1995 even the age of 50 can be extended in situations which involve a state of emergency. Since the outbreak of the Eritrean-Ethiopian war, the duration and age limits specified by law have never been respected by the government.

Related to the above issue is a very important category of exemptions that was provided by the initial national service law, Proclamation No. 11/1991, which was later abandoned by the government. The initial law exempted certain categories of people, such as married women, mothers, newly-weds and breadwinners, from the requirement of national service. For no clear reason, however, the exemption was withdrawn by Proclamation No. 71/1995, which was promulgated with the sole objective of removing the above exemptions from Proclamation No. 11/1991. Both laws were later repealed by Proclamation No. 82/1995, which did not provide the category of exemptions initially envisaged by Proclamation No. 11/1991. The only grounds of exemption envisaged by Proclamation No. 82/1995 are those stated in Article 15, which are related to physical and mental disability. In practice, however, it is a matter of routine procedure to see physically disabled individuals enlisted for national service, including military training in Sawa. Moreover, the exemption board envisaged by Articles 2(8), 14 and 15 of Proclamation No. 82/1995 is perceived by the general public as an ineffective institution, whose decisions are often manipulated by the Ministry of Defence and other high-ranking government officials. Its practice has also given rise to widespread allegations of corruption, which enables the rich and affluent to manipulate the process of recruitment for national service at the expense of the destitute who are often condemned to enduring unpaid military service.

The other important limitation imposed by the law but never respected by the government is that of duration of service. Between the initial repealed law of 1991 and the standing law of 1995 there is some difference on the length of service envisaged by each of these laws. In Proclamation No. 11/1991, the amount of time any adult member of the society should spend as part of the national service obligation is defined as a maximum of 18 months (Article 2). The duration of time envisaged by Proclamation No. 82/1995 differs from this. In order to understand this, one needs to look at the meaning of some key terminologies defined by sub-articles 2, 3, 4, and 5 of Article 2 of Proclamation No. 82/1995. Important for our understanding are the terms *national service, active national service, reserve military service and reserve army*. National service is service given by citizens both in 'active national service' and in 'reserve army.' Active national service is an 18-month service provided in accordance with Article 8 of Proclamation No. 82/1995; military training of six months and active service of 12 months. With regard to the latter component, the law says that the service to be provided is both military and development-oriented. Contrary to public understanding and belief, it is clearly indicated that the 12-month service is to be given in the defence forces, thus clearly showing that the national service is martial or military by its legal definition. This requirement is mandatory for those aged between 18 and 40.

Other important terminology includes 'reserve military service,' which is defined as service rendered by those who have accomplished the requirement of 'active national service'. The essential characteristic of this service is that it is envisaged as an obligation that has to be fulfilled during a state of emergency or in times of national mobilisation against invasion. Article 23(2) of Proclamation No. 82/1995 extends this obligation up to the age of 50 years. Article 31(1) of the same law provides a far-reaching exception to the above rule, saying that on account of certain factors the government can extend the maximum age of 50 years. It is this part of the law together with other loopholes that is frequently abused by the government. However, as a matter of general practice, even the 18-month limit envisaged by Article 8 of the same law has never been respected since the outbreak of the Eritrean-Ethiopian war. The reason put forward by the government so frequently in defence of this abusive practice is summed up in the concept of state of emergency. It will be explored in the next section.

STATE OF EMERGENCY AS AN EXCUSE

When Eritrea and Ethiopia fought a two-year devastating border conflict, almost every member of Eritrean society rallied behind the government defending the nation from what was initially seen as an invasion. The public perception about the Eritrean-Ethiopian war changed quickly after the official end of the conflict. This change of attitude was given wider currency with the emergence of the so-called reform movement of the G-15. This heralded a short-lived dawn of a new era, when questions on the need for a prolonged mobilisation of the Eritrean army began to be asked both by members of the G-15 and the public at large. Even after the silencing of the reform movement, the question of demobilisation of the large number of soldiers conscripted during and after the Eritrean-Ethiopian war continued. The issue was not taken seriously by the government, as it seemed that the government never wanted to demobilise soldiers. Contrary to popular expectation, the government came up with its own innovative delaying tactic, dubbed the Warsay-Yikealo Development Campaign (WYDC), which is in essence a way of keeping the entire able-bodied section of the society in a constant state of mobilisation.

In official narratives of the state, the WYDC was justified as a martial development plan meant to lead the nation to a period of revival after the devastating war it fought with Ethiopia from 1998 to 2000. In reality, the WYDC was a means of extending the national service programme indefinitely. The policy was introduced by the state president and approved by his cabinet in a meeting held on 7–8 May 2002 (Kibreab 2009: 44). It is important to note that the WYDC, unlike the national service programme, was not proclaimed by law, thus bringing to light the regime's contempt for a system of governance based on the rule of law. Over and above the development rhetoric apparent from the official name of the WYDC, the government frequently 'justifies' the implementation of the policy (by implication the continued state of militarisation) by linking it to a purported state of emergency in which the country finds itself. This is particularly clear from repeated government pronouncements in regard to other similar issues which are directly related to the issue of a state of emergency. For example, in response to the alarming human rights crisis and obstinate refusal to conduct general elections, the Eritrean government repeatedly cites the stalemate with Ethiopia as a 'legitimate' excuse to suspend the protection of fundamental rights and postpone the conduct of general elections indefinitely. In a televised interview of December 2011, the Eritrean president explicitly said:

> For the past fourteen years, war has been declared against this nation in different forms. We are in a state of war … not because of our own choice, but because it has been declared on us. So, war has its own laws. There are laws on how to work, organise and function in times of war. And you don't determine these laws. These are not procedures which you can administer according to your own liking. Therefore, the laws are there and we have to obey them even if we don't like it. There are some tasks we have to postpone and we do this on purpose, because we are compelled by circumstances.[5]

Since this is the most cited excuse the government uses to justify its atrocious practice associated with the continued practice of militarisation, it deserves critical analysis. In reality, does Eritrea find itself in a state of emergency after the official resolution of the Eritrean-Ethiopian war? This requires analysis from a legal point of view.

As noted in the comment of the Eritrean state president, indeed war has its own laws but such laws are of a very limited nature in that their use is strictly limited to the existence of armed conflict. It is widely accepted that the Eritrean-Ethiopian war came to an official end when the two governments signed a ceasefire in June 2000, which was followed by a comprehensive peace agreement signed in December 2000 (the so-called Algiers Agreement). Since then, there have not been major active hostilities between the two countries, apart from minor skirmishes which do not amount to a situation of a state of emergency. The peace agreement of December 2000 established two independent commissions which decided on a number of issues related to the causes and consequences of the conflict. The signing of the peace agreement and arbitral

---

[5] Interview with President Isaias Afwerki, available at http://www.youtube.com/watch?v=zy3rSMns-VA, accessed 29 December 2011.

awards given by these two commissions have thus formally concluded the conflict between the two countries.

It is true that due to the intransigence of both governments peace still remains elusive between the two countries. There are also a number of re-sidual matters that remain unresolved, and effectively the two countries are in a state of no-war no-peace. Compared to Ethiopia, the political situ-ation ensuing from the stalemate has proven much more costly to Eritrea, because the country has been ruled for the last 16 years on a constant war footing. According to applicable national and international laws, however, the stalemate with Ethiopia cannot be legally described as a situation constituting a state of emergency. There are no clearly defined statutory or institutional procedures which allow for the promulgation of a state of emergency in Eritrea. Since a state of emergency is broadly understood in terms of its direct impact on the enjoyment of fundamental rights and freedoms, it appears easier to analyse the issue from that angle – that is, by analysing the most relevant laws pertaining to limitation of fundamental rights in Eritrea. As will be seen below, this is also the most common-sense approach adopted by General Comment 29 of the UN Human Rights Committee dealing specifically with state of emergency.[6]

As with any other issue, the debate on state of emergency naturally should begin by considering applicable constitutional law provisions in Eritrea. Reserving our focus on the 1997 Constitution to the latter paragraphs in this section, we will discuss first the issue of state of emer-gency in light of laws operational in the country, by focusing on those provisions which are pertinent to the limitation of fundamental rights.

One of the most relevant laws that should be considered is the Tran-sitional Civil Code of Eritrea. The only situation where fundamental rights and freedoms can be limited is envisaged in the amended article 9(2) of the Civil Code. Accordingly, rights may be limited on the grounds of 'valid social reasons'. State of emergency (a situation necessitated by war, invasion or other emergencies) can be one such 'valid social reason' to justify the suspension of fundamental rights and freedoms. It is plau-sible to assume that such a situation may not only entail the limitation of fundamental rights and freedoms but may also include the deferral of other processes, such as scheduled elections, which are intrinsically linked with the enjoyment of fundamental rights and freedoms. As a matter of common practice, in most democratic legal systems a state of emergency is declared only for a specific period of time and when there is real and imminent threat to the life of the nation or the public at large. It is also an accepted state practice that state of emergency passes through special procedures and mechanisms before it is formally promulgated. In most cases, state of emergency is declared by a duly elected repre-sentative body or a legislative branch of government. Again, it is only plausible to argue that, in the Eritrean case, the best qualified state organ to declare a state of emergency was the now defunct National Assembly,

[6] In paragraph 2 of General Comment 29, state of emergency is implicitly defined as a measure 'derogating from the provisions of the Covenant.' See UN Human Rights Committee, UN.Doc.CCPR/C/21/Rev.1/Add.11, 31 August 2001.

an organ of the state which is defined by article 4(4) of Proclamation No. 37/1993 as the highest legal authority of the nation during the four-year transitional period envisaged by the same law.

In Proclamation No. 37/1993, state of emergency is not mentioned explicitly. Some provisions of this law that come closest to the notion of state of emergency are articles 4(5)(*b*), 4(5)(*f*), 5(4)(*a*), 5(4)(*b*) and 5(4)(*c*). In these provisions, major issues of national security, such as defending the territorial integrity and sovereignty of the nation are defined as responsibilities belonging to the National Assembly and the Cabinet of Ministers. This is a classic example where typical legislative powers seem to be nebulously shared with the executive branch of government, resulting in competing executive and legislative interests (Weldehaimanot and Mekonnen 2009). However, it is important to remember that, according to article 4(4) of Proclamation No. 37/1993, the National Assembly is defined as the highest legal authority of the nation during the four-year transitional period.[7] As a result, any overlap of power that may have existed between the National Assembly and the Cabinet of Ministers was understandably to be resolved in favour of the former.

As a matter of fact, at no point during the entire period of the conflict with Ethiopia, has the government officially proclaimed a state of emergency (either through the National Assembly or Cabinet of Ministers). Throughout the conflict, all matters of peace and war were handled by opaque executive decrees, orders and edicts emanating mainly from the office of the State President. None of these were properly approved or scrutinised by the then nominal parliament. The most important aspect, however, is that fourteen years after the official resolution of the border conflict with Ethiopia, the government cannot continuously invoke state of emergency as an excuse for its failure to respect fundamental rights and freedoms, transit the nation to a democratic system of governance, and discontinue abusive state practices, such as the indefinite military conscription of citizens under the guise of national service and/or WYDC.

Assuming that the 1997 Constitution was in force, would the argument made by the government be accepted under the constitution? State of emergency is addressed by Article 27 of the 1997 Constitution. This provision empowers the National Assembly to declare a state of emergency when public safety or the security or stability of the state is threatened by war, external invasion, civil disorder or natural disorder. For a declaration of a state of emergency, the constitution requires a resolution passed by a two-thirds majority vote of all members of the National Assembly. A state of emergency can only be declared for a period of six months (renewable only for an additional three months). As noted above, none of the requirements envisaged by Article 27 of the 1997 Constitution have been fulfilled by the Eritrean government during the war. The situation prevailing in the country also does not fit well with

---

[7] The transitional period envisaged by Proclamation No. 37/1993 has lapsed in 1997. In effect, this means that the tenure of the government in power has also lapsed in 1997. We will return to this issue with some details in our concluding chapter.

the definition of state of emergency envisaged by the 1997 Constitution. Therefore, most of the arguments made in the preceding paragraphs would also be the same if the 1997 Constitution were in force.

Finally, the issue needs to be examined in terms of relevant treaty law that is binding on Eritrea. Taking a cue from Weldehaimanot's (2011) analysis of the right to leave and return to one's own country is very helpful in this regard. Weldehaimanot's choice of the right to leave and return to one's own country is motivated by the fact that these twin rights are amongst the most abused rights in the context of the Eritrean national service programme and the *de facto* 'state of emergency' or 'limitation of rights' that has ensued as a result of the prolonged practice of indefinite military conscription. Weldehaimanot argues that, for purposes of assessing the challenge at hand, the most important international instruments binding on Eritrea are the African Charter on Human and People's Rights, the ICCPR and the Universal Declaration of Human Rights. While the first two are treaties in the proper sense of the term, the third one is a universal declaration with a status akin to customary international law (Weldehaimanot 2011: 198). Weldehaimanot's analysis is based on a thorough examination of the case law of the African Commission on Human and People's Rights, the commentaries of the monitoring body of the ICCPR (the UN Human Rights Committee) and relevant academic literature on this particular topic. Based on that, he concludes that the prevailing practice of the Eritrean government in relation to the invocation of a state of emergency or limitation of rights is far from reasonable apprehension. The practice does not correspond with what is envisaged by the above cited international instruments (ibid.: 214).

Particularly insightful for our analysis is the observation that can be made based on the requirements of the ICCPR, to which Eritrea acceded on 22 January 2002. Under this instrument, state of emergency is addressed in Article 4. The commentary developed by the UN Human Rights Committee in elaboration of this article is known as General Comment 29. In paragraph 1 of General Comment 29, the UN Human Rights Committee stresses that while states are allowed to temporarily derogate from part of their obligation through state of emergency clauses, '[t]he restoration of a state of normalcy where full respect for the Covenant can again be secured must be the predominant objective of a State party derogating from the Covenant.' In paragraph 2, the Human Rights Committee highlights that state of emergency should be 'of an exceptional and temporary nature'. It further adds:

> Before a State moves to invoke article 4, two fundamental conditions must be met: the situation must amount to a public emergency which threatens the life of the nation, and the State party must have officially proclaimed a state of emergency. The latter requirement is essential for the maintenance of the principles of legality and rule of law at times when they are most needed.

As shown above, the situation prevailing in Eritrea is not one that amounts 'to a public emergency that threatens the life of the nation'. This is so because, after the signing of the peace agreement in 2000, factually and legally speaking it is difficult to say that there is a public emergency which threatens the life of the nation.[8] Even if there was one, the government has not fulfilled the requirements envisaged by Article 4 of the ICCPR. Such requirements include, among other things, informing the international community, through the intermediary of the UN Secretary-General, of the provisions from which the Eritrean government has derogated and of the reasons by which it was actuated. These requirements are spelled out clearly in paragraphs 2, 10 and 17 of General Comment 29 in which the Human Rights Committee bolsters its argument by referring to Article 4 of the ICCPR. The fact that a state of emergency is envisaged as exceptional and temporary in nature means that its invocation for a period of sixteen years (since 1998), as done by the Eritrean government, is unacceptable. Objectively speaking, the situation in Eritrea does not amount to a state of emergency as envisaged by relevant Eritrean national laws and international treaties which are binding on the country. Therefore, the Eritrean government's continued invocation of a state of emergency has no legal basis.

The above conclusion also resonates with the observation made by the UN Special Rapporteur on the Situation of Human Rights in Eritrea. The Special Rapporteur notes that finding solutions to border disputes is important. However, she underscores that border disputes cannot be used by Eritrea as an excuse to continue to violate its human rights obligations, because the violations have in one way or another touched 'the life of almost every family' (Special Rapporteur 2013: 6, 18). Finally, it is also important to note that even in the context of a legally justifiable situation of state of emergency, there are certain fundamental rights and freedoms which must not be limited under any circumstance. As noted in paragraph 7 of General Comment 29, some of the non-derogable rights include: the right to life, prohibition of torture or cruel, inhuman or degrading punishment; the recognition of everyone as a person before the law; and freedom of thought, conscience and religion.

That the political situation prevailing in Eritrea does not amount to a state of emergency is far from being incontrovertible. In reality, under the pretext of 'renewed war' with Ethiopia, the government has effectively ruled the country for the last sixteen years under the grip of a *de facto* state of emergency. The entire society has been on a constant war footing, with virtually every adult member of the Eritrean society strictly regimented under the Ministry of Defence. Although the entire Eritrean society is severely affected by this, the brunt of the abuse is felt more deeply by the youth, whose most productive age is being wasted in indefinite and unpaid military conscription. Often times, members of the national service are subjected to numerous forms of abuses which include torture, arbitrary detention and other sorts of human rights violations. Many of them are forced to work in public projects and private enterprises owned by army commanders in situations which are characterised by Kibreab's (2009b) meticulous inquiry as forced labour.

[8] It is worth noting that Ethiopia demobilised its war army after the signing of the peace agreement.

According to a 2013 report by Human Rights Watch, the practice of forced labour that ensues from Eritrea's national service programme has now brought about serious implications for the mining activities of foreign investors, such as the Canadian Nevsun Resources, who are accused of employing a local contractor with a long track record of reliance on forced labour and conscripts of the national service programme.

There seems to be no end to the abusive practice of national service and WYDC in Eritrea. Frustrated by this, hundreds of thousands of Eritreans have fled to neighbouring countries. All border posts in the country are heavily guarded by a special force, called the border surveillance units. Citizens within the national service age margins are strictly forbidden to leave the country regardless of whether they have fulfilled the 18-month requirement or not. The border surveillance units are authorised to shoot anyone who is caught crossing the borders of the country. Therefore, many people make use of 'illegal' methods to flee the country. They pay exorbitantly prohibitive prices to smugglers. In their attempts to escape, many face violations such as killings, and in the case of women, rape and sexual violence. Most of the escapees who manage to cross the borders experience harsh conditions in refugee camps in neighbouring countries. Several other fundamental rights have also been flagrantly violated, causing immense suffering to hundreds of thousands of Eritreans. Since 2010 in particular, many Eritreans who fled the country have been targeted by a well organised ring of human traffickers based in the Sinai Desert which, according to reports by UN experts, are suspected of having links with high-ranking Eritrean government officials (Mekonnen and Estefanos 2011). In its ultimate form, the crisis has now given rise to the emergence of Eritrea as an African garrison state to which we turn our focus in the next section.

ERITREA AS AN AFRICAN GARRISON STATE

In a garrison state freedom is systematically undermined in favour of security. Those who can legally use violence, the 'specialists in violence' or the military elite, have complete control of the state in order to purportedly guarantee security. In this way, authority becomes increasingly 'dictatorial, governmentalised, centralised, integrated' (Lasswell 1941: 455). Military priorities pre-empt a larger share of a nation's resources and military values are accorded higher and higher levels of prestige. By subordinating fundamental rights and freedoms to the requirements of national security, the military elite abrogate to themselves managerial expertise over civilians' everyday life. The emergence of a garrison state is characterised by the shrinking of individual liberties, increasing governmental secrecy and an ever-growing need to defend the nation from internal and external enemies. As essential preconditions of a garrison state, these traits portend a future of unrelenting readiness for endless warfare (Lasswell 1937: Lasswell 1941; Stanley 1997: 43, 117; Esman 2012: 5-6).

Our analysis of Eritrea as a garrison state is also strengthened by a previous proposition made by Christian Bundegaard (2004), who rightly baptised Eritrea 'a battalion state'. In the account of Bundegaard, what has happened in Eritrea is 'strong politics' in the form of 'a steadfast nationalist approach,' and 'an almost "Hoxha-Albanian" perception' of the necessity of securitisation. This brought about the formation of a 'battalion state'— what we call here a garrison state—often resulting 'in the obstruction of the creation of a civil, participating, accountable, democratic culture' (Bundegaard 2004: 16). The result, again, is the conversion of what was once considered a model of an African renaissance 'into a disappointing example of a militarized police state', with its hallmark 'an obsessive securitization of the economic, social, and political development of the country' (Bundegaard 2004: 16-17).

Perhaps another insightful theoretical construct important for our discussion is biopolitics, as utilised in the Eritrean context by David O'Kane and Tricia Hepner (2009). Building on the seminal work of Agamben (1998), O'Kane and Hepner define biopolitics as the violent penetration of state power into 'the most intimate spaces of human life and consciousness in the name of development, national security and sovereignty,' the end result being excessive perversions of governance and power (ibid.: ix-xxxi, 161–162). The practices ensuing from the exercise of this particularly abusive type of power – brute force – over human life itself has rendered the Eritrean person a mere subject reduced to 'bare life' (ibid: 121). In this context, the core of the political problem in Eritrea is explained as 'valorisation of military life above all other potential ways of contributing to the nation' (ibid.: xxviii). The challenge is further expounded by Woldemikael (2009), who also utilises the concept of banality of power, borrowed from Mbembe (1992). In discussing the pervasive absolute power of the PFDJ, Woldemikael asserts that the hegemony is given effect by ruthlessly silencing any other voice that contradicts the official narrative and by creating high levels of veneration and 'fetishization' of the Eritrean state (2009: 15).

Scholars have developed various methods that help in assessing the extent to which a country is developing towards a garrison state. One such method is known as the utilisation of moral panic (Cohen 2002: 27-30). Through moral panic governments induce a state of fear in society and justify militarisation and institutions that are aimed at securitisation. Moral panic establishes and perpetuates a state whose main purpose is its defence against real and perceived enemies. For example, moral panic is instrumental in the demonisation of certain groups in a given society and in a specified period of time. Although the scapegoating of alleged societal enemies is as old as societies themselves, in the making of a garrison state moral panic plays a distinctive role. In addition to possessing absolute monopoly over violence, via utilisation of moral panic the specialists in violence also exercise a 'monopoly over opinion', with the effect of abolishing the 'free communication of fact and interpretation'. This serves as one of the most effective instruments in perpetuating a state of 'universal fear,' justifying continued militarisation—for example, by depicting members of a certain societal or political group as enemies of the state or as responsible for some national problems. The specialists in violence strengthen their 'monopoly over opinion' and its influence on moral panic particularly by fully controlling the media (Lasswell 1941: 461; Cohen 2002: 27-30).

'Moral panic' as an instrument of control

Although a number of case studies are discussed elsewhere in this work that show the extent to which Eritrea has projected towards a garrison state, the example discussed below comes as one of the latest and most authoritative trends in support of our argument. It shows how the Eritrean government frequently uses 'moral panic' to ensure that the Eritrean society is effectively mobilised on a never-ending war footing. To instil fear and panic, the specialists in violence in the Eritrean government regurgitate the possibility of renewed war and another invasion from Ethiopia. This is further supported by the often cited 'conspiracy theory' of internal and external enemies of the state. All of such pronouncements are aimed at ensuring that the society is constantly frightened by a 'siege mentality,' in other words by 'moral panic' (ICG 2010; Kibreab 2009b). Most of the time, pronouncements to this effect are made by the state president himself (the most experienced of specialists in violence in the country), either in his New Year interviews or in Independence Day speeches. The following quotation from his 2013 Independence Day speech is most illustrative:

> [T]he emerging world order under the hegemony of the USA did not leave room for Eritrea to enjoy the benefit of national sovereignty. The scenarios of fabricated border disputes and hostile attempts aimed at undermining Eritrea's sovereignty witnessed after independence were not sudden instances. And the fact that our sovereign territory has remained under occupation for about 15 years with the connivance of an external power fully attests to this. Hence, our 60-year-long struggle for independence and sovereignty has not yet come to an end ... Glory to the steadfast Eritrean people![9]

Through continued 'monopoly over opinion' and the brute force of state power, Eritrean specialists in violence have effectively used instruments of mass communication and other state resources to remain visible to the public, to depict themselves and their agencies in a positive light and to emphasise enemy discourses that justify their actions. The ultimate end-result is the emergence of Eritrea as 'a country ruled by decree,' as depicted in the words of the UN Special Rapporteur on Eritrea (2013: 8).

Militarisation of education

Education – and collective intellectual development – is one major area which has been severely affected by militarisation and in which the emerging face of a garrison state is glaringly observed (Müller 2008;

[9] President Isaias' Address on the Occasion of 22nd Independence Day Anniversary, available at http://www.shabait.com/news/local-news/13576-president-isaias-address-on-the-occasion-of-22nd-independence-day-anniversary, accessed 24 May 2013.

Schmidt 2010). Faced with an increasing evasion of national service conscription by school leavers, the Eritrean government introduced a policy that forced all high school students to enrol for their final year of secondary education in the Sawa Military Training Centre. This particularly abhorrent policy, which was announced in 2003, took effect by renaming the military training centre 'Warsay-Yikealo School.' The renaming was a diverting tactic aimed at disguising national and international pressure, caused by the ever-increasing level of militarisation and the atrocities associated with it. Once in the 'Warsay-Yikealo School,' students are treated as military conscripts and for all practical purposes they are under the jurisdiction of the Ministry of Defence, thus effectively having their activities made subject to strict military discipline (HRW 2009). Based on nuanced ethnographic data collected from Eritrean students and teachers at an earlier stage, Riggan makes one of the most poignant observations about this challenge. She concludes that in Eritrea the inevitable outcome for a student is to become a soldier, simply because the conventional purpose of schooling has been transformed into that of preparing final-year high school students for military conscription via compulsory enrolment at the Sawa Military Training Centre (Riggan 2009: 73, 90). This way, the Sawa Military Training Centre or the Warsay-Yikealo School has become the most effective instrument of societal subjugation and at the same time a blatant embodiment of Eritrea as an African garrison state in the making. In the same vein, the government's decision to close down Asmara University permanently in 2004 and put all technical colleges under military supervision, is another testimony to the glaring militarisation of Eritrean society.

Arming civilians
The government's militarisation programme has recently been expanded to include senior citizens. According to the *Indian Ocean Newsletter*, in 2012 the government distributed arms to older civilian citizens either as a result of its worry 'about a future threat from outside' or in order 'to make up for desertions from the military'. Initiated by order of the state president, this programme is implemented under the auspices of the commander of the newly formed *Hizbawi Serawit* or people's army, Major General Tekle Kiflay 'Manjus' (*Indian Ocean Newsletter* 2012).

The effect of this new militarisation strategy is alarming. Reportedly, men as old as over eighty years of age are forced to carry Kalashnikovs when they leave their homes. Elderly civilians are also compelled to participate in military training, to be prepared for something that is not explained or rationalised. The arming of the civilian population without any adequate reason given, helps to substantiate the 'moral panic' thesis, and installs a collective fear in the population.

Whatever the motives of this scheme are, its repercussions are far-reaching in that small arms and munitions have now become like any other household equipment in Eritrea. The excessive level of militarisation is also duly recognised by the UN Special Rapporteur on the Situation of Human Rights in Eritrea, who described the challenge as 'affecting the very fabric of Eritrean society, and its core unit, the family' (Special Rapporteur 2013: 17-18).

MILITARISATION OF INTERNATIONAL RELATIONS

President Isaias Afwerki's regime has effectually militarised its international relations too. Eritrea's image as 'regional spoiler' in the Horn of Africa also assumes a central place both in the militarism-totalitarianism discourse and in the emergence of Eritrea as a garrison state. Due to its belligerent foreign policy, Eritrea has now amassed unparalleled international isolation, particularly in relation to its well-established links with Somalia-based internationally abhorred personalities and radical armed groups, such as Sheikh Hassan Dahir Aweys and the Harakat al-Shabaab al-Mujahideen, mostly known by its shorthand, Al-Shabaab. Both of them are designated by the international community as 'terrorists' (Mekonnen 2009: 115-116). To a government which valorises militarism, the international repugnance attached to Aweys and Al-Shabaab is not seen as having a deterrent effect on its adventurous foreign policy. Combined with its belligerent actions against Djibouti, Eritrea's image as 'regional spoiler' has now given rise to stringent sanctions adopted in December 2009 and December 2011 by the UN Security Council.

One unique feature of the UN sanctions against Eritrea is that they were initiated by the African Union (AU), which is historically known for its stringent opposition to UN sanctions targeting African countries. In the case of Eritrea, the AU acted in an unprecedented way, signifying the deep level of indignation felt by the international community against the Eritrean government, and by implication the profoundness of the crisis Eritrea finds itself in. The first UN resolution against Eritrea (Resolution 1907) was initiated by the Inter-Governmental Authority on Development (IGAD). It was immediately backed by the AU before it was finally endorsed by the UN Security Council on 23 December 2009. It is described as the first ever to be formally initiated by the AU against one of its own member states, after the experience of apartheid in South Africa, thus becoming also one of the most exceptional resolutions in the history of the UN (Meyers 2010).

FINAL REMARKS

Eritrea emerged as an independent state after a 30-year war of liberation. In addition to this, it is located in a region that has seen constant armed conflicts for the last two centuries, a location which in itself is always prone to armed conflicts. Understandably, the prevailing level of militarisation in the country may be seen by some as of not so unique a character. In reality, however, the problem has now reached an exponential crisis level, with a detrimental effect of breaking down basic societal fabrics in the country.

The challenge of militarisation of the country began to take different shape with the start of a national service programme in the early 1990s. The programme started with relatively popular support owing to the programme's purported noble objective of national development and reconstruction. With the advent of the 1998-2000 border conflict with Ethiopia and the continued exploitation of the conflict by the government, the national service programme has now degenerated to a level which is characterised by some experts as a practice of forced labour and modern-day slavery (Kibreab 2009; Weldehaimanot 2011), thereby victimising hundreds of thousands of Eritrean youths. The overall socio-political crisis that ensued from this practice has given Eritrea peculiar characteristic features, which fit well with the theoretical construct of a garrison state, as formulated by Lasswell (1937; 1941). How sustainable the Eritrean Garrison State is will be discussed in the next and final chapter of this book.

11

Eritrea:
Towards a Transition?

INTRODUCTION

As we have seen,when the ELPF came to power in 1991 and established itself as a provisional government, hopes were high for a democratic system of governance. Over two decades later these aspirations are nothing but bleak memories. In the intervening years Eritrea has developed into one of the world's most totalitarian and human rights-abusing regimes. This is well established in the wealth of academic literature, reports of international rights groups, interviews with refugees, victims and other stakeholders, as well as decisions of regional and international semi-judicial organs that we have cited extensively throughout this work. For example, at least four major pronouncements were made against the Eritrean government at different times by the African Commission on Human and Peoples' Rights and the UN Working Group on Arbitrary Detention, as discussed in Chapter 5. These semi-judicial opinions have made it clear that the practice of the Eritrean government as related to the G-15 and the journalists of the free press, and by implication to all other victims of political persecution, is contrary to the government's commitment emanating from relevant treaty law.

As noted by the UN Special Rapporteur on the Situation of Human Rights in Eritrea, the major problem lies in the fact that 'the basic tenets of the rule of law are not respected in Eritrea owing to a centralized system of Government where decision-making powers are concentrated in the hands of the President and his close collaborators' (Special Rapporteur 2013: 8). In a similar vein, Weldehaimanot and Kesete (2012: 49) also point out that everything that now ails Eritrea is attributable mainly to the totalitarian rule of the state president, and as such the nation's predicament can be best explained in comparison with the Orwellian trajectory of *Animal Farm*. All these assertions further strengthen the argument made implicit throughout the book, based on the theoretical formulation of Harold Lasswell (1937; 1941), that Eritrea portrays several of the fundamental features of a garrison state.

In all fundamental areas, such as state institutions supporting democratic accountability, civil society, minority rights, land and language issues, prison conditions, regional and global relations, and many other pressing national issues, the performance of the Eritrean government has been proven to be lamentable. The most worrying issue is the all-encompassing human rights crisis in the country, which can only be described as having reached the level of crimes against humanity. While there are many reports that support this claim, some of which are cited elsewhere in this book, the findings recorded in the report of the UN Special Rapporteur on the Situation of Human Rights in Eritrea come as the most authoritative. A brief contextual background is in order here before discussing the relevance of the Special Rapporteur's findings to our argument and analysis.

INTERNATIONAL HUMAN RIGHTS CRITICISM OF ERITREA

Human rights abuses increased exponentially in 2001 when the Eritrean government unleashed a new campaign of attack which started with the arrest of the G-15, the journalists of the free press, student leaders and other representatives of the emerging civil society in the country. However, it took more than ten years for the human rights crisis to really grasp the attention of the international community. This happened in July 2012 at which time the UN Human Rights Council in Geneva expressed deep concern at the on-going reports of grave violations of human rights by the Eritrean authorities, and decided to appoint a special rapporteur to investigate the situation of human rights in Eritrea.[1]

Deliberations on the Eritrean human rights crisis began initially under the confidential complaints procedure of the Human Rights Council. At a later stage, however, the Council decided to discontinue reviewing the matter under the confidential complaints procedure in order to attract public consideration. This was as a result of two main factors. First, information provided by the representative of the Eritrean government during a closed meeting held on 17 September 2012 was inadequate and incomplete. Second, complaints submitted by human rights groups were 'a cause for grave concern to the extent that they may reveal a consistent pattern of gross and reliably attested violations of human rights.'[2]

The specific violations committed by the Eritrean government and condemned by the UN Human Rights Council in July 2012, necessitating the appointment of a Special Rapporteur, include the following transgressions: continued *widespread and systematic* violations of human rights and fundamental freedoms, including cases of arbitrary and extrajudicial executions, enforced disappearances, the use of torture, arbitrary and incommunicado detention without recourse to justice, and detention in inhumane and degrading conditions; forced conscription of citizens for indefinite periods of national service, whi ch could amount to forced labour, including the coercion of minors into the military. Condemned by the

---

[1] UN Human Rights Council Resolution 20/20, UN Doc.A/HRC/RES/20/20, 5 July 2012.
[2] UN Human Rights Council Resolution 21/1, UN Doc.A/HRC/RES/21/1, 27 September 2012.

Human Rights Council are other abhorrent violations, such as the shoot-to-kill practice employed on the borders of Eritrea to stop citizens attempting to flee their own country; severe restrictions on freedom of opinion and expression, freedom of information, freedom of thought, conscience and religion, and freedom of peaceful assembly and association, including the detention of journalists, human rights defenders, political actors, religious leaders and practitioners in Eritrea; and the lack of cooperation with international and regional human rights mechanisms by Eritrea.

The most important aspect of the resolution of the Human Rights Council is that for the first time the human rights crisis in Eritrea has been described by the international community as *widespread and systematic*, this being the trademark phraseology in crimes against humanity literature (Mekonnen 2009: 73-75; Cassese 2003: 64). Although the UN Human Rights Council did not use the term 'crimes against humanity' explicitly, the usage of the twin terms of 'widespread and systematic' has created a strong resonance with the language used by the international community in describing similar situations in other parts of the world. Clearly, this points to the gravity of the human rights crisis in Eritrea.

Similarly, the conclusions made by the report of the UN Special Rapporteur on Eritrea also squarely correspond to the assessment made by the Human Rights Council. Based on first-hand testimonies and interviews, the Special Rapporteur concluded that the following violations are systematically perpetrated in Eritrea: extrajudicial killings; the ruthless implementation of a shoot-to-kill policy against persons attempting to cross borders; enforced disappearances and incommunicado detention; arbitrary arrests and detentions; widespread torture, both physical and psychological, during interrogation by the police, military and security forces; inhumane prison conditions; compulsory national service of an unspecified and extended duration; lack of respect for civil liberties, including the freedoms of expression and opinion, assembly, association, religious belief and movement; discrimination against women, and sexual and gender-based violence; violation of child rights, including conscription, which has a profound impact on education; and precarious living conditions. The Special Rapporteur notes that these are the main 'reasons pushing a constant stream of Eritreans to cross the borders' (2013: 9).

In keeping with the observation made by the Human Rights Council in July 2012, the Special Rapporteur also highlights that the situation of human rights in Eritrea is worrisome. Like the Human Rights Council, the Special Rapporteur does not use the term 'crimes against humanity' explicitly. Nonetheless, the language used elsewhere in her report is indicative of the existence of a situation of a human rights crisis which amounts to crimes against humanity. For example, in paragraph 103 of the report, the Special Rapporteur notes that 'human rights violations are widespread and pervasive and affect all components of Eritrean society'. In paragraphs 48 and 51 of the same report, it is noted that 'the number of people arrested and detained without charge or due process amounts to thousands'. In paragraph 42, the Special Rapporteur cites 'widespread torture' as one of the various categories of violations that corroborate an identifiable pattern. Although international law has never sought to quantify a minimum number of casualties necessary to constitute a situation of crime against humanity, the current figures of victims given by rights groups (e.g. a minimum of 10,000 political prisoners as reported by Amnesty International in 2013), are very high. Alluding to such figures, the Special Rapporteur notes that the number of victims is estimated in thousands (Special Rapporteur 2013: 10-11). The long list of violations mentioned in paragraph 42 of the report is indicative of the fact that human rights violations are indeed perpetrated in a widespread and systematic manner, thus constituting crimes against humanity.

PERPETRATING CRIMES AGAINST HUMANITY IN ERITREA

Our conclusion on the existence of a situation amounting to crimes against humanity requires a little more analysis in order to highlight the legal and political implications for Eritrean government officials. The perpetration of crimes against humanity presupposes a deliberate government policy to commit pervasive crimes or wilful failure to prevent the commission of such crimes. This is one of the characteristic features of crimes against humanity, as widely covered in the literature on this topic (Cassese 64; Kittichaisaree 2001:97; Schabas 2001: 36; Mekonnen 2009: 73-74).

The perpetration of crimes against humanity is intentionally tolerated, condoned or acquiesced in by a government or a *de facto* authority, having the effect of a *systematic* or *widespread* practice of atrocities. 'Systematic and widespread' refers to the fact that such crimes are backed by state authorities or by leading officials of a *de facto* state-like organisation or organised political group. It also means that the practice is not limited to a random event but that it takes place as a pervasive pattern of misconduct. In other words, the crimes in question are committed on a large scale, having the 'cumulative effect of a series of inhumane acts or the singular effect of an inhumane act of extraordinary magnitude'.[3]

In our case, the Human Rights Council made one point very clear by indicating 'a cause for grave concern to the extent that' the violations committed by the Eritrean authorities 'may reveal a consistent pattern of gross and reliably attested violations of human rights'.[4] This has grave legal and political implications for the individual criminal responsibility of a range of government officials, ranking from senior to low-level positions. This means that the killings, executions, mass incarcerations, and other sorts of violations perpetrated in Eritrea can be both a matter of a permissive culture of impunity and a deliberate policy of committing international crimes or wilful failure to prevent the perpetration of such crimes.

That crimes against humanity are being perpetrated in Eritrea is less

---

[3] *Kordić and Cerkez*, International Criminal Tribunal for the former Yugoslavia (ICTY), Trial Chamber III, judgment of 26 February 2001, paragraph 179. See also *Kunarac and others*, ICTY Appeals Chamber, judgment of 12 June 2020, paragraph 95; *Jelisić*, ICTY Trial Chamber, judgment of 14 December 1999, paragraph 53.

[4] UN Human Rights Council Resolution 21/1, UN Doc.A/HRC/RES/21/1, 27 September 2012.

controvertible. In some cases, such as the persecution of the Kunama, some observers may also claim that Eritrean government officials are guilty of the crime of genocide. However, compared to other severe instances of political violence in the region, the persecution of the Kunama may not be characterised as genocide—at least in terms of the magnitude and intensity of the atrocities. The most comparable example from regional conflicts is that of the Darfur crisis in Sudan. Although Omar al-Bashir of Sudan was ultimately indicted of genocide by the International Criminal Court, the outcome of which is yet to be seen in the future, the antecedents that have led to al-Bashir's indictment were preceded by another authoritative report of UN experts which concluded that genocide was not committed in Darfur (Report of the Darfur Commission 2004: 4, 160). This underscores the fact that the aggravated criminal intention or *dolus specialis* required for the substantiation of genocide is difficult to establish. In the case of Eritrea, we believe that the challenge might be much harder. Nonetheless, this tentative observation should not be taken as in any way detracting from the gravity of the human rights violations perpetrated by Eritrean government officials against the Kunama (Mekonnen 2009: 72).

Based on the report of the Special Rapporteur on Eritrea, the Human Rights Council adopted another resolution on 14 June 2013 in which it called on the Eritrean government to immediately halt its human rights abuses and start cooperating with the international community in order to fulfil its human rights obligations. By renewing the mandate of the Special Rapporteur, the Human Rights Council also instructed the mandate holder to present her next report to the UN General Assembly.[5]

Throughout this book, we have discussed different case studies that show how abhorrent the human rights practice of the Eritrean government is. Clearly, the position of the Human Rights Council on Eritrea, although it came at a belated stage, is expected to have some contribution in resolving the human rights crisis in Eritrea. Like all previous efforts, however, it all depends not only on the good will of the Eritrean government but also on the firmness of the international community. Experience shows that the chances are slim for the Eritrean government to heed the call made by the Human Rights Council unless the government is meaningfully pressurised by the international community to that effect. As shown in the next section, the government does not even acknowledge the deep human rights crisis in the country.

ERITREA'S RESPONSE: UTTER DENIAL, SELF-DECEPTION AND A STATE OF GRAND DELUSION

Reports about human rights violations are categorically denied by the Eritrean government as unfounded fabrications. In one of several instances of blatant denials, in 2010 the state president told Al Jazeera that Eritrea is the best country in Africa. Literally, he said: 'At least we

[5] UN Human Rights Council Resolution 23/21, UN.Doc.A/HRC/RES/23/21, 14 June 2013.

will not be like Kenya, Nigeria, Ethiopia, Somalia, Sudan; we are better off. We are number one in this continent' (Al Jazeera Interview 2010). Two more recent examples are statements given to the Voice of America on two separate occasions in 2013: by the Director of the Office of the Eritrean Minister of Foreign Affairs, Mr Tsehaye Fasil, and the Eritrean Ambassador to the UK, Mr Tesfamichael Gerahtu. Commenting on the appointment and mandate of the UN Special Rapporteur on the Situation of Human Rights in Eritrea, both officials stated that grave human rights violations are not being committed in Eritrea. They described the appointment of the Special Rapporteur as a mechanism plotted to legitimise unfounded accusations made against Eritrea every now and then by the Ethiopian and US governments. Accordingly, the report of the Special Rapporteur is categorically refuted as nothing more than a vicious and 'melodramatic' account (VOA Interview 2013a; 2013b).

In addition to denying human rights violations, the government also fantasises by creating its own grand delusion. Often times, the government prides itself on achieving several of the benchmarks set by the much publicised UN Millennium Development Goals (MDGs). The eight MDGs that are set by the UN to be achieved by 2015 are: eradicating extreme hunger and poverty; achieving universal primary education; promoting gender equality and empowering women; reducing child mortality; improving maternal health; combating HIV/AIDS, malaria and other disease; ensuring environmental sustainability and developing a global partnership for development. They are accordingly numbered from MDG One to MDG Eight. Of these, Eritrea is said to be on track in achieving MDGs 2 to 7, which means all except eradicating extreme hunger and poverty (MDG 1) and developing a global partnership for development (MDG 8).[6]

The alleged achievement in the area of the MDGs does not correspond with the socio-economic reality on the ground, for example, as is articulated by newly arriving refugees in Ethiopia and Sudan, and as is widely reported by international media and reputed publicists (Hepner 2013; Kibreab 2009; HRW 2013; AI 2013). The ever-growing refugee outflow and the latest tragedy of human rights and human trafficking are just some of the few examples which run contrary to the government's claim (Mekonnen and Estefanos 2011). This issue also raises critical questions about the methodology by which the so-called achievements in MDGs were measured. Nonetheless, these 'achievements' are sometimes uncritically regurgitated even by some of the remaining UN agencies currently operating in Eritrea, apparently for fear of eviction that may ensue as a result of the unpredictable behaviour of the Eritrean government.

There are several trustworthy sources that discredit the government's inflated narrative of MDGs achievement, for example, by looking at

---

[6] Letter dated 20 October 2011 from the Permanent Representative of Eritrea to the United Nations addressed to the President of the Security Council, UN.Doc. S/2011/652, para 46; Report of the Special Rapporteur on the Situation of Human Rights in Eritrea, Sheila B. Keetharuth, UN.Doc.A/HRC/23/53, 28 May 2013, para 21.

the periodic indices of a diverse nature, which are extensively cited in Chapter 1 of this book. Some of these accounts come from UN sources. In the most cited global indicator of economic development, UNDP's *Human Development Index* (HDI), Eritrea ranks 181 in the 187 countries assessed by the report and scored an index of 0.351. This score places Eritrea not only in the category of 'low human development', but also far below the regional average for sub-Saharan Africa. According to the UNDP, the index for sub-Saharan Africa as a region has risen from 0.366 in 1980 to 0.475 in 2013.[7] This means that in 2013 Eritrea is still below the average achievement sub-Saharan Africa as a region achieved in 1980.

From other reliable global indicators on human development and security cited elsewhere in this book, perhaps the most shocking figure on Eritrea comes from the 2013 Global Hunger Index. At least for two consecutive years (2012 and 2013) Eritrea has been ranked second from last in the list of countries assessed by the report. Globally, Eritrea is one of only three countries which have "extremely alarming" levels of hunger. The other two countries are Burundi and Comoros. Eritrea is preceded only by Burundi.[8] How is it then possible that Eritrea is achieving marvellous accomplishments in the area of the MDGs, as frequently propagandised by the government?

Moreover, the observation made by the Human Rights Council about the alarming number of civilians fleeing Eritrea as a result of grave human rights violations does not fit well with the 'success story' propagandised by the Eritrean government and other sources. On the particular issue of MDGs, the Human Rights Council explicitly stressed that 'sustainable social changes are linked with the establishment of a conducive political and legal environment'.[9] Indeed, as articulated by Amartya Sen's (1999) much celebrated 'development as freedom' argument, development in its broader sense is hardly achievable in an environment which is inherently antithetical to human freedom—freedom in the broader context of the term as discussed throughout this book.

The government's empty rhetoric on MDGs and other achievements in the area of socio-economic rights was exposed in its worst form in the context of the Lampedusa tragedy on 3 October 2013 which involved an accident at sea that claimed the lives of more than 360 African refugees trying to cross the Mediterranean with the objective of entering Europe via Italy.[10] The overwhelming majority of the victims were Eritreans. Of about 155 survivors, only one was non-Eritrean, according to Italian

---

[7] United Nations Development Programme (UNDP), 'Human Development Index 2013', available at http://hdr.undp.org/en/reports/global/hdr2013/, accessed 1 July 2013.
[8] Global Hunger Index, http://www.ifpri.org/sites/default/files/publications/ghi13.pdf, accessed 21 October 2013, p. 14.
[9] UN Human Rights Council, Resolution 23/21, UN.Doc.A/HRC/RES/23/21, 14 June 2013.
[10] VOA, Interview with Aba Mussie Zerai (in Tigrinya), available at http://tigrigna.voanews.com/content/lampadusa-eritreans-/1771140.html, 16 October 2013.

government sources.[11] The accident was so shocking and unique that it focused unprecedented global attention on the plight of Eritrean refugees and the alarming level of insecurity in Eritrea. The tragedy was covered for several days by leading media outlets, such as BBC, CNN and others. The site where the dead bodies were recovered from the sea was officially visited by the Italian prime minster (Enrico Letta) and the president of the European Commission (José Manuel Barroso), drawing wider attention to the catastrophe.

In the aftermath of the Lampedusa tragedy, Frontex, UNHCR and Fortress Europe published revealing statistics. Out of a total number of 30,100 people who have crossed by sea to Italy in the year 2013 (up to September), 3000 were Somalis, 7500 were Syrians and 7500 were Eritreans.[12] Somalia and Syria are countries which are ridden by ongoing armed conflicts and many have asked what 'peaceful' Eritrea was doing at the top of the statistics if things were really as flowery as the Eritrean government MDG reports depict them to be?

To the surprise of many, the Eritrean Embassy in Italy had the following to say about the Lampedusa tragedy in which context it is easy to discern the looming humanitarian crisis in Eritrea: 'What is tormenting is the fact that we are witnessing such a huge loss of life in a non-armed conflict, a loss that can only be imagined in a situation of armed conflict.'[13] Again, the core question to be asked here is: If the level of achievement in human development and human security is as bright as is depicted in the other Eritrean Government reports (and some other reports the veracity of which is difficult to articulate), then why are Eritreans fleeing the country in such huge numbers and risking such unfathomable levels of hazard?

In reference to the Lampedusa tragedy and in a vivid observation highlighting the looming humanitarian crisis in Eritrea, *The Economist* reported as follows:

> The main reason for the mass flight is that a growing number of Eritreans feel they are living in a prison camp, rivalled—some say—only by North Korea. All males up to the age of 50 have to do national service on starvation wages in an army whose senior ranks are brutal and corrupt. Up to the age of 65 men must continue to serve for periods every year in the "popular army", even though life expectancy hovers at only 61.[14]

Seen against such credible reports, which depict a dire socio-economic and politico-legal crisis in the country, stories of MDG achievement emanating from the Eritrean Government and other sources remain hardly convincing.

[11] Police Headquarters in Agrigento, "List of Lampedusa Survivors," available at http://download.repubblica.it/pdf/2013/cronaca/sopravvissuti_lampedusa.pdf, 4 October 2013.
[12] As cited in *BBC News*, "Italy to hold state funeral for shipwreck migrants," available at: http://www.bbc.co.uk/news/world-europe-24456058, 9 October 2013.
[13] Press Release of the Eritrean Embassy in Italy (in Tigrinya), dated 9 October 2013, on file with authors.
[14] *The Economist*, "Why They Leave," http://www.economist.com/news/middle-east-and-africa/21587844-eritreans-are-taking-seas-because-worsening-conditions-home-why-they, 12 October 2013.

TOWARDS A TRANSITION

What the future holds for Eritrea cannot be precisely spelled out. Accurate predictions in this regard are fraught with ambiguities. While a detailed analysis on this issue may go beyond the immediate objectives of this book, some tentative indications can be marked out briefly about potential political scenarios for the country. At least five major possibilities can be mentioned. One possibility is a coup d'état by the army. The potential for this cannot be underestimated as witnessed in the failed coup of 21 January 2013, which is now widely known as the Forto Operation among exiled activists and political groups. In the government's narrative, however, it was a non-event (Asmerom 2013; ICG 2013). Another much less likely scenario is the possibility of regime change by armed opposition groups based in Ethiopia (and with tactical support from Ethiopia). These groups are in their own constant process of fragmentation. How long it will take them to muster themselves as a formidable force is yet to be seen. Between the first two scenarios lies a third possibility, which includes unpredictable traces, such as the cause of death of the state president due to illness or a freak assassination. The fourth possibility is the kind of popular uprising seen in the Arab Spring. Given the extremely closed political situation in the country, the likelihood of this is probably not foreseeable in the near future. Negotiated transition instigated by the military leadership is the fifth possibility. This appears the most lenient of all the options, even to the Eritrean regime itself. As seen in many other situations, it may also be the most prudent option for Eritrea's future stability, although there are still insurmountable challenges. Perhaps the most plausible of all scenarios is a combination of some of the above.

President Isaias Afwerki does not seem to be concerned enough about the future of the country or its people. There are currently no indications that the government will make itself amenable to a negotiated transition. One main reason for this is that transition to democracy may entail individual and collective accountability for abuses that have been committed since 1991, or even during the era of liberation struggle. Accountability may take prosecutorial or non-prosecutorial form. The government (mainly the state president) is not willing to face this, even in its lenient form, namely, the type of truth and reconciliation initiative with conditional amnesty as the major incentive for negotiated transition. President Isaias Afwerki does not seem to be willing to face any sort of accountability for past or current abuses. Understandably, he has much to fear from his past misconduct. But most of all, he does not seem to be adequately pressurised to accept the terms and conditions of a negotiated transition. That is why he has repeatedly frustrated any initiative aimed at transitioning the country to democracy. Unless he feels real pressure that threatens the core of his power base, he is unlikely to come to the negotiating table.

On this particular issue, Eritrean activists and political groups in the diaspora are divided across the spectrum. There is, however, one fundamental assumption with which, we assume, many would agree. Much as the brutality of the PFDJ regime is despised, it seems hardly possible to imagine a stable future for Eritrea without its involvement in the processes of political transformation. It seems that Eritrea's stability concerns are too complicated to be handled without the PFDJ, especially considering the ever-fragmented existence of exiled Eritrean political groups and activists, and the ever-lingering fault lines in Eritrean society. The latest developments in the diaspora communities indicate that, in addition to the most prominent highland-lowland, Tigrinya-minority, Christian-Muslim divide, there is friction newly resurfacing (with alarming levels of animosity) within the highland Hamasien-Akele Guzay dichotomy. All these factors allude to the intricacies the Eritrean society has to go through in the forthcoming era of 'the second republic'. Eritrea is at a more critical juncture than at any other time in its history. Over its uncertain future hangs the proverbial 'Sword of Damocles'. The onset of a large-scale tragedy can only be averted by a delicate balancing of the interests of all political forces with a stake in the country's future.

In the absence of obvious widespread armed violence, the political crisis in Eritrea is sometimes misunderstood and its threat to local and regional stability underestimated. Also frequently overlooked is the imperceptible hollowing out of state structures that is gradually occurring out of public-international view, as a consequence of the progressive entrenchment of informal individual networks close to the state president (ICG 2010; ICG 2013). The ramifications of this latent fermentation of instability are appearing gradually, for example, as manifested in the failed coup of 21 January 2013—an event which was preceded by several other important events in 2012, making the year *The President's Annus Horribilis* (worst year) (ICG 2013: 6). Only closer scrutiny can avoid the tendency to respond to the symptoms rather than the deep-rooted causes of the crises.

In the short to medium term, a combination of solutions suggested by different actors needs to be taken into consideration. For our purposes, some of the recommendations suggested by the UN Special Rapporteur on Eritrea (2013) and by the ICG's 2013 report appear plausible. While the need to cater for Eritrea's internal and external stability concerns is a very important variable in the equation, the responsibility of the international community to suppress the perpetration of widespread human rights violations cannot be understated. As the UN Special Rapporteur on Eritrea underscores, 'real change would require a fundamental reform process transforming the current culture of rights denial into one anchored in the rule of law and in respect for and the realization of all human rights and human dignity.' This involves mainly keeping 'Eritrea under close scrutiny until meaningful change is evident in the country (Special Rapporteur 2013: 18, 21). The possibility of prosecuting the most responsible perpetrators of human rights violations before the International Criminal Court may be fraught with procedural difficulties. As a result, other international punitive measures may have to be applied to pressurise a meaningful change of behaviour on the part of Eritrean government officials. In this regard, the imposition of stricter sanctions, particularly focusing on the internal human rights crisis, can be seen as one of the possible punitive measures that can be adopted by the international community.

CONCLUSION: THE ERITREAN SECOND REPUBLIC

It seems clear that the Eritrean Garrison State – in the long run – is not sustainable. It will eventually collapse due to economic, social and political pressure from internal and external forces. It is, however, unclear what will come after Isaias Afwerki; the most likely scenario is a military take-over. No doubt the post-Isaias transitional period will be challenging, and international observers warn of a possible state collapse and ensuing conflict in the country. The two most challenging issues Eritreans have to handle is how to deal with the massive and widespread human rights atrocities committed by the EPLF/PFDJ regime post-1991 (so-called transitional justice mechanisms), and second, how to reconfigure the Eritrean state and central government in order to regain legitimacy and support for the fragmented and highly heterogeneous Eritrean communities.

The 'Eritrean second republic' must be based on the rule of law, human rights and democracy, and perpetrators of the abuse of human rights ought to be held accountable for the crimes against humanity conducted under President Isaias Afwerki. Likewise, the new republic must establish a governance system that accommodates all ethnic and political groups in Eritrea, with a particular emphasis on the protection and acceptance of minority rights. What type of autonomy system Eritrea should adopt – under a federal or unitary state – will be the key issue to tackle in the immediate post-Isaias period. Hopefully, the Eritrean actors driving the transition will be able to reach a consensus on this issue; if not we fear a relapse into turmoil and violence.

The Eritrean transition will in this regard be hugely challenging and complex; the plight of the Eritrean people seems thus to be never-ending.

Postscript

ERITREA – RENEWED INTERNATIONAL ENGAGEMENT
TO SUSTAIN CONTROL AT HOME

Since publication of the first edition of this book, developments inside Eritrea have continued along the same trajectories as before: sustained restrictions on civil and political liberties, reports of widespread and systematic human rights abuses, and a continued exodus of its population being disbursed as refugees across the globe. The regime has, however, opened up and re-engaged internationally, as a response to three key factors: increasing pressure for human rights accountability, which it has tried to counter; a new constellation of geo-politics in the Horn of Africa/ Gulf of Aden; and European countries' interests in stemming Eritrean migration and flight to Europe, which it has made an effort to cash in on. This postscript to the second edition of the book provides a summary of key developments that have taken place in Eritrea since 2014 and up to early 2017. The most important developments under discussion include:

- the establishment in June 2014 of the United Nations Commission of Inquiry on Human Rights Violations in Eritrea (COI), and the publication of its major reports in June 2015 and June 2016;

- the mobilisation of the Eritrean diaspora against the human rights violations back home;

- renewed international dialogue with the Eritrean regime;

- and the new geo-political dynamics in the Horn of Africa and the Gulf of Aden region – transcending the Middle East and East Africa.

THE UN COMMISSION OF INQUIRY: IMPUNITY NO MORE?

In June 2014, the UN Human Rights Council decided to establish a commission of inquiry on Eritrea.[1] This was a clear indication of a heightened concern on the part of the Council, in other words the international community, on the deteriorating situation inside the country. It followed the publication of two major reports by the UN Special Rapporteur on the Situation of Human Rights in Eritrea, who not only depicted a very sad state of affairs but also called for increased international scrutiny of Eritrea.[2] Establishing a commission of inquiry is the utmost level of implied criticism against a government, a prelude to initiating criminal prosecution under the International Criminal Court (ICC). During a two-year mandate period, the COI published two separate reports, in June 2015 and June 2016, which can be considered the most authoritative accounts, from an international law perspective, on the situation of human rights in Eritrea.[3]

The tentative conclusion about crimes against humanity made in the first edition of this book was supported and verified by the COI. This means that in relation to the human rights situation in Eritrea, for the first time, the international community began to speak in terms of crimes against humanity – which is one step closer to ensuring accountability for the gross human rights violations committed. This was a game changer in many ways, but mainly on account of the most important recommendation the COI made in its second report, which calls on the UN Security Council to refer the human rights situation in Eritrea to the Prosecutor of the ICC – with the aim of ending impunity for human rights violations in the country (Second Report of the COI, para. 132). However, given the prevailing deep-seated antagonism between Africa and the ICC, the likelihood of this recommendation becoming a concrete action remains to be seen (Mekonnen and Sereke 2017).

Nevertheless, the boldness demonstrated by the COI in terms of recommending the highest level of accountability mechanism available under international criminal law was remarkable. In its second report of June 2016, the COI unequivocally concluded: 'crimes against humanity, namely, enslavement, imprisonment, enforced disappearance, torture, other inhumane acts, persecution, rape and murder, have been committed in Eritrea since 1991' (Second Report of the COI, p. 1 and paras. 59–95). Further, the COI identified the following government organs and

---

[1] Human Rights Council Res. A/HRC/RES/26/24, 27 June 2014, para. 7.
[2] See *First Report of the Special Rapporteur on the Situation of Human Rights in Eritrea, Sheila B. Keetharuth*, A/HRC/23/53, 28 May 2013 [hereinafter 'First Keetharuth Report']; *Second Report of the Special Rapporteur on the Situation of Human Rights in Eritrea, Sheila B. Keetharuth*, A/HRC/26/45, 13 May 2014 [hereinafter 'Second Keetharuth Report'].
[3] *First Report of the UN Commission of Inquiry on Human Rights in Eritrea*, A/HRC/29/42, 4 June 2015 [hereinafter 'First COI Report Short Version']; *Second Report of the UN Commission of Inquiry on Human Rights in Eritrea*, A/HRC/32/47, 8 June 2016 [hereinafter 'Second COI Report Short Version'].
[3] According to the *Advanced Practitioner's Handbook*.

officials as the main perpetrators of the said violations: the Eritrean Defence Forces, in particular the Eritrean Army; the National Security Office; the Eritrean Police Forces; the Ministry of Information; the Ministry of Justice; the Ministry of Defence; the People's Front for Democracy and Justice (PFDJ); the Office of the President; and the President (First Report of the COI, para. 23). Identification of the most responsible state organs comes as another grave accusation against the Eritrean ruling clique.

There are two other important observations, among several others, about the establishment of the COI and its reports that warrant a brief presentation. First, the COI was established in a context that does not involve any of the classic factors for the establishment of commissions of inquiry, such as armed conflicts, internal disturbances and natural disasters (Harvard Humanitarian Initiative 2015). In this sense, Eritrea became the second country (next to North Korea) for which a commission of inquiry was established by the Human Rights Council in the absence of the so-called 'classic factors'. Moreover, at the time of writing, Eritrea is the only country in Africa in which there is an on-going situation of crimes against humanity officially verified as such by the UN. Although there are other sad situations of human rights violations in Africa, such as those of Burundi and South Sudan, none of these are as yet officially acknowledged by the UN as constituting crimes against humanity.

Secondly, in its 2016 report, the COI made specific recommendations, calling on the African Union (AU) to establish appropriate accountability mechanisms under its aegis, supported by the international community (Second Report of the COI, para. 133). This recommendation was adopted possibly with a view to providing a counter-balance to any objection that might arise from some African countries (given the deep-seated animosity between Africa and the ICC), should the situation in Eritrea ultimately be referred to the Prosecutor of the ICC by the UN Security, as recommended by the COI.

In this case, it can be argued that Eritrea may soon become another litmus test for the newly developing Pan-African norm of collective military cooperation, encapsulated in the concept of the African Peace and Security Architecture (APSA) (Tieku, Obi and Scorgie-Potier 2014; Tieku 2013; Murithi 2014). Introduced at the time of the formal transformation of the Organisation of African Unity (OAU) to the AU, APSA is the trigger mechanism for military intervention by the AU in another African country, should a situation that violates any of the prohibitions stipulated in the Constitutive Act of the AU arise – mainly those related to peace and security, including gross human rights violations. In order to give meaningful effect to AU's renewed interest in collective security, Article 4(*h*) of the Constitutive Act of the AU explicitly enshrined the new legislative concept of 'the right of intervention' (Kioko 2003), which provides for:

> the right of the Union to intervene in a Member State pursuant to a decision of the Assembly in respect of grave circumstances, namely: war crimes, genocide and crimes against humanity as well as a serious threat to legitimate order to restore peace and stability to the Member State of the Union upon the recommendation of the Peace and Security Council.

The right of intervention envisaged in the above provision requires putting into effect the whole concept of APSA, at the heart of which lies a Pan-African collective military cooperation, the so-called African Standby Force (ASF), that is, AU's newly established 'armed wing'.[4] Whether the AU will take such draconian measures against the Eritrean regime is yet to be seen. However, with the kind of solid findings on the issue of crimes against humanity made by the COI, and given the kind of political will that should come on the part of the AU, such a possibility cannot be ignored. For example, the January 2017 pro-active engagement of the AU (through ECOWAS) in the post-election crisis of The Gambia – leading to the exceptional measure of compelling the former Gambian dictator to hand over power – is a most important lesson in this regard (AU Communiqué 2017; Joint Declaration of AU, ECOWAS and UN 2017).

THE GALVANISATION OF EXILED PRO-DEMOCRACY GROUPS

The establishment of the COI and the publication of its ground-breaking reports have galvanised the pro-democracy agenda of Eritrean diaspora grassroots movements as never before. This was unequivocally witnessed in two major demonstrations that took place in Geneva in June 2015 and June 2016, with replica demonstrations in Addis Ababa, New York and Tel Aviv, and other smaller demonstrations in capitals across Europe. Focus is given here mainly to the Geneva Mass Rallies of 2015 and 2016 on two major grounds. First, these were demonstrations held in front of the UN Office at Geneva (UNOG), which hosts the UN Human Rights Council by which the COI was mandated. So, for many Eritreans, Geneva is the equivalent of the headquarters of the COI. Indeed, Geneva became a semi-judicial forum in which justice for crimes against humanity in Eritrea was partially served by the combined effect of the two COI reports and the two Geneva Mass Rallies.

Secondly, the first Geneva Mass Rally of 26 June 2015 was the largest ever demonstration condemning human rights violations in Eritrea since the advent of the Eritrean regime to power in 1991.[5] More than 5,000 pro-democracy demonstrators rallied under the banner 'End Impunity

[4] As yet, ASF is not fully operational. In terms of operational structure, it is designed not as a single constituent army, but rather as an army composed of standby multidisciplinary contingents, based on existing African regional groupings or Regional Economic Communities (RECs) or Regional Mechanisms (RMs), such as the Economic Community of West African States (ECOWAS) (Mekonnen 2017b).

[5] On the same day the first Geneva Mass Rally took place another huge demonstration by Eritreans living in Ethiopia was also staged in Addis Ababa, in front of the AU headquarters. Naturally, since Ethiopia is a country seen as the arch-enemy of Eritrea, questions can be asked about the demonstration that took place in Addis Ababa. In contrast, the greatest advantage of the Geneva Mass Rally was that it was free from such pre-conceived biases. See the activity report of the organising committee of the first Geneva Mass Rally (in Tigrinya), available at http://hidri.net/wp-content/uploads/2015/07/Final-Report-Long-Version-2.0.pdf.

in Eritrea!' Demonstrators (Eritrean and non-Eritreans) flocked from all parts of the world, some even travelling from countries thousands of miles away, such as Australia and North America. The number recorded in 2015 was by far exceeded on 23 June 2016 at the second Geneva Mass Rally, which brought together more than 12,000 demonstrators.[6] Compared to two other similar demonstrations, staged by pro-Eritrean government groups around the same time and in the same venue, the demonstrations by pro-human rights groups managed to rally more support and set a broader agenda.

Apart from staging the Geneva Mass Rallies, Eritrean diaspora grassroots movements have also played a key role in the collection of numerous written testimonies that formed part of the core information analysed by the COI, leading to the robust finding of the COI that crimes against humanity have been committed in Eritrea since 1991. One of the most important examples in this regard is a joint task force that was established by three exiled grassroots movements known as the Eritrean Solidarity Movement for National Salvation (ESMNS); the Eritrean Youth Solidarity for Change – North America (EYSC-NA); and the Eritrean Law Society (ELS).[7]

The entire COI process and the Geneva Mass Rallies have clearly demonstrated one fundamental reality: that the balance of power between Eritrean pro-democracy and pro-regime elements is shifting meaningfully towards the former. It is likely that this trajectory of increased support to the pro-democracy diaspora lobby will continue; however, how this may be converted into meaningful action to change the conditions back home and to instigate a transition towards democracy in Eritrea is still unclear.

There was, however, one major shortcoming of the COI. This relates to the manner in which the COI interpreted its mandate. When writing its report of June 2015, the COI adopted a narrow interpretation of its mandate, precluding it from making a definitive finding on the issue of crimes against humanity. This meant waiting unnecessarily for another year before a definitive finding was to be made on the issue. In our view, this was erroneous. The COI had the spacious jurisprudential room to adopt a wider interpretation of its mandate, and thus to allow itself the task of making a definitive finding on the issue of crimes against humanity at the time when it published its first report in June 2015 (Mekonnen 2017a).

Prolongation of the COI's mandate by another year made it possible

---

[6] Information about the Geneva Mass Rallies is based on first-hand knowledge of Daniel Mekonnen, who served as chairperson of the seven-member coordinating committee that was entrusted with organising the first Geneva Mass Rally of 23 June 2015. He also collaborated as a non-committee member with the other coordinating committee that organised the second Geneva Mass Rally of 26 June 2016.

[7] Representing the Eritrean Law Society (ELS), Daniel Mekonnen served as a member of the joint task force. ELS is the only professional association of Eritrean lawyers, working from exile due to the extremely closed political situation in Eritrea. Several of its members are victims of abuses committed by the Eritrean government.

for the Eritrean regime to launch an orchestrated counteroffensive diplomatic assault, winning some support base in Geneva and New York. For a regime that was shocked by the first report of the COI, launching a concerted diplomatic campaign was the only way out. It seemed this worked in some ways. This is better understood in the context of the ever-changing diplomatic winds of the Human Rights Council, which is also affected by developments at the General Assembly and the Security Council in New York. As is generally known, the Human Rights Council is a political body. Thus, unlike a judicial body, its decision-making process is strongly influenced by political interests subject to fluctuating geo-political and other considerations, such as the flight of tens of thousands of Eritreans to Europe.[8]

GEOPOLITICS AND RENEWED INTERNATIONAL DIALOGUE

In the period under review (from 2014 to 2017), the Eritrean government was also seen to be moving, albeit at a very slow pace, from its self-imposed and prolonged international isolation. There are several factors that account for this change. One is related to the outbreak of civil war in March 2015 in Yemen, a neighbouring country of Eritrea on the Western coast of the Red Sea. At the time of writing, Yemen continues to experience a devastating civil war, between two major groups, each receiving varying levels of support from regional allies in the Arabian Peninsula.

Joined by other regional allies (Gulf countries), Saudi Arabia took a stand in favour of one of the warring parties in the Yemeni civil war. This gave rise to the formation of a military pact between the Saudi Arabia-led coalition of Gulf States and the Eritrean regime, due to Eritrea's strategic importance for the conflict in Yemen. Ultimately, the Eritrean regime agreed to give access to Eritrean airspace, territorial waters and some military bases (especially the Port of Assab) for use by the Saudi-led coalition.[9] This provided the Eritrean regime with a dual benefit: alleged financial revenue in the form of rental of the Port of Assab, and a much-needed boost in its regional and international diplomacy.

For obvious reasons, winning the support and sympathy of Saudi Arabia is very helpful in terms of winning the support, albeit indirectly, also of its Western allies. In this way the Eritrean regime seems to be gradually turning from its prolonged regional and international isolation. In that sense, it can also be argued that the Eritrean President has once

[8] One recent example is a highly polarised debate at the UN General Assembly, from December 2016, which was called to vote on a report emanating from the Human Rights Council, dealing with sexual orientation and gender identity. See General Assembly Plenary 71st Session, 65th Meeting (AM), 'General Assembly Adopts 50 Third Committee Resolutions, as Diverging Views on Sexual Orientation, Gender Identity Animate Voting', 19 December 2016, http://www.un.org/press/en/2016/ga11879.doc.htm.

[9] The Saudi-led coalition, which includes nine Middle Eastern countries, advances a military operation known as Operation Decisive Storm (ostensibly fighting the causes of instability in Yemen) (STRATFOR 2015).

again manoeuvred into a position of geo-political relevance, perhaps at the cost of Ethiopia in terms of the bilateral power-balance between the two countries. However, due to the regime's (especially the President's) erratic behaviour, no one can predict how long this new relationship will last. One only needs to remember that at the very start of the Yemeni civil war in 2015, Eritrea was said to have been supporting the other part of the conflict, namely Houthi fighters, who are believed to be allies of Iran (Saudi Arabia's arch-enemy). This level of unpredictability means that no one can be sure what may transpire in Eritrea in due course.

On the other hand, due to the ever-worsening refugee crisis in Europe, some European governments (and also the European Union) were also sending signals for renewed diplomatic relationships with the Eritrean regime. As a result of the influx of Eritrean refugees to Europe, many governments reviewed their policies towards Eritrea in the interest of curbing migration to Europe. What makes this problematic is that it comes in the context of a very strong conclusion by the COI on the on-going situation of crimes against humanity. As is generally known, crimes against humanity are one of the three major categories of crimes that fall under the exclusive jurisdiction of the ICC: the other two being genocide and war crimes. Seen from this angle, the latest 'change of heart' by some European governments may prove problematic.

While there are different moves by the various countries in this regard, the most important change is that of the EU. In December 2015, the EU formalised the donation of a new package of 'development aid', amounting to €200 million, to Eritrea (European Commission 2015). It is clear that money is being sent to Eritrea without adequate monitoring strings attached to it, as stipulated in Article 9 of the Cotonou Agreement, the main treaty document that governs EU development cooperation with the developing world.[10] More than that, what makes the new agreement different from previous such dealings is that it makes specific reference to the objective of stemming migration from Eritrea (supposedly by easing the root causes of migration in Eritrea).[11]

Thus, there is a clear link between the EU's migration-related concerns – Eritrea being a major source of refugees to Europe – and its desire to continue supporting the Eritrean regime, regardless of the formidable conclusion of the COI on the issue of crimes against humanity. In the long run, this may have long-reaching ramifications on the credibility of the EU and its commitment towards accountability for crimes against humanity. Among other things, it has the danger of cultivating a sense of cynicism on the part of the Eritrean government, premised on the

[10] For instance, Sub-article 1 of the same provision provides: 'Cooperation shall be directed towards sustainable development centred on the human person, who is the main protagonist and beneficiary of development; this entails respect for and promotion of all human rights. *Respect for all human rights and fundamental freedoms*, including respect for fundamental social rights, *democracy based on the rule of law* and transparent and accountable governance are an integral part of sustainable development' [emphasis added].
[11] See http://uk.reuters.com/article/uk-europe-migrants-eritrea-idUKKCN0RH1MU20150917.

conviction of the latter that in spite of its despicable record on human rights, it has the privilege of being taken seriously as a reliable ally (Mekonnen 2016a; Mekonnen 2016b).

As part of its effort to break out of a prolonged international isolation, the Eritrean regime has also announced promises to limit the national service programme to its original maximum period of 18 months (Reuters 2016). This promise was followed by a proposed increase of salary to national service conscripts. Information obtained from people who have fled the country in recent months indicates that none of these promises have been fulfilled in a meaningful way. Moreover, with the revenue generated from the mining sector, the Eritrean economy is believed to have revived over the last few years. This has however not brought any change in the everyday life of ordinary Eritreans.

CHANGE TO COME?

Although the Eritrean regime seems to signal an interest in changing its policies and opening up, little seems to translate into concrete actions. Eritrea needs fundamental political change, not mere superficial remedies, which can be likened to short-term painkillers and have no meaningful effect on the debilitating political bankruptcy of the Eritrean regime.

In the light of this, the concluding observations and assessments we made in the last chapter of our book (Chapter 11) still hold very true. Perhaps one new additional element needs to be stressed, the level of societal anxiety experienced within Eritrea over the last couple of years. Over and above a worsening political situation, economic hardship is reaching exponential levels, worsened also by a predatory currency regulation introduced at the end of 2015. These days Eritreans are not even allowed to carry in their hands more than Nakfa 5,000 a month (roughly equivalent to US$250).[12]

Partly disguised as a means to stabilise the local market, which was struck by free-falling inflation of the national currency (Nakfa), the other objective of the new currency regulation was to satisfy the apparently insatiable appetite of the government to control every aspect of life in Eritrean society. However, the population is no longer taking it quietly. Information obtained from Eritreans who left the country as late as January 2017 indicates that the long reigning societal fear of the regime seems to be cracking, so much so that ordinary Eritreans are no longer frightened of venting their frustration against the regime in a number of ways considered previously as unimaginable (such as angered utterances in non-private conversations). If anything, this is indicative of the fact that the regime cannot sustain its grip on power the way it has been doing for so long, and the much-anticipated arrival of the second Eritrean republic may indeed happen sooner than expected.

[12] Legal Notice No. 124/2015 (4 November 2015).

Bibliography

Aalen, Lovise and Kjetil Tronvoll. 2009. The end of democracy? Ethiopia's return to authoritarianism. *Review of African Political Economy* 36, (120).

Agamben, Giorgio [trans. Daniel Heller-Roazen]. 1998. *Homo Sacer: Sovereign Power and Bare Life*. Stanford, CA: Stanford University Press.

Amnesty International. 2002. *Eritrea: Arbitrary detention of government critics and journalists*. London: Amnesty International.

—. 2004. *Eritrea – 'You have no right to ask'. Government resist scrutiny on human rights*. London: Amnesty International.

—. 2005. *Eritrea: Religious Persecution*. London: Amnesty International.

—. 2008a. *Egypt. Deadly journeys through the desert*. London: Amnesty International.

— 2008b. Eritrea Amnesty International Report 2008. in *The State of the World's Human Rights*, edited by Amnesty International. London: Amnesty International.

—. 2012. *Amnesty International Report 2012: The State of the World's Human Rights*. London: Amnesty International.

—. 2013. *Eritrea: Twenty Years of Independence, but still no Freedom*. London: Amnesty International.

Asmeron, Girma. 2013. Ambassador Girma Asmerom's reflections on the so-called 'attempted coup d'état' in Eritrea, 26 January 2013, available at http://www.dehai.org/archives/dehai_news_archive/2013/jan/0139.html

AU. 2017. AU Communiqué on the post-election situation in The Gambia (PSC/PR/COMM. (DCXLVII), 13 January 2017, available at http://www.peaceau.org/uploads/647.psc.comm.gambia.13.01.2017-1.pdf.

Bailliett, Cecilia M. 2007. Examining Sexual Violence in the Military within the Context of Eritrean Asylum Claims Presented in Norway. *International Journal of Refugee Law* 19: 471-510.

Banakar, Reza and Max Travers. 2005. *Theories and Method in Socio-Legal Research*. Oxford: Hart Publishing.

Bariagaber, Assefaw. 2006. *Eritrea: Challenges and crisis of a new state*. London: WRITENET.

Bengali, Shashank. 2009. Eritrea: Africa's version of North Korea? *The Christian Science Monitor*, 10 November, available at http://www.csmonitor.com/World/Africa/2009/1110/p06s12-woaf.html.

Bernal, Victoria. 2013. Please forget democracy and justice: Eritrean politics and the powers of humour. *American Ethnologist* 40(2): 300-309.

Bertelsmann Stiftung. 2010. *Bertelsmann Transformation Index 2010: Eritrea Country Report*. Gütersloh: Bertelsmann Stiftung.

Beyene, Teame. 2001. The Eritrean judiciary: Struggling for independence, May 2001, available at http://papers.ssrn.com/sol3/papers.cfm?abstract_id=1723868, accessed 12 December 2012.

BIA. 2008. *Country of Information Report Eritrea*. London: Border and Immigration Agency, Home Office, UK Government.

Bondestam, Lars. 1989. *Eritrea med rätt til självbestämmande (Eritrea - The right to self-determination)* Lysekil: Clavis.

BosNewsLife. 2013. Eritrea turned into 'giant prison' as president celebrates 20th anniversary, available at http://www.bosnewslife.com/28974-eritrea-turned-into-giant-prison-as-president-celebrates-20th-anniversary.

Bozzini, David. 2011. Low-tech surveillance and the despotic state in Eritrea. *Surveillance & Society* 9(1/2): 93-113.

Bundegaard, Christian. 2004. *The Battalion State: Securitization and Nation-Building in Eritrea*. Programme for Strategic and International Studies Occasional Paper I Number 2/2004. Zurich: Swiss Federal Institute of Technology.

Cassese, Antonio. 2003. *International Criminal Law*. Oxford: Oxford University Press.

Cliffe, Lionel and Basil Davidson (eds). 1988. *The long struggle of Eritrea for independence and constructive peace*. Nottingham: Spokesman.

Cohen, Stanley. 2002. *Folk Devils and Moral Panics*. London, Routledge.

Connell, Dan. 1993. *Against All Odds. A Chronicle of the Eritrean Revolution*. Lawrenceville, NJ: Red Sea Press.

—. 1997. New Challenges in post-war Eritrea. *Eritrean Studies Review* 2:129-159.

—. 2001. Inside the EPLF: The origins of the 'People's Party' and its role in the liberation of Eritrea. *Review of African Political Economy*: 345-364.

—. 2005. *Conversations with Eritrean Political Prisoners*. Trenton, NJ: Africa World Press.

—. 2005. Eritrea: On a slow fuse. in *Battling Terrorism in the Horn of Africa*, edited by Robert I. Rotberg. pp. 64-92. Cambridge, MA and Washington DC: World Peace Foundation and Brookings Institution Press.

—. 2007. Country Report - Eritrea. in *Countries at the Crossroads 2007*, edited by Freedom House. Washington DC: Freedom House.

—. 2011. Country Report - Eritrea. in *Countries at the Crossroads*, edited by Freedom House. Washington DC: Freedom House.

CORC. 2007. The Kunama. p. 6 in *COR Center Refugee Backgrounder*. Washington DC: Cultural Orientation Resource Center, Center for Applied Linguistics.

Cotterrell, Roger (2007). Sociology of law. In *Encyclopedia of Law and Society: American and Global Perspectives*, edited by David S. Clark, pp. 1414-1421. Thousand Oaks, CA: Sage Publications.

Davenport, Christian (ed.). 2000. *Paths to State Repression: Human Rights Violations and Contentious Politics*. Lanham, MD: Rowman and Littlefield.

Eide, Asbjørn. 2001. Cultural rights as individual human rights. In *Economic, Social and Cultural Rights*, edited by Asbjørn Eide, Catarina Krause, and Allan Rosas. pp. 289-301. Dordrecht, Boston, MA and London: Martinus Nijhoff.

EPLF. 1994. *A National Charter for Eritrea, for a Democratic, Just and Prosperous Future*. Nacfa: EPLF.

Erlich, Haggai. 1996. *Ras Alula and the Scramble for Africa. A political biography: Ethiopia and Eritrea 1875–1897*. Lawrenceville, NJ: Red Sea Press.

Esman, Milton J. 2012. *The Emerging American Garrison State*, Basingstoke: Palgrave Macmillan.

European Commission. 2015. EU Announces Support for Poverty Eradication in Eritrea, 11 December 2015, http://europa.eu/rapid/press-release_IP-15-6298_en.htm.

Favali, Lyda and Roy Pateman. 2003. *Blood, Land, and Sex. Legal and political pluralism in Eritrea*. Bloomington and Indianapolis, IN: Indiana University Press.

Fegley, Randall. 1995. *Eritrea*. Oxford: Clio Press.

Firebrace, James and Stuart Holland. 1987. *Never Kneel Down. Drought, development and liberation in Eritrea*. Nottingham: Spokesman.

Freedom House 2011, Worst of the Worst 2011: the world's most repressive societies, available at http://www.freedomhouse.org/sites/default/files/WorstOfTheWorst2011.pdf.

Friedrich, Carl, Michel Curtis and Benjamin Barber. 1969. *Totalitarianism in Perspective: Three Views*. New York: Praeger.

Friedrich, Carl and Zbigniew Brzezinski. 1956. *Totalitarian Dictatorship and Autocracy*. Cambridge, MA: Harvard University Press.

Gaim, Eyassu. 1993. *The Eritrean Question. The conflict between the right of self-determination and the interests of states*. Uppsala: Uppsala University/ Justus forlag.

Gates, Bill. 2013. Public Speech by Bill Gates on World Health Initiatives and Philanthropy, University of South Wales, 28 May 2013, available at https:// www.youtube.com/watch?feature=player_embedded&v=qROud0hQUYw.

Gebre-Medhin, Jordan. 1989. *Peasants and nationalism in Eritrea. A critique of Ethiopian studies*. Lawrenceville, NJ: Red Sea Press.

Gebremedhin, Yohannes. 2004. *The challenges of a society in transition*. Trenton, NJ: Red Sea Press.

Gilkes, Patrick. 1983. Centralism and the Ethiopian PMAC. in *Nationalism and Self Determination in the Horn of Africa*, edited by Ioan M. Lewis. London: Ithaca Press.

—. 2005. Violence and identity along the Eritrean-Ethiopian border. in *Unfinished Business. Ethiopia and Eritrea at War*, edited by Dominique Jacquin-Berdal and Martin Plaut. pp. 229-253. Lawrenceville, NJ: Red Sea Press.

Gottesman, Les. 1998. *To Fight and Learn. The praxis and promise of literacy in Eritrea's independence war*. Lawrenceville, NJ: Red Sea Press.

Guardian. 2009. Eritrea: The world's biggest prison. 17 April 2009, available at http://www.guardian.co.uk/commentisfree/2009/apr/17/eritrea-human-rights.

Gurr, Ted R. 1988. War, revolution, and the growth of the coercive state. *Comparative Political Studies* 21(45): 45-65.

Habte Selassie, Bereket. 1998. Creating a Constitution for Eritrea. *Journal of Democracy* 9:164-174.

—. 2003. *The Making of the Eritrean Constitution: The Dialectic of Process and Substance*. Trenton, NJ: Africa World Press.

Hagos, Berhan. 2013. Yemane Gebreab: Let us read it; let us understand it!, 26 June 2013, available at http://www.asmarino.com/articles/1800--yemane-gebreab-let-us-read-it-let-us-understand-it.

Hagos, Mulubrhan Berhe. 2009. *The Laws of the Forefathers in View of Modern Standards on Gender Equality* [Book in Tigrinya]. Asmara: Aman Printing Press.

Harvard Humanitarian Initiative, Program on Humanitarian Policy and Conflict Research (HPCR). 2015. *Advanced Practitioner's Handbook on Commissions of Inquiry* (2015).

Hedru, Debessay. 2003. Eritrea: Transition to dictatorship, 1991–2003. *Review of African Political Economy* 30:435-444.

Hepner, Tricia Redecker. 2009. *Soldiers, Martyrs, Traitors, and Exiles: Political Conflict in Eritrea and the Diaspora*. Philadelphia: University of Pennsylvania Press.

—. 2013. Militarization, generational conflict, and the Eritrean refugee crisis. in *African Childhoods: Peacebuilding, Education, and Development in the Youngest Continent*, edited by Marisa O. Ensor, pp. 152-175. New York: Palgrave Macmillan.

Hirt, Nicole. 2010. Eritrea. in *Africa Yearbook*, edited by Henning Melber and Klaas van Walraven, pp. 301-309. Leiden: Brill Academic Publishers.

Hirt, Nicole and Mohammad Abdulkader S. 2013. 'Dreams don't come true in Eritrea': Anomie and family disintegration due to the structural militarization of society. *Journal of Modern African Studies* 51(1): 139-168.

Human Rights Watch. 2009. Eritrea Country Summary. in *World Report 2009: Events of 2008*, edited by Human Rights Watch. pp. 66-70. New York and Washington DC: Human Rights Watch.

Indian Ocean Newsletter. 2012. Issayas Afeworki arms the elderly. No. 1340, 22 September 2012, available at http://www.africaintelligence.com/ION/politics-power/2012/09/22/issayas-afeworki-arms-the-elderly,107884087-ART.

International Crisis Group. 2010. *Eritrea: The Siege State*. Brussels: International Crisis Group.

—. 2013. *Eritrea: Scenarios for Future Transition*. Africa Report No. 200, 28 March 2013, Brussels: International Crisis Group.

Iovane, Massimo. 2007. The universality of human rights and the international protection of cultural diversity: Some theoretical and practical considerations. *International Journal on Minority and Group Rights* 14: 231-262.

Iyob, Ruth. 1995. *The Eritrean Struggle for Independence. Domination, resistance, nationalism 1941–1993*. Cambridge: Cambridge University Press.

Jembere, Aberra. 1998. *Legal History of Ethiopia 1434–1974: Some aspects of substantive and procedural laws*. Rotterdam and Leiden: Erasmus Universiteit and Afrika-Studiecentrum.

Joint Declaration on the Political Situation in The Gambia, issued on 21 January 2017, by the Economic Community of West African States, the African Union and the United Nations, available at https://www.un.org/sg/en/content/note-correspondents/2017-01-21/note-correspondents-joint-declaration-political-situation.

Joireman, Sandra Fullerton. 1996. The minefield of land reform: Comments on the Eritrean land proclamation. *African Affairs* 95.

—. 2001. Inherited legal systems and effective rule of law: Africa and the colonial legacy. *Journal of Modern African Studies* 39: 571-596.

Keika, Omar M., and Ghidewon A. Asmerom. n.d. Eritrean Customary Laws (ECL) and the Constitution. p. 34: Dehai Constitution Discussion.

Kibreab, Gaim. 2008. *Critical Reflections on the Eritrean War of Independence*. Lawrenceville, NJ: Red Sea Press.

—. 2009a. *Eritrea: A Dream Deferred*. Woodbridge, UK: James Currey.

—. 2009b. Forced labour in Eritrea. *Journal of Modern African Studies* 47: 41-72.

King, John C. 2000. Exploring the ameliorating effects of democracy on political repression: Cross-national evidence. in *Paths to State Repression: Human Rights Violations and Contentious Politics*, edited by Christian Davenport, pp. 217-239. Lanham, MD: Rowman and Littlefield.

Kioko, Ben. 2003. The right of intervention under the African Union's Constitutive Act: From non-interference to non-intervention. *International Review of the Red Cross* 85 (852): 807- 825.

Kittichaisaree, Kriangsak. 2001. *International Criminal Law*. Oxford: Oxford University Press.

Lasswell, Harold. 1941: The garrison state. *American Journal of Sociology* 46 (4): 455-468.

Lasswell, Harold. 1937. Sino-Japanese conflict: The garrison state v. the civilian state. *China Quarterly* 643-649.

—. 1941: The garrison state. *American Journal of Sociology* 46 (4): 455-468.

Linz, Juan J. 2000. *Totalitarian and Authoritarian Regimes*. Boulder, CO: Lynne Rienner.

Longrigg, Stephen H. 1945. *A Short History of Eritrea*. Oxford: Clarendon Press.

Lussier, Dominique. 1997. Local prohibitions, memory and political judgement among the Kunama: An Eritrean case study. in *Ethiopia in Broader Perspective, Papers of the XIIIth International Conference of Ethiopian Studies*, edited by Katsuyoshi Fukui, Eisei Kurimoto, and Masayoshi Shigeta. pp. 441-455. Kyoto: Shokado Book Sellers.

Markakis, John. 1990. *National and class conflict in the Horn of Africa*. London: Zed Books.

Mbembe, Achille. 1992. The banality of power and the aesthetics of vulgarity in the postcolony. *Public Culture* 4(2): 1-30.

McDougall, Gay J. 2007. Minorities, poverty and the millennium development goals: Assessing global issues. *International Journal on Minority and Group Rights* 14: 333-355.

Media24.com. 2009. Eritrea: Held hostage. Documentary, October 2009, available at http://www.a24media.com/index.php/component/content/article/90-films/743-eritrea-a-nation-held-hostage?directory=867.

Medhanie, Tesfatsion. 1994. *Eritrea and neighbours in the 'New World Order'. Geopolitics, democracy and 'Islamic fundamentalism'*. Münster and Hamburg: Lit Verlag.

—. 2008. Constitution-making, legitimacy and regional integration: An approach to Eritrea's predicament and relations with Ethiopia. in *DIIPER Research Series Working Paper*. pp. 36. Aalborg: Aalborg University.

Mehreteab, Amanuel. 2001. Renewed demobilization in Eritrea. *Bonn International Centre for Conversion Bulletin* 1.

Mekonnen, Daniel R. 2017a (forthcoming). The case for crimes against humanity in Eritrea: Assessing the reports of the two UN fact finding missions. *Journal of International Humanitarian Legal Studies*, pp. N/A.

Mekonnen, Daniel R. 2017b (forthcoming). Other international military headquarters: African Union. In *The Handbook of the Law of Visiting Forces*, edited by Deter Fleck. pp. N/A. Oxford University Press, 2nd rev edn.

Mekonnen, Daniel R. 2016a. Eritrea at the centre of the international migration crisis. *International Affairs Forum* 1(1): 72–73.

Mekonnen, Daniel R. 2016b. The Valetta Summit and the Eritrean refugee crisis. *Horn of Africa Bulletin* 28(5): 28–33.

Mekonnen, Daniel R. and Sereke, Wegi. 2017. Prosecuting Sinai trafficking: An overview of options. In *Human Trafficking and Trauma in the Digital Era: The on-going tragedy of the trade in refugees from Eritrea,* edited by Mirjam van Reisen and Munyaradzi Mawere. Langaa RPCIG: Cameroon, pp. 466-498.

Mekonnen, Daniel R. 2006. The reply of the Eritrean Government to ACHPR's landmark ruling on Eritrea: A critical appraisal. *Journal for Juridical Science* 31(2): 26-56.

—. 2009. *Transitional Justice: Framing a Model for Eritrea.* Saarbrucken: VDM Verlag.

Mekonnen, Daniel R. and Meron Estefanos. 2011. From Sawa to the Sinai Desert: The Eritrean tragedy of human trafficking. SSRN Working Paper Series.

Mengisteab, Kidane, and Okbazghi Yohannes. 2005. *Anatomy of an African tragedy: Political, economic and foreign policy crisis in post-independence Eritrea.* Trenton, NJ: Red Sea Press.

Meyers, Nathaniel. 2010. Africa's North Korea: Inside Eritrea's open-air prison. *Foreign Policy,* July/August 2010, available at http://www.foreignpolicy.com/articles/2010/06/21/africas_north_korea?page=0,0.

Miran, Jonathan. 2007 Power with Pashas: The anatomy of Na'ib autonomy in Ottoman Eritrea (17thC-19th C). *Eritrean Studies Review* 5(1): 33-88.

Mohammad, Abdulkader Saleh. 2013. *The Saho of Eritrea: Ethnic Identity and National Consciousness.* Münster and Berlin: Lit-Verlag.

Molidor, Christian. 2001. The Kunama of Eritrea. in *One,* New York: Catholic Near East Welfare Association.

Müller, Tanja R. 2008. Bare life and the developmental state: Implications of the militarisation of higher education in Eritrea. *Journal of Modern African Studies* 46: 111-131.

—. 2012. Beyond the siege state: Tracing hybridity during a recent visit to Eritrea. *Review of African Political Economy* 39(133): 451-464.

Murithi, Tim. 2014. *The Handbook of Africa's International Relations.* Routledge Publishing.

Nadel, Siegfried F. 1944. *Races and tribes of Eritrea.* Asmara: British Military Administration.

Naty, Alexander. 1998. *The Discourse on environment and ecology among the Kunama people of Eritrea.* in V.R.F. Series. Tokyo: Institute of Developing Economics.

—. 2001. Memories of the Kunama of Eritrea towards Italian colonialism. *Africa [Rome]* 56: 573-589.

—. 2002a. Environment, society and the state in Western Eritrea. *Africa* 72: 569-597.

—. 2002b. Potential conflicts in the former Gash-Setit region, western Eritrea: Threats to peace and security. in *Organisation for Social Science Research in Eastern and Southern Africa (OSSREA).* http://www.ossrea.net/announcements/alexander,pdf, accessed 20 March 2003.

—. 2004. Political and cultural history of the Kunama people. www.deqebat.com: Dekebat, Eritrea.

Negash, Tekeste. 1987. *Italian colonialism in Eritrea, 1882–1941. Policies, praxis and impact.* Uppsala: Department of History, Uppsala University.

—. 1997. *Eritrea and Ethiopia. The federal experience.* Uppsala: Nordic Africa Institute.

Negash, Tekeste and Kjetil Tronvoll. 2000. *Brothers at war: Making sense of the Eritrean-Ethiopian war.* Oxford and Athens, OH: James Currey and Ohio University Press.

Normark, Sture. 1972. Sociala Förändringar i Kunamasamhället (Social change in the Kunama community). p. 47 in *Sociologiska Institutionen, Avd. för Socialantropologi*. Department of Social Anthropology, Lund University, Lund, Sweden.

Novak, Manfred. 2005. *UN Covenant on Civil and Political Rights: CCPR Commentary* (2nd revised edition), Kiel: N.P. Engel.

Nystuen, Gro and Kjetil Tronvoll. 2008. The Eritrean-Ethiopian peace agreement: Exploring the limits of law. *Nordic Journal of Human Rights* 26.

Obama, Barack, 2012. Remarks by the President to the Clinton Global Initiative, Sheraton New York Hotel and Towers, 25 September 2012, available at http://www.whitehouse.gov/the-press-office/2012/09/25/remarks-president-clinton-global-initiative.

Ogbazghi, Petros B. 2011. Personal rule in Africa: the case of Eritrea. *African Studies Quarterly* 12(2): 1-25.

O'Kane, David, and Tricia Redeker Hepner. 2009. Introduction: Biopolitics, militarism and development in contemporary Eritrea. in *Biopolitics, Militarism, and Development: Eritrea in the Twentieth Century*, edited by David O'Kane and Tricia Redeker Hepner, pp. 159-170. London: Berghan Books.

Pateman, Roy. 1990. *Eritrea. Even the stones are burning*. Lawrenceville, NJ: Red Sea Press.

Pausewang, Siegfried. 1993. The outlook for democracy in Eritrea. in *The Referendum on Independence for Eritrea. Report of the Norwegian Observer Group in UNOVER*, edited by Siegfried Pausewang and Astri Suhrke. pp. 59-64. Oslo: Norwegian Institute of Human Rights.

Pausewang, Siegfried and Astri Suhrke (eds). 1993. *The Referendum on Independence for Eritrea. Report of the Norwegian Observer Group in UNOVER*. Oslo: Norwegian Institute of Human Rights, University of Oslo.

Plaut, Martin. 2002. The birth of the Eritrean reform movement. *Review of African Political Economy* 29: 119-124.

Pool, David. 1997. Eritrea: Towards unity in diversity. London: Minority Rights Group.

—. 2001. *From Guerillas to Government: The Eritrean People's Liberation Front*. Oxford: James Currey.

Prunier, Gérard. 2010. Eritrea and its discontents. Speech delivered at the Conference of the Association for the Study of the Middle East and Africa (ASMEA), 5 November 2010.

Raji, Ahmed. 2010. The Lost Rainbow, www.awate.com.

Reid, Richard. 2011. *Frontiers of Violence in Northeast Africa*. Oxford: Oxford University Press.

—. 2009. The politics of silence: interpreting apparent stasis in contemporary Eritrea. *Review of African Political Economy* 36(120): 209-221.

Report of the International Commission of Enquiry on Darfur to the United Nations Secretary-General Pursuant to Security Council Resolution 1564 (2004), 25 January 2005.

Report of the Monitoring Group on Somalia and Eritrea, Pursuant to UN Security Council Resolutions 751 (1992) and 1907 (2009), 18 July 2011.

Report of the Secretary-General on the Rule of Law and Transitional Justice in Conflict and Post-Conflict Societies, UN.Doc.S/2004/616/, 24 August 2004.

Reporters Without Borders. 2008. *Freedom of the press worldwide in 2008*. Paris: Reporters Without Borders.

Reuters, 'Eritrea won't shorten national service despite migration fears', 25 February 2016, http://www.reuters.com/article/us-eritrea-politics-insight-idUSKCN0VY0M5.

Rickett, Oscar. 2013. Eritrea has failed to realize its revolutionary dream, 3 July 2013, available at http://www.vice.com/en_uk/read/a-revolutionary-dream-turned-sour-eritrea-at-20.

Riggan, Jennifer. 2009. Avoiding wastage by making soldiers: Technologies of the state and the imagination of the educated nation. in *Biopolitics, Militarism, and Development: Eritrea in the Twentieth Century*, edited by David O'Kane and Tricia Redeker Hepner, pp. 72-91. London: Berghan Books.

Rosen, Richard A. 1999. Constitutional process, constitutionalism, and the Eritrean experience. *North Carolina Journal of International Law and Commercial Regulations* 24:263-311.

—. 2001. Theory in practice: Code drafting in Eritrea. *North Carolina Journal of International Law and Commercial Regulations* 27:67-93.

Schabas, William. 2001. *An Introduction to the International Criminal Court*. Cambridge: Cambridge University Press.

Scharf, Michael P. 1996. Swapping amnesty for peace: Was there a duty to prosecute international crimes in Haiti? *Texas Journal of International Law* 31: 1-41.

Schmidt, Peter R. 2010. Postcolonial silencing, intellectuals, and the state: views from Eritrea. *African Affairs*, 109, (435): 293-313.

Schmidt, Eric. 2013. AFP. 2013. Google boss sees autocrats' pushback against Internet, 26 April, available at https://www.google.com/hostednews/afp/article/ALeqM5hrr3zDLsd8lts93Q-nn7yytRcs0A?docId=CNG.48a9bb5618bba18381d9fab36c912d5b.

Sen, Armatya. 1999. *Development as Freedom*. Oxford: Oxford University Press.

Shinn, David H. 2010. Challenges to peace and stability in the Horn of Africa. Paper presented at the World Affairs Council of Northern California, 12 March.

Smith, J. A. Clarence. 1955. Human rights in Eritrea. *Modern Law Review* 18:484-486.

Soudan, François. 2010. 'Érythrée: La Corée du Nord de l'Afrique. *Jeune Afrique*, 17 March, available at http://www.jeuneafrique.com/Articles/Dossier/ARTJAJA2565p022-028.xml0/usa-corruption-islamisme-electionla-coree-du-nord-de-l-afrique.html.

Stanley, Jay (ed.). 1997. *Essays on the Garrison State*. Piscataway, NJ: Transaction Publishers.

STRATFOR. 2015. 'The Emirati Navy arrives in Eritrea', 29 October 2015, https://www.stratfor.com/analysis/emirati-navy-arrives-eritrea.

Tadesse, Medhane and John Young. 2003. TPLF: Reform or decline? *Review of African Political Economy* 30 (97): 389-403.

Travers, Max. 2009. *Understanding Law and Society*. London: Routledge-Cavendish.

Tieku, Thomas Kwasi, Obi, Cyril, and Scorgie-Porter, Lindsay. 2014. The African Peace and Security Architecture: Introduction to the Special Issue. *African Conflict and Peacebuilding Review* 4(2): 1-10.

Tieku, Thomas Kwasi. 2013. African Union in *Responding to Conflict in Africa: The United Nations and Regional Organizations*, edited by Jane Boulden. pp. 33-50. Palgrave Macmillan.

Trevaskis, G. K. N. 1960. *Eritrea. A colony in transition: 1941–52*. London, New York and Toronto: Oxford University Press.

Tronvoll, Kjetil. 1993a. Issues affecting a peaceful development of independent Eritrea. in *The Referendum on Independence for Eritrea*, edited by Siegfried Pausewang and Astrid Surkhe. Oslo: Norwegian Institute of Human Rights, University of Oslo.

—. 1993b. The meaning of the referendum to highland peasants. in *The Referendum on Independence for Eritrea*, edited by Siegfried Pausewang and Astrid Surkhe. Oslo: Norwegian Institute of Human Rights, University of Oslo.

—. 1994. Camel-dance and balloting – The Afar factor in the referendum. in *Post-graduate Students' Yearbook (Hovedfagsstudentenes Årbok)*. pp. 208-220. Oslo: Department and Museum of Anthropology.

—. 1996. The Eritrean referendum: Peasant voices. *Eritrean Studies Review* 1: 23-68.

—. 1997. *Election observation report from the Maekel Zoba election in Eritrea, 1 March 1997*. Pp. 27. Oslo: Norwegian Institute of Human Rights, University of Oslo.

—. 1998a. *Mai Weini. A highland village in Eritrea. A study of the people, their livelihood, and land tenure during times of turbulence*. Lawrenceville, NJ: Red Sea Press.

—. 1998b. The process of nation-building in post-war Eritrea: Created from below or directed from above? *Journal of Modern African Studies* 36:461-82.

—. 2000. *Meret Shehena*, 'Brothers' Land': S.F. Nadel's *Land Tenure on the Eritrean Plateau* revisited. *Africa* 70: 595-613.

—. 2009a. Ambiguous elections: The influence of 'non-electoral' politics on Ethiopia's democratisation. *Journal of Modern African Studies* 47.

—. 2009b. *War and the politics of identity in Ethiopia. The making of enemies and allies in the Horn of Africa*. Oxford: James Currey.

UN Commission of Inquiry. First Report of the UN Commission of Inquiry on Human Rights in Eritrea (Short Version), UN.Doc.A/HRC/29/42, 4 June 2015.

UN Commission of Inquiry. First Report of the Detailed Findings of the UN Commission of Inquiry on Human Rights in Eritrea, A/HRC/29/CRP.1, 5 June 2015.

UN Commission of Inquiry. Second Report of the UN Commission of Inquiry on Human Rights in Eritrea, UN.Doc.A/HRC/32/47, 8 June 2016.

UN Special Rapporteur. Report of UN Special Rapporteur on the Situation of Human Rights in Eritrea, Sheila B. Keetharuth, UN.Doc.A/HRC/26/45, 13 May 2014.

UN Special Rapporteur. 2013. *Report of the UN Special Rapporteur on the Situation of Human Rights in Eritrea*, Sheila B. Keetharuth, UN.Doc.A/HRC/23/53, 28 May 2013.

UNHCR. 2004. *UNHCR position on return of rejected asylum seekers to Eritrea*. p. 7. Geneva: United Nations High Commissioner for Refugees.

US CIS. 2003. *RIG Query – Eritrea*. Washington DC: United States Citizenship and Immigration Services.

USSD. 2001. *Country Report on Human Rights Practices in Eritrea for year 2000*. Washington DC: US State Department.

—. 2002. *Country Report on Human Rights Practices in Eritrea for year 2001*. Washington DC: US State Department.

—.   2003. *Country Report on Human Rights Practices in Eritrea for year 2002.* Washington DC: US State Department.

—.   2007a. *Eritrea. Country Report on Human Rights Practices – 2006.* Washington DC: US State Department, Bureau of Democracy, Human Rights, and Labour.

—.   2008a. *Eritrea – Country Report on Human Rights Practices 2007.* Washington DC: US State Department, Bureau of Democracy, Human Rights, and Labour.

—.   2008b. *Eritrea: International Religious Freedom Report 2008.* Washington DC: US State Department, Bureau of Democracy, Human Rights, and Labour.

—.   2009. *Eritrea – Country Report on Human Rights Practices in 2008.* Washington DC: US State Department, Bureau of Democracy, Human Rights, and Labour.

—.   2010. *Eritrea: International Religious Freedom Report 2010.* Washington DC: US State Department, Bureau of Democracy, Human Rights, and Labour.

—.   2011. *Country Reports on Human Rights Practices.* Washington DC: US State Department, Bureau of Democracy, Human Rights, and Labour.

Vaughan, Sarah and Kjetil Tronvoll. 2003. *The Culture of Power in Contemporary Ethiopian Political Life.* Stockholm: SIDA Studies.

Venosa, Joseph L. 2007. Faith in the Nation: Examining the Contributions of Eritrean Muslims in the Nationalist Movement, 1946-1961. Master of Arts (MA) Thesis, Ohio University, International Studies - African Studies.

Welde Giorgis, Andebrhan. 2010. Nation building, state construction and development in Africa: The case of Eritrea, Bonn: Friedrich-Ebert-Stiftung Study Paper.

Weldehaimanot, Simon M. 2011. The right to leave and its ramifications in Eritrea. *East African Journal of Peace & Human Rights* 17(1): 195-226.

—.   2009. Eritrea: Constitutional, legislative and administrative provisions concerning indigenous peoples. in *The Constitutional and Legislative Protection of the Rights of Indigenous Peoples: Country Reports*, compiled by International Labour Organization and the African Commission on Human and Peoples Rights, pp. 1-60. Pretoria: Centre for Human Rights.

Weldehaimanot, Simon M., and Semere Kesete. 2012. Rubbishing: A wrong approach to Eritrea/Ethiopia union. *Review of African Political Economy* 39(131): 45-62.

Weldehaimanot, Simon M. and Daniel R. Mekonnen. 2009. The nebulous law-making process in Eritrea. *Journal of African Law* 53(2): 171-193.

—.   2012. Favourable awards to trans-boundary indigenous peoples. *Australian Indigenous Law Review* 16 (1): 60-76.

Woldemikael, Tekle M. 2003. Language, education, and public policy in Eritrea. *African Studies Review* 46: 117-136.

World Bank. 2001. Eritrea: The process of capturing indigenous knowledge. in The World Bank, *IK Notes*. p. 4. Washington DC: Knowledge and Learning Centre, Africa Region, World Bank.

Yohannes, Zemhret. 1996. Nation-building and constitution-making in Eritrea. *Eritrean Studies Review* 1: 155-165.

Østebø, Terje. 2008. *Localising Salafism: Religious change among Oromo Muslims in Bale, Ethiopia.* Stockholm: University of Stockholm.

Index

EASTERN AFRICAN STUDIES

These titles published in the United States and Canada by Ohio University Press

www.ingramcontent.com/pod-product-compliance
Lightning Source LLC
Chambersburg PA
CBHW050353270326
41926CB00016B/3724